It Doesn't Have to Be That Way

It Doesn't Have to Be That Way

How to Divorce Without Destroying Your Family or Bankrupting Yourself

Laura A. Wasser

St. Martin's Press
New York

www.stmartins.com

Design by Phil Mazzone

Library of Congress Cataloging-in-Publication Data

Wasser, Laura A.
It doesn't have to be that way : how to divorce without destroying your family or bankrupting yourself / Laura Wasser. — First edition.
pages cm.
ISBN 978-1-250-02978-2 (hardcover)
ISBN 978-1-250-02977-5 (e-book)
1. Divorce—Law and legislation—United States—Popular works. 2. Divorce suits—United States—Popular works. 3. Divorced people—United States—Handbooks, manuals, etc. I. Title.
KF535.Z9W325 2013
346.7301'66—dc23

2013014469

St. Martin's Press books may be purchased for educational, business, or promotional use. For information on bulk purchases, please contact Macmillan Corporate and Premium Sales Department at 1-800-221-7945, extension 5442, or write specialmarkets@macmillan.com.

First Edition: October 2013

10 9 8 7 6 5 4 3 2 1

AUTHOR'S NOTE

This book is intended as a resource, and offers guidance and information for individuals going through the process of separation and divorce. Examples of typical (and sometimes rather unique) situations and solutions to common problems are included for illustrative purposes only. The names and characteristics of all clients and others mentioned in the book have been changed to protect their privacy and their identities.

If the reader needs advice concerning the evaluation or management of specific legal or financial concerns, including bankruptcy, estate, or tax matters, he or she should seek the help of a licensed, knowledgeable professional.

To my parents, Bunny and Dennis Wasser, who gave me roots and wings

CONTENTS

It Doesn't Have to Be That Way

INTRODUCTION

Welcome to Divorce in the Twenty-first Century

Marriage is not a noun, it's a verb. It's not something you have... It is a choice you make over and over again.

—BARBARA DE ANGELIS

I have been a practicing Family Law attorney for nearly two decades. I am also the daughter of one of the country's preeminent divorce lawyers. You could say that Family Law runs in my family. Both the law and the practice have definitely evolved quite a bit since I was a kid—even since I started practicing law. Some of the change has been for the better and some for the worse. But I think the time has come to share information about what should be a new approach to revising your relationship—whether it's a marriage, a registered domestic partnership, or cohabitation with or without children.

In the twenty-first century, people tend to couple up and have kids a bit later in life than they did a generation ago. Many people today are better communicators, better educated, and for the most part more litigation-savvy than their forebears—thanks to the proliferation of fender benders, landlord-tenant disputes, wrongful termination suits, and a rise in general litigiousness. We have also been more exposed to divorce—almost all of us have experienced it in some way, shape, or form. If your own parents remained happily married for the long haul, perhaps your partner's did not. If both of you are the children of intact homes, it would be almost weird if no friends, friends' parents, siblings, aunts, or uncles ever went through a breakup to which you were exposed, albeit tangentially. This experience, paired with the technological advances of the twenty-first century, has the average splitting couple poised to experience a far better breakup than couples of generations past—basically, a breakup that promises healthier children, fuller bank accounts, and intact personal integrity.

It's All Good

It was the early 2000s. I was representing the bass player for an alternative rock band—I'll call him Zack—and we were on the phone going over the settlement offer sent to my office by Zack's wife's attorney. It was about 10:00 in the morning. As I presented my analysis of the first couple of terms, I heard on the other end of the line an unmistakable bubbling sound. "Dude," I asked incredulously, "are you taking a bong hit?"

Silence. Heavy exhalation from the receiver—a long sigh ending in "Yeahhhhh."

"You cannot take a bong hit while you are on the phone with your divorce attorney," I said somewhat sternly.

Another long silence. "Dude," he replied (it is either a blessing or a curse that I often still speak like a fourteen-year-old skate punk and am responded to in kind), "is there a better time to take a bong hit than when on the phone with my divorce attorney?"

I thought about this for a moment. It seemed a reasonable question.

"I make good money doing a job I love," Zack went on. "I have a couple of awesome kids, and even though she is being kind of a bitch right now, their mom is actually a pretty good mom. This isn't the greatest time—hence the wake and bake—but it's going to get better. Everyone is healthy, I've got arms and legs, and I can play my bass. It's all good."

Now, I am in no way proposing that twenty-first-century divorce is best handled while stoned. But I did have to admire my client's Zen attitude toward the process. This is a lawsuit like no other you will ever go through. (At least one hopes so.) It is a legal and business transaction taking place in your family—right inside, precisely at the heart of it. Interestingly, the last time you went through a similar transaction was when you got married, but back then, you were likely thinking about what flavor cake to order, how your dress would fit, or exactly what would or would not be appropriate for the bachelor party. You were almost certainly not focused on the fact that you were about to enter into a legal contract with someone, nor were you pondering what the ramifications of that contract would be. Unless you had entered into a prenuptial agreement, the rights and responsibilities of getting married were likely not explained to you. Sure, you were clear about "to have and to hold, in sickness and in health," but had you considered the extent to which the state would control how you would spend your money if you and your spouse were to separate in the future? Doubtful. They don't really put that out there when you're about to walk down the aisle to the strains of Pachelbel's Canon in D.

It is certainly true that we are a more sophisticated generation than those before us when it comes to familiarity with divorce. Beyond the firsthand experience, we grew up with movies like *Kramer vs. Kramer* and *Stepmom* and with television shows like *Who's the Boss?* and *My Two Dads*. So we are aware that not all families look the same and that some marriages do not last forever. Nevertheless, if it were up to me, marrying couples would be required to take some kind of an entry-level course. But that's another book.

Marriage is a contract. Every relationship, in fact, is a deal. Each person expects something from the other in exchange for whatever each is bringing to the table. It can be as simple as the fact that one person is the provider and the other is the aesthetically pleasing subservient. Or, one half of the couple might be the "fun one" and the other the voice of reason. Generally, there is a list of things for which each party is responsible, so if and when the responsibility changes by virtue of time or circumstance, it means the contract terms have also changed, and that must be addressed. If the provider is no longer able to provide the unlimited credit card spending at Prada, Chanel, Gucci, and Hermès, the aesthetically pleasing subservient may not be feeling as subservient as he or she was before, nor as eager to please. The deal has changed. Not every couple is able to adjust to that or to weather the storm. Love may not always conquer all.

A new deal must be negotiated. That can be in the context of the relationship or in the context of a breakup. Although your head should be clear and ready to address the issues that arise, developing my pot-smoking client's mentality might not be a bad idea. It's all good.

Generation Gap

Tap tap tap. It was my father, knocking on the door of my office. He is the founding partner of the law firm where I work, and he is my father, two titles that give him every right to come into my office, even when I am meeting with a client. But it was probably not beside the point that at the time, the client with whom I was meeting was a rising star among film actresses and drop-dead gorgeous to boot.

My father is a very prominent lawyer, one of the best known of the Hollywood divorce lawyers, highly respected and indeed celebrated both inside and outside the legal community. "The Silver Fox," as we call him, is a wonderful-looking man, and he was dressed for work the way most people probably think prominent partners of big law firms should dress—looking very distinguished indeed in an elegant suit, with a silk tie, cuff links, and butter-soft Italian shoes. I was wearing a black mini sweater dress and Alaïa platform ankle boots. My father came in, and although he did not know who the actress was—exactly—he knew she was someone, and she's hot. He chatted her up and took his leave.

"It's so nice that you let your father work here," the actress said when my dad had departed. As far as she was concerned, I was dressed for work; my father was costumed in some Hollywood idea of what the head of a prominent law firm should look like.

But I'll bet you that if you stand my father and me side by side and ask most people which of us looks like the divorce lawyer, ninety-nine out of a hundred will point to the guy in the suit. Old perceptions die hard.

That's true of just about everything having to do with divorce. The fact is that now, in ending a marriage or dissolving a relationship—as in everything else—there's a whole new way of doing it and a whole new generation in charge of getting it done. It's a change that is way more than clothing-deep. Yet my guess is that most people reading this right now still harbor an old idea of divorce—and probably of divorce lawyers—left over from our parents' generation.

That's too bad because divorce, never a happy episode, can today be a better process resulting in a better outcome than at any time in history. Enough has changed in a generation, and a sufficient range of tools is now available to the parties to a divorce to make the dissolution of your marriage or partnership smooth, expedient, cost-effective, low-stress, and as amicable as your goodwill or your perseverance allows. In short, divorce today can be, if not almost-good, at least good enough to keep yourself, your sanity, your wallet, and your dignity intact—and your children safe, sound, and emotionally healthy.

This book tells how.

This Is Not Your Parents' Divorce

What is different from a generation ago? Family law, the body of laws governing domestic relations, has undergone a profound and dramatic change, propelled by and reflecting equally profound and dramatic changes in the social reality of relationships. A case I recently handled sums up what I mean.

We'll call them Melissa and Jennifer. They had been registered domestic partners under California law for well more than a decade. They had two children, a son and a daughter born two years apart, both now in school. The women had contrived a somewhat elaborate formula for conceiving the kids. To ensure that the children would have the same "father," they used a single sperm donor for both pregnancies. But then they went a step further. Melissa contributed the egg that would become their son, but after fertilization, it was placed for gestation into Jennifer's uterus. Two years later, it was the other way around: Jennifer's egg, fertilized by the sperm donor, went into Melissa's uterus, and it was Melissa who gave birth to their daughter.

If the formula seemed a bit of a reach—if it seemed to some that the couple was using it to make a "statement"—it was nevertheless a way for both women to experience pregnancy and childbirth and to make their two children truly the offspring of them both. In any event, it was their choice, their uteri, and their family.

And when their relationship unraveled, as relationships can, and the couple decided to separate, a similarly well-planned and lovingly thought-out process governed the issues of custody and child care. On those subjects, the two women were in fairly harmonious agreement.

Other issues proved thornier, however—namely, money. As is typical in many states that recognize domestic partnerships, the money earned by Melissa during the course of the partnership was to be equally divided in the event of a separation. But since federal law at the time did not as yet recognize same-sex marriage or its joint-property provisions, she could end up having to pay federal gift taxes on the amount she was giving to Jennifer. At the going rate at the time, that would mean she would be almost doubling her property award—which Melissa did not find acceptable. Her only out would be to pay a lower lump-sum payment, which was not acceptable to Jennifer. So the case went to court.

The judge hearing the case was an older man—old enough, in fact, to be the grandfather of the couple's children, and the way in which those children came into the world seemed to transfix the judge's mind to the extent that it became a sticking point in the proceeding. Befuddled by the formula the women had devised, hung up on the lengths to which they had gone to ensure their kids' origins, fascinated and at the same time repelled by a situation utterly foreign to his experience, he simply could not get past what he persisted in calling the couple's "lifestyle."

His emphasis on this issue was irrelevant and wide of the mark, as both lawyers agreed, and the judge's insistence on raising it was both time-consuming and offensive. It was Melissa who first hit the bursting point, proposing to Jennifer that the two take their fate out of the hands of a guy who struck her as very much a caricature of the quirky judges on *The Good Wife.* He simply could not get his head around who they were as people and what they had at stake. Melissa and Jennifer were not comfortable with this person making decisions that would affect their lives—lives he clearly did not understand. Instead, the couple agreed to go to mediation to settle the issue on their own.

And that's exactly what happened.

To me, this case seemed to exemplify the disconnect between outmoded perceptions and current reality when it comes to relationships and their dissolution. To oversimplify a bit: On one side was the generation the judge embodied, still clinging to the idea that "family" means father, mother, two kids, refrigerator, and split-level—a template that was never as pervasive as claimed but that served as a kind of Madison Avenue standard for many years. On the other side was a family configuration that shattered that notion noisily and then had the temerity to break up and seek resolution in the law, which, by the time the twenty-first century rolled around, in fact protected the new configuration.

Social Revolution, Legal Evolution

The irony is that it was the judge's generation, the generation that has trouble getting its head around the new definition of families, that set in motion the social changes that did the redefining. They were the folks who roiled the world with the sexual revolution, the women's movement, the movements for civil rights and gay rights. Those forces transformed our social fabric, our economy, our politics, our demographics, the way we live, our attitudes about what counts and what works—and what doesn't—in coming together as a couple and being part of a family. Family law *had to* evolve to accommodate that revolution. After all, the life of the law is experience; it exists in a context. And the context, after a generation of social revolution, constituted a whole new ball game when it came to defining and dissolving relationships.

Our parents married because it was what you did at a certain time of life. It was expected; people who did not marry were somehow on the fringe. Similarly, couples stayed together because it was thought you shouldn't give up easily or perhaps because you shouldn't expect too much. Gender roles to a great extent still reflected the idea of a family as an economic unit in which the division of labor assigned to one spouse—typically, the male husband—the task of earning income, and to the other spouse—the female wife—the job of maintaining the household. Interracial couples were oddities, typically confined to specific neighborhoods of big cities. Nonheterosexual individuals—and certainly nonheterosexual relationships—were still in the closet a generation ago; in fact, it wasn't until 2003 that so-called "sodomy laws," effectively outlawing homosexual activity, were struck down by the Supreme Court.

Now look. Gender roles are out the window, mothers are no longer willing to deny themselves careers, fathers are no longer willing to play a secondary parental role, and instead of looking for partners in an economic unit, people seek a soul mate in a relationship aimed at personal fulfillment, married or not. You can literally see the change if, like me, the first thing you do on Sunday mornings is peruse the Vows page—that is, the wedding announcements—in *The New York Times* Style section. What not all that long ago was a review of both parties' prep schools, lineage, and connections has morphed into narratives of how the couple met, fell in love, and made their relationship work well enough to decide to marry.

Today, as often as not, the couples on the Vows page are mixed-race or same-sex—or both. This should not be a surprise. The fastest growing segment of the U.S. population is people who identify themselves as mixed-race—like, for example, President Barack Obama—and interracial and interethnic unions are on the rise.

So are same-sex unions, as gay marriage becomes law in state after state and soon perhaps, depending on the Supreme Court, everywhere. And by "everywhere," I mean not just in the hip neighborhoods of major cities on the two coasts, but in suburbs and small rural towns as well—unheard of a generation ago.

When our generation marries, it's usually far later than when our parents did, although we are sexually active at a far younger age. Yet the truth is that marriage is on the downswing among us; today, almost half of American adults—44 percent—are unmarried. That doesn't mean they are un-"together"; at the start of 2013, seven million Americans were living in couple relationships without benefit of a marriage certificate.[1] Coincident with those statistics, as *The New York Times* reported in 2012, is that "53 percent of all children born to women under thirty"[2] are born out of wedlock. These young mothers may eventually marry, but they are unlikely to marry the fathers of these babies.

The bottom line is that the Norman Rockwell vision of the traditional nuclear family has simply been sidelined by this generation. What served as a romanticized—almost deified—standard for our parents, their parents, and their grandparents before them is a social relic to us, who are totally at ease with blended families, same-sex or mixed-race couples, adoptions, surrogacy, families in which no one looks like anyone else.

But in all the discussion—celebratory to some, a bit threatening to others—about the proliferation of different types of relationships and family configurations, the one thing that hasn't been addressed very fully is the inevitability of breakups in both the relationships and the families. So let me put it on the record: It is precisely and indisputably inevitable that the more relationships there are, the more relationship dissolutions there will be. When our parents' generation was breaking down all those barriers between people, they may have neglected to look ahead to that inevitability, but it is here now, and it is here to stay.

Relationships end. Our generation accepts that. Relationships unravel or hit a wall or sometimes blow up. What was once wonderful

---

1 "Unmarried Spouses Have a Way With Words," Elizabeth Weil, *The New York Times*, January 4, 2013.

2 "For Younger Mothers, Out-of-Wedlock Births Are the New Normal," KJ Dell'Antonia, *The New York Times*, February 19, 2012.

turns sour. Or we change, and what worked before doesn't make us happy or fulfill us anymore. And our generation is fine with that. We're okay with ending what doesn't work and moving on. We do not believe that it is good for anyone or in anyone's self-interest to persist in a situation that is limiting or oppressive or, God knows, abusive. We won't accept a situation that in any way, shape, or form curbs an individual's control over his or her life.

But there are consequences. Certainly where children are concerned, the consequences can at times be costly, difficult, even ugly. It doesn't matter whether you are married or not, either. Child support and custody law work exactly the same for the unmarried as for those with a marriage certificate, or civilly joined, or domestically partnered, or none of the above. In the twenty-first century, the breakup is as much a fact of the new relationship reality as are the varied options for getting together.

The law recognizes all of it. The social revolution that prompted this new relationship reality also spurred changes in family law that enable us to dissolve those relationships when we feel we must—consequences and all.

No-fault

The great change in family law triggered by our parents' relationship revolution was no-fault divorce, first enacted in the United States in California in 1970 and last in New York as recently as 2010. No-fault took the stigma and the scandal out of divorce and put an end to the infantile legal fictions couples were forced to profess—in what one California judge called a "melancholy charade"—to prove adultery or cruelty, the allowable causes, under prior law, for dissolving a marriage.

To "prove" a client's case, for example, lawyers would hire private gumshoes to trail a cheating spouse into a motel, the seedier the better, so as to burst in on the adulterous couple, flashbulbs popping, to gather photographic evidence of infidelity. Often, if there was no adultery, it would be staged, and a down-at-the-heels actor or actress would be hired to impersonate the "correspondent" in order to provide photographic evidence. In other words, otherwise reputable people who simply wanted to divorce each other would collude in choreographing a dismally unethical pantomime so they could get out of a marriage that had become oppressive to one or the other or both.

No-fault divorce laws liberated grown men and women from this demeaning evidentiary nightmare—of which today's Photoshop and digitization would make a mockery in any event. It freed couples from having to sling mud at each other. Today, nobody has to charge anybody with wrongdoing, much less prove it, in order to dissolve a relationship.

What this means in practical terms is that if you feel anger, or resentment, or the need to vent your spleen against a spouse or partner, you have to leave those feelings at the courthouse door. Family law judges are not there to adjudicate emotions but to preside over an equitable settlement, and your personal grievances may just be irrelevant. You're ready to give the judge a mouthful about the low character of your soon-to-be-ex-spouse? Forget it. Not here. You consider your wife slovenly and are ready to assert that her household negligence will affect the kids? Short of abuse, she still has rights and responsibilities as a parent. You've decided your husband is a jerk who will never hold down a job and boy, are you sorry you married him? The judge doesn't want to hear it because it's just not pertinent to the issues before him or her, which are child custody, division of assets and liabilities, and financial arrangements. You'll be instructed to save your rants for your therapist or your lawyer or lunch with your best friend. But keep them out of court.

No-fault changed everything. Reflecting the shifting gender roles of the times, the expanding notion of marriage, and the rising insistence on equal parental rights and responsibilities, it empowered both parties in a relationship, treating both as equally entitled and equally accountable. After all, it took two of you to get into this relationship, and it will take two of you to get out of it.

Divorce in the Twenty-first Century

So why is our mind-set regarding divorce still locked in the perceptions of a generation ago? Why are we still in thrall to an outdated, outmoded view of divorce that has outlived any claim to reality—the notion that this process is about character and behavior and blame, when it is really about protecting rights and assigning responsibilities while undoing a civilly authorized family structure?

The outdated perception is bolstered by the long-running soap opera that is our celebrity culture, which loves nothing better than the breakups of the rich and famous. We thrill to divorces that drag on for months or years, to headlines about her telling her lawyer to "squeeze him for every penny" and him telling his lawyer to "not give her one red cent." We're titillated by the drama of these unapproachably beautiful people flailing about financially and emotionally—with the images and sound track of divorce scandals from a generation ago.

But the perception these images reinforce has significant and sometimes dire consequences. It makes people—maybe you're among them—afraid, angry, and anxious when they even think about divorce. It burdens this already ponderous decision and difficult process with more stress. There is probably no such thing as a good divorce, but clinging to this old idea of how relationships are unraveled can make a bad thing even worse.

For the truth is that there is a whole new way to dissolve your relationship—really a whole new choice of ways to do it. The evolution in family law has been accompanied by advances in mediation, collaborative practice, and self-representation, by the development of support and counseling practices, and by a substantive body of data on the impact of dissolution, direct and indirect, on all parties. And there is a whole new cadre of divorce lawyers—like me—who know how to help their clients navigate this new territory and emerge from it strong in mind, spirit, and resources and eager to move on to the next stage of their lives.

As you'll learn in this book.

Me and Divorce

What credentials do I offer that qualify me to guide you through this territory?

For one thing, I am a child of divorce. My parents split when I was sixteen and my kid brother was thirteen. I have said there is probably no such thing as a good divorce, but my parents' divorce was as close as you can get; in fact, it was pretty nearly a very, very good divorce. It's the example I hold in my head as a goal for all my clients; in fact, it's probably the reason I chose to practice family law.

Why was their divorce so good? My father was already an experienced divorce lawyer at the time who knew how he did *not* want the divorce to proceed; my mother held a law degree, worked in politics, and knew a good deal about the art of compromise; and—if you'll forgive me for saying so—my mother and father are exceptional people. From the outset and all the way through to this day, it was clear that what both of them cared about above everything was us, their kids, and assuring us that we were now and always would be a family. They trusted each other in this if in nothing else. I'll give you just one example of how that played out.

Some years after the split, my mother happily entered into another relationship with a lovely man who was also more than capable of supporting her financially—and who was eager to do so. Yet my father made no move to change the terms of the spousal support agreed to in their divorce settlement. The support he provided enhanced my mother's own earnings and enabled her to be financially independent. He knew that was important to her, and it was important to him that she retain that sense of independence for her own sake and that of our family. There was no way he would risk poisoning an amicable divorce or upsetting the family stability both of them worked hard to maintain just to save a few bucks. Nothing was worth such a risk.

In time, my mother and Howard married, and my father stopped paying spousal support. But I think of his example often when I hear a client suggesting a way to get or save a few more dollars in the settlement and insisting he or she deserves it. Maybe, but I ask the client to think also about the cost of going after more money—the effect on the ex, with whom you'll be linked through your children for the rest of your life; the effect on those children; the effect on the family that you keep insisting to your children will remain a family no matter what. Maybe it's worth it, but maybe the example of my parents' divorce is a better guide.

In any event, their divorce is my reference point, the headwater of my approach to dissolving relationships. I think it's a better source than the kind of acrimonious divorce we hear about all too often.

I also bring to bear in writing this book the credential of motherhood. I have two sons, each by a different father, and I coparent with both fathers pretty much around the clock. I admit that I often draw on what my clients do to remind myself what *not* to do in dealing with my own exes.

The bottom line is that I have experienced the many permutations of breakups, transitions, and the blended family personally as well as professionally. I know what it is like to have multifamily Thanksgivings. I am familiar with the rushed text messages about whose turn it is to pick up whom from where and drive them somewhere else. I am skilled at divvying up the school photos among several sets of grandparents, and I have mastered the ability to attend preschool orientation with one son's father and back-to-school night with the other's.

I am not a divorce-monger. I'm a sucker for a good love story and I tear up at weddings along with everybody else. I also know how hard people work to try to repair relationships that have gone bad or have ceased to be fulfilling; there is virtually no client I have represented who has not been through some form of counseling or therapy or consultation with a member of the clergy or all of the above, and I respect and applaud those efforts. In fact, I often urge—and sometimes insist—that a couple make one more try. I mean, if it's not his/her shit, it will be someone else's.

But I believe wholeheartedly that once the decision has been made, the legal system of the twenty-first century is particularly well equipped to treat the decision honorably and to ensure that both partners emerge from the process with their dignity, their children, and their wallets whole—pretty quickly and smoothly, too.

That's what I'm going to show you in this book. It will guide you through every step of the process—from first saying the word "divorce" out loud to walking away with a final settlement. I'll show you at each stage what's real about today's process—and how that may differ from your perception and from the way things used to be—and I'll offer suggestions for the best way to come through each stage as the master of your own destiny. At the end, my hope is that you and your children, if you have them, will emerge safe, sound, financially secure, and prepared to take up the next challenge of your lives.

How NOT to Divorce Gracefully

Michelle was Stanley's second wife, and the marriage had proven to be a major mistake from the start. Although the level of acrimony was high, Stanley was prepared to be financially generous just to end the relationship; his main objective in the proceedings was to ensure that his collections of art and wine remained intact. The final divorce decree reflected that; Michelle was awarded plenty of money but had no claim to the art or the wine.

On the day the property division takes place following a divorce decree, lawyers for the parties often oversee the actual

moving out. In this case, since Stanley had repaired to his summer home during the proceedings, it was Michelle who was actually taking her stuff and getting out, and I was the low-level lawyer on Stanley's team assigned to supervise the move—yeah, that's why I got a law degree—so I was the one who first noticed what she had done. At some tremendous effort, she had managed to steam the labels off all of the several hundred bottles in Stanley's prestigious wine collection, thereby of course rendering the collection worthless in the global wine market.

So she reaped a kind of mean pleasure from the divorce, along with a fairly fat paycheck. For Stanley, the loss was only money, of which he had plenty. "Wine is for drinking," he said.

And he proceeded to do just that each night for the next several years, even hosting "What's-that-wine?" dinner parties where guests with sophisticated palates enjoyed Stanley's chef's fine cuisine while they tried to figure out what they may have been drinking. Think of it as an older generation's version of "It's all good. . . ."

I

How Do You Know?

OLIVER ROSE: I think you owe me a solid reason. I worked my ass off for you and the kids to have a nice life, and you owe me a reason that makes sense. I want to hear it.
BARBARA ROSE: Because. When I watch you eat, when I see you asleep, when I look at you lately, I just want to smash your face in.

—*THE WAR OF THE ROSES*

It is not always so cut-and-dried. A woman I'll call Lisa phoned my office asking if she could come in for a preliminary consultation. It happens all the time. A relationship has gone sour in a big way, and even though the person has not yet said the word "divorce" or even the word "separation" aloud, he or she nonetheless wonders if it might be a good idea get some guidance on what's what.

I certainly understand the impulse. For one thing, I've been in those exact same shoes: pretty sure this wasn't working out but not yet really at the point of calling it quits. And for a lot of people, a first meeting with a lawyer—no pressure, nothing to sign—is an integral part of the process. There's something about sitting face-to-face with an attorney in an office that enables people to come to grips with the very idea of divorce—or to reconsider the idea. Like a number of my colleagues—not all—I offer that preliminary consultation for free. I'll ask a few questions, deliver what I call my Family Law 101 lecture, and let the prospective client size me up as well.

That's just what happened with Lisa. As do so many of the people who ask for a preliminary consultation, Lisa began by saying how strange it felt to be sitting in a divorce lawyer's office at all. It was "surreal," she said—"unbelievable" to be in this situation and to be actually uttering the word "divorce." It just didn't fit with the way she thought about herself and her life. Then she talked a little about her husband, her children, and her circumstances. I told her some facts about financial settlements and custody agreements under California law. We shook hands, she said she still wasn't sure she was ready to go forward, and she left.

A year later, Lisa scheduled another appointment. We talked about what had changed in a year—very little—and I answered some more questions about finances and custody. Lisa sighed and said she still wasn't sure she was ready, and again we shook hands before she left.

Once a year for the next three years—a total of five years in all—Lisa came into my office to reiterate her story and listen to me reiterate my Family Law 101 lecture. By year three, we were hugging good-bye, and in year four, we showed each other photos of our children. Finally, in year five, Lisa said she was ready to dissolve her marriage, retained the firm, and asked me to begin proceedings.

Five years from the preliminary consultation to the decision to separate may be a record for my law office, but it is not a particularly long time for a marriage to unravel. The rarity is the sudden epiphany or single turning point showing you with dramatic clarity that your marriage is over, although that does happen. Most relationships hover on a precipice for years before one party or the other finally decides it is time to jump, and coming to the decision isn't easy. The expectations you assumed when you entered into the relationship and the responsibilities you have as a partner in the life and family the two of you have created loom large. You're aware that any and every action you take can have a ripple effect on those expectations and responsibilities—and on other people—and you want to tread carefully. You are right to do so.

First, Get Some Counseling

BERNARD: Joan, let me ask you something. All that work I did at the end of our marriage, making dinners, cleaning up, being more attentive. It never was going to make a difference, was it? You were leaving no matter what. . . .
JOAN: You never made a dinner.
BERNARD: I made burgers that time you had pneumonia.

—THE SQUID AND THE WHALE

People get married because they fall in love. They get divorced, however, for one of three reasons.

One reason—and it is perhaps the most compelling driver of divorce—is unacceptable behavior on the part of one or the other partner. Abuse—physical or psychological—tops the list, but excessive or out-of-control drinking, drugs, gambling, serial or random adultery, or resorting to prostitutes all qualify.

One caveat here: People can and do change their behavior. As the affected but powerless spouse, you may be able to spur your badly behaving spouse to do just that. I know of a number of instances where ultimatums have been issued—e.g., "Either you go to rehab or I am out"—and the situations have been resolved and the marriages saved. The key is to be particularly clear-eyed in facing the reality of your partner's behavior. How many chances has he or she squandered? What is the real likelihood of a change this time? How far are you willing to go to help? What line can't you cross? But once you're sure in your mind about the answers to these questions, it can be well worth it to try again to save the relationship.

The second major reason for divorce is the proverbial inability to communicate; you just don't get each other anymore. Except for exchanging logistical details about who has to pick up whom from soccer practice and when the dry cleaning is supposed to be ready, you no longer even have much to say to each other. There are no more of those deep, endless conversations that used to keep you up til two in the morning; now when you converse, you find you're talking past each other.

The third reason people split up is that they grow apart. It happens—period. You get older, and your interests and goals change. Or one of you falls in love with someone else. Or you both do. Or you simply fall out of love with each other and do not want to be together as a couple anymore.

In all three cases, before you say the word "divorce" aloud, it is important that you make the effort to go to couples counseling first. After all, coming together was a major step; so is splitting apart, and the feelings you once had for each other should not be set aside lightly. If there's still something there—if there's enough there—don't you owe it to yourself, not to mention to each other, to see if you can salvage and revive it? If there's a chance of that, counseling is likely to find it, and once it has been identified, you can decide if it's worth pursuing.

When my significant other and I were going through a difficult time, we found ourselves arguing loudly, frequently, and ineffectually. He got so aggravated so much of the time that he would literally pivot on his heel and walk out of the room. (Yes, I have that effect on people.) What infuriated him was what he saw as my tendency to treat every argument as a courtroom battle and to turn into, basically, the prosecutor.

A few sessions of therapy were immediately helpful: He *could not* leave—that's simply not allowed in counseling—and I was checked each time I started to litigate our issues. Once we were both talking like normal people and listening to each other, we worked it out.

The idea in counseling is to sit down with an unbiased third party to whom you both can express grievances in the presence of the other. That unbiased third party might be a qualified Marriage-Family-Child counselor (MFCC) or a psychiatrist or a psychologist or a social worker or the clergyperson of your choice. You meet in a room containing just the three of you, with no distractions, and with time enough for both of you to have your say.

Sometimes, just the act of venting is helpful. Counseling provides a safe haven for precisely that kind of free-ranging release: You can say things in the therapist's office, with the therapist present, that would be incendiary or hurtful in your living room. And often when you let 'er rip, you get all sorts of things off your chest and out of the way. I have known couples who realized it was time to quit therapy when the issues they were venting about were down to minor matters—in one case, her distaste for the way he had "decorated" his man cave and his annoyance that she had signed up for yet another evening course at the local college. That couple figured that "if this is what we're venting about, we must be okay," and they sure didn't need to pay a therapist to adjudicate those low-level issues. They stayed together and routinely turned to a therapist when the high-level issues threatened to get out of hand again.

It is the safe-haven aspect of counseling and the presence of the third party that make it so effective and important. Both ensure that each of you can be heard, and qualified couples counselors know what to do with what they hear. They can help you cut through the resentments that have built up and find a renewed civility with each other—useful whether you end up dissolving your relationship or not. They can also pinpoint suggestions and recommend tools that open a valve through which you may be reminded of why you got together in the first place. In a great many cases, it's a matter of finding ways to spark a sex life that has become routine, infrequent, and unfulfilling. There are counselors for that, too, and such renewal is often enough to move you to a reconciliation.

There is even a case to be made that any couple that can afford the luxury of counseling should indulge in it. Just as you go to the gym regularly to keep your body fit, regular couples counseling can keep your relationship fit as well.

But for couples in difficulty or on the brink, counseling is essential. What you must understand about it is that it can be hard work. The operating motto for counseling, however, is that if a relationship can work, you should work for it. Things may never be as fresh and rosy as they were when you first came together—that kind of passionate excitement does fade—but you did marry each other, and maybe it was meant to be. If so, counseling can help you rediscover the reasons.

Couples counseling gets many couples back together. But not all, and not always. For your own sake and that of your children, however, I recommend it—I almost insist on it—as the first step for anyone unhappy in a relationship. The truth is, however, that the great preponderance of prospective clients who come to my office for a preliminary consultation have gone the couples-counseling route already—and in their case, it has failed. They've made the attempt and exhausted the possibilities—in fact, the counseling may have helped clarify their thinking—and they are ready now to dissolve their relationship and move on.

As a part of this soul-searching, indulge me in something. Make a list of at least five things your spouse or your marriage holds you back from—things that you would really like to be doing. Items on the list can be as simple as sleeping with others, working out more, or spending more time with friends, or as complex as getting a degree, finally seeing April in Paris, or learning ancient Greek. Put the list aside; we'll get back to it in chapter 15.

It's Time

New Year's Day, and the resolutions are as numerous as the hangovers. Lots of people resolve to lose ten pounds. One of my clients resolved to shed a hundred and sixty pounds—her husband. A lot of people feel a similar impulse.

It is why January is such a big month for divorce lawyers. People emerge from the holiday season swearing that come hell or high water, they are not going to spend another Thanksgiving/Christmas/Chanukah/Kwanzaa/you-name-it with their in-laws. They are not going to go through another overpriced family vacation during which they have to put on a good front for the sake of the children who see right through it and are surly and undisciplined anyway. Another connubial New Year's Eve kiss, trying to feel party-ish and hopeful while contemplating yet another year in a relationship that has ceased to be fulfilling or make either of you happy, is just one kiss too many. My office is flooded with phone calls on January 2: A lot of unhappy wives and husbands figure that if they start now, they can have a new life by the time the holidays roll around again.

And a funny thing happens. Once people you know start to get divorced, you think about it, too. It's why divorces come in clusters within prescribed communities. One person in the women's book club announces she is splitting from her husband, and before you know it, two more have done the same. Or somebody in the lunch crowd at the office gets divorced and has to spend lunch hour at his lawyer's, and pretty soon a couple of other folks have followed suit. It's almost as if divorce were catching. More likely, once one person in your circle does it, you see that it is possible—specifically, that it's possible for someone like yourself. It's not so "surreal," as Lisa felt at first, after all. Then the discontent that has been festering in you comes to the surface, and making a change, frightening as it is, becomes something you feel you can do, too. You just feel the time has come.

How do you *know* it's time to end your marriage? There's a simple answer to that question. It's time to dissolve a relationship when the pain or oppression of being in it exceeds the fear or anxiety of being on your own. Unfortunately, no one and nothing on this earth can tell you when you've reached that tipping point. Not your best friend, not your accountant or lawyer, not your mother, not a *Cosmopolitan* magazine quiz or a checklist or, heaven knows, a book can decide this for you. What *this* book can do, however, is tell you some things you should not leave out of your consideration when you are toting up both the pain of staying and the fear of going and weighing the one against the other to decide if it's your time to move forward.

Sometimes, to be sure, life gives you an unmistakable sign. A client of mine returned from shopping at the mall to find her husband on the receiving end of a blow job from their nanny while the couple's four-year-old twins napped in the next room. She said that once the initial shock had worn off, she considered the incident her get-out-of-jail-free card.

State of the Law

The fear of being on your own is the fear of the unknown, and you can eliminate some of it at your computer or by heading to the nearest library. Family law is a matter of state jurisdiction in the United States, and you will want to find out some basics about the law in your state—specifically, the laws concerning your children and those concerning finances.

But perhaps the first thing you need to find out is how your state deals with the issue of fault. No-fault divorce, premised on the idea that both partners assume equal blame for the failure of the marriage, is now enshrined in the family law books of all fifty states. In many of the fifty, however, spouses can choose to proceed on either a fault-based or no-fault basis, and the choice will often depend on how the no-fault concept is applied in your particular state. In my home state of California, for example, no-fault is almost an absolute. This means that a judge asked to rule on, say, the division of community property will not even consider complaints about a spouse's serial adultery or lengthy, drug-induced absences from the family home. It is all just an even-steven split down the middle. In New York, by contrast, such factors may be brought forward in a hearing over equitable distribution of assets even if the divorce is by mutual consent.

The laws regarding a couple's date of separation also differ from state to state. What must you do to ensure that you are legally separated? Does this stop the clock on the length of time you will pay or receive support? How about accruing joint income? If you believe you are separated and have communicated this to your spouse, can he or she dispute the separation? How must your behavior match your intent? These are all valid queries and not so simple to answer without specifics.

You should also find out if yours is a community property state or an equitable distribution state. Most states are the latter, which means that the property you acquired as a couple during your marriage will be divided between you upon your divorce based on a number of "equitable factors"—namely, the length of the marriage and the relative value of the financial contribution each of you made, including the value of being a homemaker.

Only nine states are community property states. They are mostly in the West because the community property concept comes to us from Mexico and before that from Spain via the conquistadors. Under the community property rule, property acquired during the marriage is owned jointly by both spouses and is evenly divided in a divorce. The idea is that both partners contributed equally to the creation of the household or family, and each should therefore retain an equal portion.

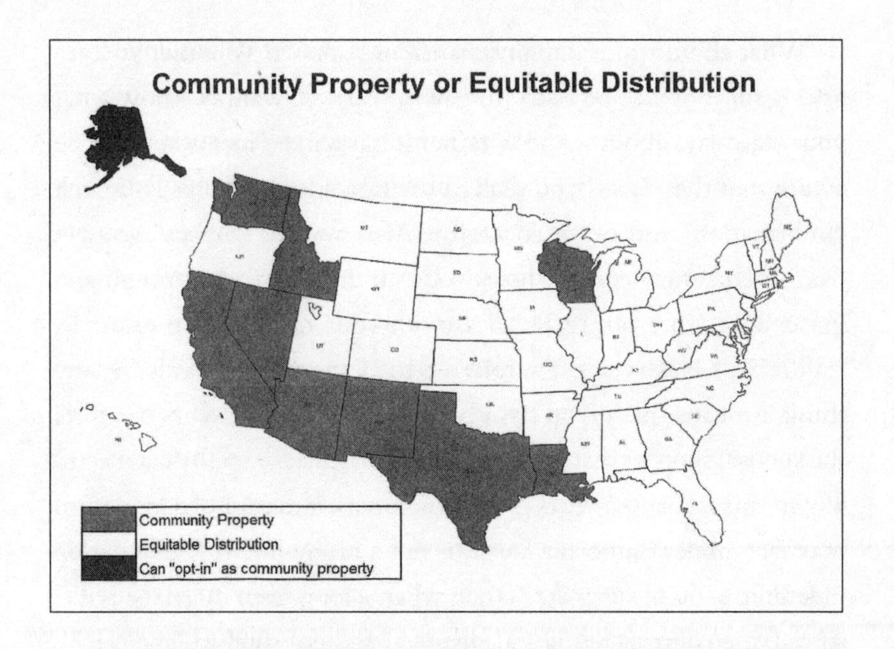

The Nine Community Property States—Plus Alaska

Arizona

California

Idaho

Louisiana

Nevada

New Mexico

Texas

Washington

Wisconsin

Alaska is an opt-in community property state: Property is separate unless both parties opt for a community property agreement.

What about spousal maintenance or support? Whether you are asking for it or will be asked to pay it, you will want to know what your state says about it and whether it has a fixed formula for it. Be aware that the "facts" you read in the tabloids about this issue, the "information" you get at cocktail parties, and the "advice" you get from friends may contain holes you can drive a truck through and inaccuracies that can really mess with your mind. As an example, California has what is often referred to as the "ten-year rule." Many think it means that if you have been married for ten years or more, the spousal support that is ordered will continue for life. What it actually means is that ten years is the benchmark indicator of a long-term marriage under California law. It is not a bright-line rule mandating indefinite spousal support. Rather, when a long-term marriage is dissolved, the court *retains jurisdiction* over spousal support, and it may choose not to provide a cutoff date for that support during the initial divorce proceeding. But the court can and will revisit the issue.

There are other key questions about spousal support, and before you proceed with dissolution, you would do well to know the answers for your state. For example, you will want to find out how spousal support is calculated in your state—namely, is it based on marital lifestyle or on the income of the higher-earning spouse? If both of you work, is the lesser-earning spouse nevertheless eligible for spousal support? What happens if there's a change of circumstance? That is, suppose the higher-earning spouse loses or quits his or her job or retires completely; what effect will that changed circumstance have on the spousal support issue? Or what if the lower-earning party is just rejoining the workforce at the time you split up? What happens then?

Again, don't trust your friends, married or divorced, to know the answers to these questions. If you cannot find the answers online, it may be time for a preliminary consultation with a divorce lawyer.

If you have kids, you should also find out the basics of child custody arrangements and child support. What do your state's laws say about shared or joint custody and about how long child support must be supplied? Not surprisingly, anything having to do with kids tends to be the thorniest of issues in dissolving a marriage, certainly the most fraught and anxiety-producing, and often the most contentious. The more you can find out ahead of time about how child support is calculated in your state and, if possible, how the judges in your jurisdiction make the decisions they make on the subject, the better off you will be—and the better off your kids will be.

Here is a checklist of legal topics you would do well to check up on as you contemplate dissolving your marriage. Knowing the basics will throw a lot of light on that unknown you may be heading into up ahead.

The State of the Law in Your State: The Basics

Custody

Date of separation

Community property vs. equitable distribution

Child support

Spousal support (alimony)

Fault

Process period: how long from start to finish?

Testamentary provisions: should you change your will, adjust your trust

Can You Afford to Split Up?

It's an important question. To be weighed against the psychological costs of remaining in the relationship are the financial costs of dissolving it. They can be substantial.

There are two categories of cost. One is the up-front cost of the proceedings: attorney's fees and court costs. The other cost category is what you will have to pay or to live on as a result of the divorce. It is wise to try to get a handle on both—in a sense, to estimate a budget for your divorce—before you set it in motion.

Lawyers typically demand a retainer in advance; their hourly fees and other costs—copies, answering your questions over the phone, filing expenses—are taken out of this retainer until it is used up.

If both you and your partner earn incomes, you are likely to share the legal costs, with the higher-earning party probably contributing to the other's fees. In some cases, who pays the legal costs is a matter for discussion, mediation, or a court ruling.

Yes, lawyer's fees are high. I believe we are worth the training, expertise, and experience we bring to our clients' cases. I will also say this: The less contentious the proceedings, the faster they will go, and since we are paid for our time, the less you will pay. If you and your spouse can agree ahead of time on such basics as custody and support, you can lower your legal fees significantly.

Remember: The more acrimony, argument, and angst, the more money your attorney makes. We profit from your inability to resolve issues. Think about that. Some family law attorneys are responsible about this fact; some are not. I often tell clients that I have a nice house, my kids' private school tuition is paid, and I prefer not to make more money arguing about issues that can be easily solved.

How can you estimate what the divorce will do to your household finances? Without knowing precisely how much you will have to pay or how much you will be awarded in support, that is difficult to calculate, but you can estimate it. Start with your monthly net salary or wages and any income you may receive above that. Based on your library or online research, add what you think your spousal support payments will be, or subtract what you expect the support payments to cost you. Ditto for monthly child support. Add it up, then subtract what you think you'll have to pay in income tax. The result is at least a guesstimate of what you'll have to work with.

Out of this, you'll need to pay all your estimated expenses. Tally them up. You'll have household expenses, including mortgage or rent, utilities, food and clothing for all of you. Health care expenses are relentless—either for insurance or for doctor visits and medicines, or both. If you have a car, you'll need to pay operating and maintenance costs; don't forget insurance. Kids in school? Even in public schools, there are all sorts of costs for supplies, field trips, and events.

You should also think about your tax liability once you are filing as a head of household and no longer as married, filing jointly. Spousal support is taxable for the receiving spouse, tax-deductible for the payer. It usually works exactly the opposite with child support; the receiving spouse pays no tax on child support income, and the payments are not tax-deductible for the paying spouse.

And what if you add it all up and decide that you simply cannot afford to divorce? I have seen it happen. Are you then "condemned," as some of our parents were, to staying together indefinitely in what is likely to be increasing misery? Because the whole thrust of this book is that no one has to do that ever again, the answer is an emphatic *no*!

It is up to you. Pay each other the courtesy of complete honesty and realize that you are in this together, and that your choice is (a) to put up with it and deaden your soul, seeking solace in philandering and/or drinking yourself into a stupor to avoid going home, or (b) to figure out a way that you can both have a better life while being legally and financially tied to each other.

It is in your hands, and it is within your power. All you have to do is think a little bit differently, risk being unorthodox, and be absolutely clear about what you do and do not want.

I am one lawyer who is glad to sit down with a couple and draw up an agreement for changing their lives while living under the same roof. Such an agreement is fairly common for couples who intend to divorce but who, for one reason or another, can't manage to separate physically just yet—more on this in chapter 4. It works also for couples who just cannot divorce but who are no longer willing to "stay together," and I've worked with a number of clients to give legal validity to the modus operandi that works for them. Typically, such a plan will specify the living arrangements and determine how finances will be shared, and it will prescribe emotional and physical boundaries as needed. It might lay out a schedule—who is responsible for the kids on which days, or who has access to which rooms, or the computer, or the TV on which nights.

At the same time, you both might want to lay out a plan that would make it possible to revisit the dissolution issue in a stated amount of time—a year, say, or three years, or five. Such a plan might detail how to share your earnings so that you save or raise enough money to go through with a divorce; it might assign work or fund-raising responsibilities to each partner. The point is that there are ways to change a marriage you cannot afford to dissolve, and they are limited only by your imagination and by your willingness to take charge. Dissolving a relationship, whatever form it takes, is your process. The more substantially you involve yourself in it, the better your lives will be.

The Right Time to Dissolve Your Marriage

Assuming you believe you can afford to dissolve your marriage, when is the right time to do so? Notice I say "the right time," not "a good time." There is really no good time to get divorced, but given your situation, and given whatever stage of life your kids are at, and given your state's laws and the legal options available to you, there is some relatively better moment to go through this, and that's what we'll call the right time for you.

There is an exception to this, of course, and that's in the case of unacceptable behavior. Certainly if there is physical abuse, but also in the case of a spouse acting irresponsibly—unrestrained drinking, or use of illegal drugs, or gambling away the kids' college fund at the blackjack tables—just get out, especially if you have children. But failing such an exigency, it is a good idea to pick your moment.

It is not an easy calculation. The ideal moment is before things have gotten so bad that civility has been lost, and while there is still sufficient time for the process to play out amicably and well—and for you to create a new life. Finding that moment will depend on a few factors.

You want to dissolve this relationship before you've gone past some irrevocable turn in the road—e.g., before you feel really suffocated or before it gets ugly or before you do something you'll regret. Remember that you did once love this person, and you do not want to get to a point where you hate him or her. True, he has never, ever learned to put the toilet seat down, or she is congenitally incapable of capping the toothpaste, but you do not want to find yourself staring at the sleeping frame of your spouse or partner and contemplating suffocation by pillow. You also don't want to get so frustrated and distressed that you simply take your kids and a suitcase and flee mindlessly, thereby possibly harming your chances for the kind of adult, amicable dissolution of this marriage that you and your family deserve.

If and when you feel your irritation level grabbing you by the throat, or if you hear yourself vowing inwardly, "One more time, and I'll throttle him/her," it is time to cut your losses and put an end to the relationship.

You also want to do this at a point in your life when you will have enough time and energy and wherewithal to carve out a new life for yourself. Maybe you hope to meet someone you can share your life with again, and maybe you'd like to have more children. You don't want to become so embittered or burned out that you will have no further interest in finding somebody else or will have lost the ability to respond if someone comes into your life.

Maybe you have had enough of being part of a couple and yearn to live independently. That will take some adjusting, and you probably want to get started on it sooner rather than later.

And of course you want to do this at a time that is best for your kids, if you have kids—best in terms of their state of mind and emotions, and best also in terms of navigating through the milestones of their lives. If your child is starring in the school play or putting together a project for the science fair—or both—you probably do not want to add any more pressures to the burden she or he is already carrying.

Of course, with kids as with adults, there is no good time for divorce. Your kid is going through a phase? Bad time to divorce. Going through puberty? Really bad time. On the other hand, what's a good time? And of course, the current state of your marriage is also having an unwelcome impact on your kids. So as you weigh what's good for your kids—or at least fair to them—in calculating the right time for you to begin divorce proceedings, you will need to juggle numerous considerations. At a minimum, your aim is to look for the least bad moment, or for a time when you will be best able to mitigate the repercussions your kids will experience.

A Demanding Process

The process you are about to go through asks a lot of both partners in the relationship. There's little room for cutting corners. It is going to absorb a substantial amount of your time, so in calculating when to divorce, keep in mind that once you set the process in motion, you are going to be even more busy than usual for the duration of the proceedings.

The process is also emotionally draining. The reality of not being part of a couple is often more complex to deal with than you might have thought—even if it's welcome. Suddenly sleeping alone, with no one around to take care of you in big and small ways, and no one there to talk to when you have something to say: It can be baffling at first, and it can feel lonely. The dissolution process also tends to dredge up all sorts of memories, good and bad, as well as resentment and discontentment you thought you buried long ago. It can stir guilt, sorrow, and a range of regrets. Bottom line: This is a profound change; don't underestimate what it might take to go through it.

There are also physically demanding chores ahead. Moving, for one. If you're the one leaving the joint home, you are almost certainly going from a bigger to a smaller space; it will be an adjustment. If you're the one staying, you will now be living with half of what you were accustomed to: half the pictures on the walls, half the DVDs, half the plants. And of course, you'll be living on half the money.

Through all this, you'll be expected to participate fully in the legal process of dissolving your marriage. It can be a time-consuming, energy-sapping process, but, as this book cannot emphasize enough, it's essential for your sake and that of your children that you be very present in the process, respond to its demands, and call the shots as best you can. It makes no sense to try to turn over all responsibility to your lawyer, who is in any case utterly dependent on what you provide: statements, records, data, the numbers, the narrative. It's up to you to corral all this material and to fulfill your role as a player in the dissolution proceedings.

Is there an ideal time to divorce? If you're the higher-earning spouse, and your income has seen no major upward spikes this year, and you haven't been married that long, and there are no kids, then now may be an opportune moment to end this relationship and move on. By the same token, if you're the lower-earning spouse in a comfortably well-off couple, and you've been married ten years, and you're in your thirties, and the children are well along in school and have stalwart friendships and understanding teachers, and if it's the end of the school year and summer vacation is about to start, then now may be a good time to begin the end of your marriage—especially if you want to be sure not to go through yet another holiday season like last year's.

IN BRIEF

You know you're ready to dissolve your relationship when the pain or oppression of being in it exceeds the fear or anxiety of being on your own. But to crystallize your thinking on the matter, be sure to do the following:

1. Seek counseling—together if you can, on your own if that doesn't work.
2. Get information on the basics of divorce in your state: the fault issue, date of separation, community property or equitable distribution, alimony and child support, custody, the process, testamentary provisions.
3. Calculate your financial situation.
4. Figure out the timing that makes sense for all parties.

2

Getting Started on Ending It

Amicable, cost-effective dissolutions are today possible in a way they have not been before. The evolution of family law and the social changes that have prompted that evolution have arrived at a point where you can do this, unpleasant as it may be, in a mature, businesslike, yet caring way. You win. So does your spouse or partner. And so do your children.

It starts with the very first time you make it clear that you want or are considering or believe it is time to break up—finally and permanently.

We've all heard stories of absurd and awful breakup announcements; our popular culture is filled with them. In an episode of *Sex and the City,* Berger, one of Carrie's boyfriends, tells her he is splitting up with her on a Post-it note stuck to the refrigerator. In the movie *Up in the Air,* George Clooney's character's young sidekick, Natalie, laments that her significant other has announced their separation via text message. Actress Minnie Driver swears she first found out Matt Damon was ending their romance when he confided it to Oprah Winfrey and her fifteen million television viewers, and Hollywood is rife with gossip about this or that celebrity learning his or her marriage had ended when it was "reported" on TMZ. The day cannot be far distant when people will learn of the end of their relationship when their partner changes his or her status on Facebook: One day you're "in a relationship," the next day "it's complicated," and by day three, you find you're "separated."

We laugh at these stories for good reason: They're ludicrous. We are talking about a life-changing and in some instances a life-defining event, and the idea that someone would give notice of such an event in an offhand way or turn it into tabloid fodder to hurt a spouse's career—or advance one's own—stretches credulity right into the realm of the funny. Of course, some people just *are* offhand or vindictive when they break up with a partner; but then, some people jump out of airplanes wearing webbed wingsuits, and you don't have to follow them there.

Nor should you follow them to using the breakup of the central relationship of your life as a weapon. Whether you aim for it or not, the dissolution of the relationship is going to hurt you both; using the opening shot as target practice gains nothing and almost invariably backfires.

I can't stress enough the central fact about that opening conversation about ending your marriage or partnership—namely, that the way it goes down is likely to be the way the rest of the dissolution goes. Therefore, your objective should be to begin as you mean to go on, and for both of you, that should mean acting like grown-ups caught up in one of life's difficult situations.

In truth, that first discussion is a strategic moment coming at a critical juncture. I don't mean this as a comment on anyone's state of mind or emotions; if you know you're ready for the discussion, you have no doubt been dealing with both for some time. In some way, by having reached the decision you've reached, you have also achieved some resolution of feelings and thoughts, although clearly they will continue to affect your actions. Rather, I am speaking here of the civil and legal structure of your life. Where that is concerned, basically everything is going to be different from this moment forward, so you must proceed in a way that can produce the greatest advantage for you over the long term. And in ending a relationship, the greatest advantage for you is the most amicable resolution. It is unfailingly the most cost-effective, the least tough on the emotions, the easiest on the nerves, the least harmful to the kids, and the most likely to prepare you to get on with the next phase of your life. Achieving such a resolution starts in the dissolution discussion.

One big reason amity produces advantage is money. The cost of a divorce is directly proportional to rancor. The fiercer the rancor, the higher the cost; conversely, the more courteous the proceedings, the cheaper—also the quicker, which is of course part of why it costs less. The reason for all this is self-evident: Where there is rancor, every aspect of the proceedings will become a battlefield; every issue will be grounds for contest. The opposing lawyers, each paid to be an advocate for his or her client, will do their jobs and wrangle over every point—and the meter will kick up a notch with every argument.

It's a choice you make early on. I suppose one of the worst choices I have ever heard about was when the wife, who became my client, answered the door on Valentine's Day to see a deliveryman carrying a box big enough to contain a passel of long-stemmed roses. Long-stemmed roses they indeed were—dead ones. Among their stems, speared onto a thorn, was a court summons announcing that my client was being sued for divorce.

There was no reason for this vindictive action. No tactical advantage was gained by it. It was pure pettiness—a puerile move that poisoned the divorce proceedings from that moment forward, caused everybody more misery than necessary, and, because it signaled conflict at every step of the process, ended by making the divorce far more costly, financially and in every other way, than it ever needed to be.

It is with the aim of avoiding that sort of proceeding and ensuring instead an amicable, cost-effective dissolution that you should address your announcement to your spouse or partner with civility and rationality at the very least, and with courtesy and even grace if possible.

Process and Jurisdiction

Let's define some terms and understand some facts about the legal process. It starts when you or your lawyer files what is officially known as a Summons and Petition for divorce with the appropriate court in your chosen jurisdiction. That makes you the petitioner—or plaintiff—in the process.

The petition papers contain whatever information is required by the statutes of the particular jurisdiction in which the papers are filed. Typically, that will include your name and that of your spouse, your children's names and the dates of their birth, the date of your marriage or of your registration of domestic partnership, and the date of your separation. It will also outline your preliminary requests concerning the custody of the kids, spousal support, division of the estate, and who should pay the attorneys' fees. In other words, it's an initial staking out of your position, all subject to change and/or negotiation.

A court clerk stamps the petition. A lawsuit has been initiated. A copy of the petition must then be served on your spouse, the respondent—or defendant—in the case. This is called service of process, and there are a couple of ways to do it. If jurisdiction is not an issue, you may present the petition to your spouse, the respondent/defendant, in an informal manner and ask that he or she sign an acknowledgment of receipt. For my clients, I typically do this in a letter that includes a stamped, self-addressed envelope. When we get back the signed acknowledgment of receipt, that means the respondent has accepted the court's jurisdiction, and we are ready to roll.

The other, more formal way to effectuate service is the way we always see it done in the movies; it is called personal service. You should check what qualifies as personal service in your jurisdiction, but in most jurisdictions, it doesn't necessarily have to be executed by a professional process server. Your papers can be served by anyone over the age of eighteen who is not a party to the action; that means: not you. The personal server signs a proof of service swearing on pain of perjury that he or she identified the respondent and served him or her the papers on such-and-such a date at such-and-such a time and in such-and-such a place. Like acknowledgment of receipt in informal service of process discussed above, proof of service in personal service starts the divorce ball rolling.

It rolls first to something called ATROs, Automatic Temporary Restraining Orders. ATROs automatically and temporarily restrain you or your spouse from taking your children out of the state without the consent of the other parent and from any action involving money or property that is outside the normal transactions of your daily life. That means no big-ticket purchases, no changing names on accounts, no putting the weekend house on the market, no major charitable contributions, no borrowing against or cashing in an insurance policy, and the like. Among other implications, this suggests that if you have any of those activities in mind, you should get them out of the way before you file and serve the divorce petition.

You have filed, served or been served, and been temporarily restrained. What comes next? If you have been served—if you're the respondent—do you need to respond? Check the petition; normally, it will state you have thirty days to respond. Most lawyers don't stick to that thirty days, so don't worry about it, but you might want to take the first step and request an extension from your spouse or your spouse's lawyer. Why? Even though thirty days sounds like plenty of time, it can take that long or even longer to wrap your head around the idea of divorce, hire a lawyer, deal with your emotions, and find your feet. It's a big step; give yourself time.

Jurisdiction

Jurisdiction, or the venue of the action, can be an issue, so addressing it is the one thing you need to settle in your mind even before you have the one-on-one breakup conversation with your spouse. Jurisdiction is where the case is going to be heard. It should be where you lived during your marriage. If you have more than one residence, look at where your kids go to school, where you file state taxes, which state has issued your driver's license, and where your bank accounts are domiciled. In fact, satisfying yourself that you are filing for divorce in the jurisdiction that makes most sense for you is the one reason you might want to put off the one-on-one discussion; it's an argument for filing first, talking later. Here's why.

While in ideal circumstances couples divorce where they live, and hire lawyers or mediators whose offices are convenient for both to get to, the fact is that the filing jurisdiction will influence the outcome of every issue that may arise in the divorce proceeding—child custody, child support, spousal support, division of property. That's why it is so important to know your own state's practices concerning the key issues.

There are cases in which "forum shopping," as it is called, is tried. It happened to a client of mine, a pro basketball player. He was the father of four children and although not married to their mother, lived with them all in Texas. Their life as a family was there; they lived in a large house in a lovely neighborhood, and the kids were all enrolled in local schools. Although California was my client's place of work, he owned no property in the state, and his family rarely came to visit him here.

But when some problems surfaced in the relationship, his partner suggested that he rent a house in California so that the whole family could spend the summer there while the two worked out their relationship problems. My client did just that, and after three months in residence in the state, his partner filed a paternity suit against him. She didn't want to work out their difficulties after all; she wanted out of the relationship, with the kind of sizable support award California was far more likely to deliver than Texas, and then she wanted to go back home with the money.

And she seemed to have a case, too. Three months' residence is all that is required to sue for paternity in California, and she had enrolled the kids in schools for the coming fall term as further evidence that the Golden State was now her home. But the California judge ruled that the appropriate jurisdiction for this action was indeed Texas, where the children had attended school and where the majority of the family's activities and expenditures had taken place. In short, the judge saw through this as a clear case of forum shopping.

You can imagine the welcome the woman got from her local Texas family law court when she and the children returned home.

If you choose a different jurisdiction from your obvious home state, and you file before discussing the filing with your spouse, then instead of the one-on-one conversation, your announcement that you want a divorce will arrive in a lawyer's letter or when the process server shows up at the door. Not great, but not as bad as a Post-it or text message. Still, even if this coldly legalistic format is the first inkling your spouse has that you want a divorce, there is a right way to go about it and a wrong way, and I cannot emphasize enough how important it is to set the tone by doing this the right way.

It means if you're doing it via process service, choose the manner of the process and the server very carefully. That was not the case with a woman I know who asked her mother to serve the papers. The mother loathed her son-in-law and couldn't wait to slap the papers into his hand, announcing with relish and a smug grin: "You've been served." It was an emotionally satisfying moment of schadenfreude for Mom but not so good, as it turned out, for the wife; the husband was unable to muster much goodwill toward his soon-to-be-ex, and the divorce dragged on for years.

And if you're announcing by letter, which I think is by far the best way to articulate your intentions to your spouse, do it as informally and as civilly as possible. I've mentioned that my preferred practice in these instances is to send a letter containing the stamped copy of the petition to the respondent. But the letter gets downright chatty—well, for a lawyer. I introduce myself as the petitioner's attorney and affirm that the petitioner has filed for divorce. I explain that he or she has asked me to write to notify you, the respondent, of this filing rather than having you served by a process server. This is because the petitioner, your spouse and my client, really wants to dissolve this union in an amicable and cost-effective way. Please therefore sign this acknowledgment, return it in the enclosed stamped and self-addressed envelope, and ask your lawyer to call me. If we do not receive the acknowledgment by a certain date, then more formal means of service will be necessary. This can be an unpleasant experience, which our client wants to avoid.

Stern, but it certainly beats dead roses or a smirking mother-in-law.

Well Begun Is Half Done

Preferably, any and all of these legal actions will have been preceded by a one-on-one conversation—most likely, more than one. But the exchange between the two of you in which you first speak of divorce is a strategic moment. What you say at this moment and how you say it can establish the tenor of the entire proceeding to come and can affect both the results and the price each of you pays. One thing that can be really instrumental at this strategic moment, the thing that can establish a prevailing direction that will be most advantageous to you and your children, is for the two of you to determine that you will take control of the process as a team—i.e., that you will depart your relationship as a united twosome, which is presumably the same way you entered it.

Why is this so important? If you want to be masters of your destiny, you need to take it out of the hands of the lawyers. I am not antilawyer, as you may well imagine. I believe the law is a noble profession, that family law is a practice at the very core of our social fabric, and that the presence of lawyers in a dissolution proceeding is advisable nine times out of ten. But it is not the lawyers' divorce; it is yours, and it's up to you to define your objectives and control the process if you want to divide and conquer.

There is a popular perception that divorce lawyers relish an adversarial dissolution proceeding because, presumably, they get to strut their stuff in a public hearing and charge even higher hourly fees to the next client.

Not this lawyer. Not the other partners and associates in my firm. Not the vast majority of my colleagues who specialize, as I do, in family law. In fact, the popular perception could not be further from the truth, which is that nobody really gains from the kind of knock-down, drag-out spite fests that titillate the popular imagination. For sheer financial self-interest, nothing serves lawyers better than shepherding clients as smoothly and as quickly as possible through amicable, cost-effective dissolutions in which custody and support arrangements are split as evenly as possible. Those are the cases that result in further referrals, and it's those ongoing referrals that produce material success for lawyers.

But as attorneys, we are required to take one side, that of our client. By definition and by the rules of professional conduct, we are there to advocate for the interests of our client against those of the other lawyer's client, and if you leave us to our own devices, we may have no choice but to bring up issues you may not want brought up and/or to raise arguments on your behalf that you don't find at all beneficial. Again, that may not be the best way to achieve the most amicable and most cost-effective dissolution you can possibly get. So it is up to you, the client, to set the parameters for the kind of advocacy you want and to control the process, reining in your lawyer when necessary. If you and your spouse or partner can agree from the outset that you will do this—that you will present a united front to your lawyers—you will, among other results, help your lawyers achieve the kind of dissolution you want.

And as every lawyer—and every writer—knows, language is key, in this first discussion and throughout the process. Imagine that you and your spouse are sitting down at the kitchen table, opposite each other, to have the discussion. Your spouse goes first. "I want you to know that my aim is to nail you to the wall," says your partner of X number of years. "My fervent desire is to crush you, and to that end, I have hired the most punishing ballbuster of a lawyer I could find and have instructed him to leave no stone unturned—I don't care what it costs or how long it takes—to reduce you to pulp."

It is probably fair to say that your first response to these words would be to put up your dukes and prepare for a fight. Your second response would be to lash out with one or both of said dukes to crush your spouse right back. Punch and counterpunch, and pretty soon, this divorce is spinning out of control.

Try imagining you hear this instead: "I want us to do this the right way. You are the father/mother of my children, and I will always care for you. You have been my lover, my best friend, and my support. You know me better than anyone, and I would like to preserve some part of our history and good feelings for each other. I hope we can always remain united for the sake of our children and ourselves, and I hope we can control this process toward that end."

Since chances are that is the language you would rather hear, that is also the language you should use when you talk about dissolving your marriage. The language alone, in my view, can get you more than halfway to where you want to be when this marriage is dissolved.

The Agenda

There is a range of issues you and your spouse should address when you begin to talk about dissolving your relationship—everything from who gets the custom-made dining table to when to break the news to the in-laws to who keeps the Netflix account. But which issues you tackle and how you tackle them are likely to depend on where you are in the process—how far along toward dissolution you have traveled. If dissolution is still a new idea, or if it is one you have only "discussed" with yourself in your own head, your agenda is likely to be quite different from what it might contain if the two of you have been mulling the idea over for years.

So here is a best-case checklist—the items you ideally want to address before you begin the legal phase of your dissolution. The more items on this checklist the two of you can settle—the fuller your joint game plan—the better. If you hit a stumbling block, table it and move on. Some issues will be stickier than others for either or both of you. Don't get hung up on them; push on to the next.

Timing. As I noted back in chapter 1, there can be better and worse times to dissolve a marriage—better for the kids when they're not in school, worse for financial reasons to split around tax time, maybe not good right now because one spouse's parent is ill.

I recall a recent instance in which the couple had agreed that the marriage was over and had pretty much settled how they would handle the key issues. But before any petition was filed, the husband received a much-longed-for promotion at work. The promotion elevated him to an executive, highly public position in which it would have been "unseemly"—his word—to be seen to be going through a divorce proceeding. Could his wife agree to wait?

It was certainly to her financial advantage to do so. She didn't even have to use the postponement as a bargaining chip; the promotion meant a huge jump in her husband's compensation, which would translate into considerably more spousal support for her. What she did negotiate was the length of the postponement, agreeing to stay married for another six months—for both, a better time for the divorce.

Timing may not be everything in life, but it can be important. It's worth considering.

Date of separation. If you did your homework as recommended back in chapter 1, you should know the rules about the date of separation in your state. It's essential to understand what sorts of things the official date of separation triggers and how it may affect each partner's claims on property or liability for debt. In states like California and Pennsylvania, for example, anything you do from which you derive income is considered your separate property from the date of separation, and the income is solely yours. If you find a dollar, buy the ticket, and win the lottery the day after your date of separation, it's all yours—your separate property. By the same token, any money you spend will be charged to you as a separate property obligation.

Once you and your spouse have determined a date of separation, it's a good idea to declare same, to issue a statement to your spouse saying that by your understanding, the marriage is irremediable as of Month X, Date Y, Year Z. Once that's done, you also need to act separated—that is, in a manner that demonstrates that you both believe the marriage can no longer be redeemed. If you separate and then go to counseling together, that sends the message that you're really not sure the marriage is over; your behavior is in fact signaling that you're trying to reconcile. So state the date of separation and act separated, and if by some chance, you do reconcile, you won't have lost anything.

A well-known California case illustrates what I mean. The couple had agreed to separate, and the husband moved out, taking up residence in a rented houseboat while his wife and young son continued to live in the family home. The separated spouses led distinctly separate lives—the husband even began dating someone fairly seriously—but every Sunday without fail, he returned to the family home for a visit. He spent time with his son, his wife cooked dinner for all three of them, and, because the houseboat lacked a washer and dryer, she did her putatively soon-to-be-ex-husband's laundry.

This went on for a few years, and it prompted the wife's attorney to argue, successfully, that because the Sunday routine gave "reasonable belief" that the two were not separated, the wife was entitled to her share of the community property the husband had earned over the period she was cooking his Sunday dinner and doing his laundry. And so the judge ruled.

The case offers clear and fair warning: Once you declare your date of separation, your behavior must be consistent with the declaration, so it is important to address this issue and agree on a date that both of you can live with. Some couples even enter into date-of-separation agreements so there is no question about either's intent.

Custody. This is by any measure the most substantive, the most gut-wrenching, and potentially the most harrowing issue in the dissolution of a relationship—and one we will look at in detail later on in this book. Obviously, you are both invested to the hilt and with every fiber of your being in your children; the self-interest of each of you is what is best for them. But, of course, people have different views of what constitutes their children's best interests. I have seen parents use their kids as pawns in a divorce proceeding while assuring themselves it is for the sake of the children. I have also seen the angriest and most spiteful of warring spouses stop grinding axes, lay down their cudgels, and agree calmly to a custody plan. That's a better way.

The courts just about everywhere now hold the child's best interests as the standard for determining custody arrangements, and most states see the child's best interests served by as much frequent and continuous contact as possible between the two parents, favoring neither one. If you can map out your joint custody plan before you file for divorce, as so many of my clients do, you will be well on your way to the kind of amicable, cost-effective resolution that will be in the best interests of all of you.

Support. The same can be said for this often thorny, certainly vital issue. If you can reason together about the financial resources each of you may need, it will establish a sound footing for what is to come. If you can actually agree on figures, that's of course even better.

Property. Maybe you each grab a different colored pad of Post-its and you walk through the house together, with each of you slapping your Post-its on the things you want to claim. Or perhaps you video the property together, then watch the video separately, each of you calling dibs as you see fit. It's what the lawyers will do anyway, at high hourly rates, so you might as well steal a march on them and at least inventory the property. The more claims you can agree to before you get to court, the cheaper and smoother your final dissolution will be.

Mediation? Finally, do you want to go through the dissolution process with lawyers before a judge or via mediation—either just the two of you before a mediator, or the two of you plus your lawyers before a mediator? In the latter case, the lawyers do the mediating, but you are there to add, subtract, or modify as you see fit. Each of these three options has its pros and cons, and it makes sense to discuss which option may be right for you.

In general, the distinctive benefits of mediation are that you have the opportunity fully to have your say about what matters to you (a judge is likely to cut you off and suggest you stop wasting time) and that, while each of you loses something, if it works, it can be cheaper and faster than going to court—i.e., it all just gets done, without the almost frighteningly ponderous solemnity of a courtroom. Moreover, as mediators very often are retired judges with considerable experience, they may be able to advise you on how your case may fare if you end up going to court.

The potential downside of mediation is that it could blow up in your face or end in an unresolvable impasse. If that happens, you'll probably have to go to court anyway, only by now, each side knows the other's arguments. Thanks to what is known as the mediation privilege, however, most of what is said during mediation is not admissible in court. It means you cannot argue that you know your spouse will settle for one weekend a month in the custody arrangement because he said so in the mediation proceedings that failed. Court is a whole new ball game, and such a claim is inadmissible and therefore irrelevant.

But the two of you will need to reach a resolution somehow—via mediation or in court. Start off on the same page now, and you can avoid some unpleasant surprises later.

Walking the Talk

Getting it right starts with you at the very outset of the process, but keeping it right may not be that easy. As the process moves forward, unanticipated issues may surface, as may irritants and annoyances. At some point, one or both of you may lose it. That's the time to grit your teeth and get back to behaving as if you are half of an amicable process.

The apt phrase is to "walk the talk." You started by declaring you both wanted to do this right. You wanted an amicable process that would keep you both whole, financially and emotionally, and would leave each of you with your dignity intact. If or when your spouse or partner strays from that path, it's a signal to you to stick to it with even more determination. Continue to act as if the process is still amicable, and it will typically revert to that in short order.

One tool that has worked for a number of my clients is to keep a journal that starts with a declaration of principles—your own statement of what you would like the dissolution process to be. As you go through the process, your journal entries enable you to remind yourself of what you set out to do—stay amicable, control the process, be fair, aim for cost-effectiveness—and can help you both stick to those principles.

IN BRIEF

The most amicable resolution is the most advantageous, and it starts here. Announcing a divorce with civility and respect can go a long way toward achieving a process and resolution that save you money and angst down the road.

1. Consider whether to petition for divorce via a letter to be acknowledged or service of process.
2. Petitioning for dissolution triggers Automatic Temporary Restraining Orders, so consider handling any matters that will be restrained before filing the petition.
3. The jurisdiction in which you file will influence the outcome of every issue that may arise in the divorce proceeding—child custody, child support, spousal support, division of property—so beware of forum shopping and know the laws in your jurisdiction.
4. In the dissolution conversation with your spouse or partner, watch your language; it will likely set the tone for the entire process and resolution. Two wrongs do not make a right.
5. Conversation checklist: timing, date of separation, custody, support, division of property, whether to use professionals to help with administration and process or employ a do-it-yourself method. If using professionals, whether to try mediation or not.

3

"We Need to Talk . . ."

It wasn't so long ago that divorce wasn't really talked about—except perhaps in lawyers' offices and in the pages of Hollywood gossip magazines. A generation back, dissolving your marriage marked you not necessarily with shame but almost surely as an object of sympathy and failure. Either way, it was a matter of "the less said on the subject the better," leaving others to assume causes and surmise details however they chose. If and when you did talk about your divorce, you probably talked nasty. Remember that divorce was universally fault-based back then. To justify the divorce, you pretty much had to hurl accusations or, at the very least, articulate irreparable injuries or unbridgeable divisions between you and your spouse.

That day is past. You don't have to solicit sympathy anymore, and you don't have to kick ass to do it. Divorce happens. And it happens a lot.

Which doesn't mean that it's now a breeze to sit down with family, friends, coworkers, or—worst of all—your children and talk about divorce. It isn't. But if there is a new set of challenges when it comes to telling others you are splitting up, there are also some powerful new tools for addressing the challenges.

Granted, the tenor of the discussion has changed radically. One of the stunning side effects of the prevalence of divorce today—and of the round-the-clock attention to celebrity divorce—is that the whole subject has become not just common but communal. There's so much divorce—among the rich and powerful, in the neighborhood, in the media, in the air—that everyone is an expert on the subject. One result is that *your* divorce, which is probably one of the most traumatic events in your life to this point, is also public property. Just about everyone you know will perceive himself or herself as a stakeholder in the dissolution of your relationship, entitled and empowered to offer advice, instruction, and insight ad nauseam.

Your divorce is and isn't public property. Yes, you want the understanding of your neighbors and the world at large. You certainly crave the support and help of your friends and family, and in due course, you are going to need to reach out to them in very material and substantive ways, as chapter 5 will make clear. On the other hand, there are at least some aspects of your divorce that you may want to keep private and personal and absolutely yours alone, or between you and your soon-to-be-ex, or at least in the family. In this you have an edge that was not available to previous generations—namely, that precisely because the subject is no longer hush-hush and no longer all about fault, you can control the narrative.

Simply put, when it comes to sitting down and telling others of your divorce—your children, family, friends, and coworkers, in that order—you are in charge. You write the script. You dictate the level of plot detail, and you define the characterizations. You also determine how, when, where, and to whom you present the account you've constructed—and how much of it you will reveal to each of those audiences.

With that power comes responsibility—actually, a twofold responsibility. Responsibility number one is to think before you speak and to weigh the impact of what you're about to say on your life and the lives of your children and other family members. The other responsibility is, as far as possible and as best you can, to do the thinking and create the narrative as a couple. Certainly, you and your spouse or partner should together determine what you will say to each audience and when and how to say it, deciding as much of this as you can in tandem at least and in harmony at best. The aim is a united front—conceptually if not physically. The one time when it should probably be both—when the two of you ought to be physically together as well as conceptually united—is when speaking to the most important of your audiences, your children. Even feuding spouses should come together at this time to achieve a united front, even if it is only temporary. In my experience, the most bitterly adversarial couples are indeed able to put aside their vitriol at this time, albeit briefly, out of parental concern for their children. Most of them, anyway.

But maybe you just cannot hack being in the same room together—even when it comes to telling your kids you are splitting. Maybe you are too angry or too disgusted or too afraid you will be unable to maintain control if you actually have to deal with each other. So presenting a physical united front is out. Still, make sure you build a united front in the script you write, and that each of you delivers the script as written. Even if you have to do the composing through intermediaries, agree on what you are going to say to your children and stick to it. Sending disparate or opposing messages to your children at this time can be downright damaging to them; allowing such damage would be simply inexcusable.

The good news is that you don't have to go into this scriptwriting exercise cold. One of the other great advantages of divorcing in the twenty-first century rather than the twentieth is that you can draw upon decades of experience, study, and trial and error about how to construct and present the narrative you control. Want to cause the least damage or disruption to people you love? Of course you do. You also want to invite the least scrutiny from all the others who need to know you are splitting up. You're in luck: There is a veritable industry of consulting psychologists, sociologists, and other experts—including family lawyers—who have learned a great deal about how to deliver this notification to achieve those very aims. And all of that information, insight, and wisdom are available to you at the click of a mouse, the end of a phone connection, or in an expert consultant's office.

This expertise is for real; that is, it works. It is why some courts, at later stages of the divorce process, will *require* the intervention of a licensed marriage and family therapist, or a trained psychologist, or a licensed custody expert. But why wait? There is no reason not to seek out this expertise at the very start of the process, and if you are particularly concerned about the effect of your announcement on any of your audiences, there is every reason to do just that.

For nothing can change the fact that telling others that you are splitting up will affect them. There's a simple reason for this: Your divorce means change for them as well as for you. Nowhere near as profound a change, to be sure, but change nevertheless. And change can bring discomfort. Much of the time, it represents loss. It is often stressful, sometimes downright scary. Different people will react to the change you're bringing them in different ways, but the one thing you can be sure of is that they will react.

Children First

BERNARD: Your mom and I, we're going to separate. I've got you Tuesday, Wednesday, and every other Thursday.
WALT, AGED 16: And what about the cat?
JOAN: The cat!
BERNARD: We didn't discuss the cat.

—THE SQUID AND THE WHALE

To no one will the change be more important than to your children; on no one will its impact be more profound. They are your most important audience, and they are the first people you tell.

Really first. You don't want them to find out in any other way, from anybody else. I know a couple who agreed to separate and decided to wait to do so until their kids' school year had come to an end. But the kids somehow caught sight of their father in the company of the woman for whom he was leaving his wife, and the sight left them perplexed and somewhat frightened. When their mother learned of it, it was left to her to "admit" the separation, which she did in the car on the way home from school as she puffed nervously on a cigarette—after having given up smoking a decade before. Nobody came out of that one unscathed.

I have heard some amazing stories about how my contemporaries learned a generation ago that their parents were getting a divorce. My friend Roger learned it at breakfast one morning when he was nine after he had a friend sleep over. "By the way," said his mother, as his father sipped coffee, "Daddy and I are getting divorced. Go out and play."

My friend Kate was twelve, the middle child of three girls, when her mother called her daughters together, sat them down, and proceeded to deliver herself of a rant about their good-for-nothing father. She had married him only for security, she told them, but since he was such a loser, she was divorcing him, and they should consider themselves lucky. They didn't. And the overload of damaging details about their father actually sent them rebounding to him in sympathy.

Try not to go to either of these moronic extremes: Don't slough it off and don't expound your grievances. And certainly don't turn the telling into yet another competitive weapon against your spouse. This moment really does have to be about *them*. The kids. The change that's coming in *their* lives. They are going to be okay—if you make it okay for them. The point is to show that you are there for them in this as in all things.

Prepare well to bring this off. The right expert or experts—psychologist, family lawyer, therapist—can help you arm yourself with advice about how and when to have this conversation with your children and about the answers you're going to need to bring to the discussion. The first question your children are likely to ask, for example, is why you're splitting up, and the truth is that the two of you may have very different views on that. Yet you'll need an answer that balances honesty with reassurance, that expresses both in terms that are pertinent to your situation and your children, and that in some way demonstrates that you're still a family. It's not so easy, and an expert may be able to help.

The right expert can also alert you to the signals to look for when you have the conversation—signals about the concerns your children, depending on their age, may not be able to articulate in words. Make a cheat sheet—bullet points for the emotional and even legal answers to the questions they are bound to ask and the concerns you intuit.

The exact content of those questions and concerns will vary, depending first and foremost on their age—that is, their level of cognitive development and coping skills. Your task may be easiest with preschool kids. Obviously, their cognitive comprehension is limited, and their coping skills are as yet minimal. They are also tiny little egocentrics. The boundaries of their world are parents and self; they need to know this will not change.

Kids in the six-year-old to eight-year-old range are a tougher nut to crack. The change they confront is likely to be their first experience of grief, and they may well feel angry about it. Also, acting out is a real possibility at this age; it's the kids' way of venting, and it's a distress signal. Pay attention to it as best you can, but certainly, with this age group, patience is a virtue.

Older kids and adolescents presumably have better developed coping skills, but grief and anger are also possible reactions from them. They tend to be focused on their own emerging identities and will likely respond to the news of divorce in those terms. I was sixteen when my parents told me they were getting divorced, and my head was totally elsewhere. I don't mean to suggest I didn't care; of course I did. But their marriage and its dissolution were the past, and I was hell-bent on my future.

But at any age, of course, divorce hurts kids. That is why the core message at any age is reassurance—that both of you will always love them, and that the dissolution of your relationship is not about them or in any way their fault. They are not to blame. Our parents lived in a more narcissistic era; they married younger and often sowed their wild oats in their thirties and forties, post-dissolution. For better or worse, we are of the generation of helicopter parents, hovering over our children and overprotecting their every move. While this doesn't mean staying together for their benefit, it is essential to handle communication with them during a breakup with grace and compassion.

At any age, kids' main concern is going to be how your split will affect them. Your split undermines their security—emotional and physical—and what they will be looking for from you is some kind of certainty: that both of you are still in their lives, that you are all still a family unit and will be such a unit forever, only in a different household arrangement from the one they're used to.

The blow to their emotional security often expresses itself in worries about logistics. Where will they sleep? Will there be a bedroom for them at the other house? Who will pick them up from school? What will be the impact on their daily lives?—whether daily life means who their babysitter is or where they will study for their SATs. All their questions deserve calm, clear answers; calmness and clarity alone can go a long way toward reassuring them and providing the certainty they seek.

Many kids worry about how they'll deal with telling their schoolmates what's happening; you might want to assure them that you will do this with them—even, for very young kids, *for* them.

The key to addressing their pain and worry reassuringly is to pay attention not just to the words you speak but to how you present yourselves as you speak them. "Careful the things you do," in the lyrics of the Stephen Sondheim song; "Children will see and learn." If you can exemplify a united front—the reassurance that the family unit persists—in your behavior both toward the children and with each other, your body language can speak for you just as persuasively as your words. Maybe more so.

Set a time. Pick the right place where everyone can be comfortable. Allow no interruptions. Turn off phones, tablets, computers, televisions—all *devices*. Keep it simple. Let it go on as long as they need it to. Be expansive in answering their questions about what it will mean for them; show that you've thought about all this, that you're concerned for them. Be honest. No mind games. No tricks. Let them know you will keep the burden off them: You will handle all the particulars; they should go on with their lives.

Don't break down; maintain control. In every way, you want to model what you are telling them—that you have it all worked out, that you will make sure everything is okay, that you've got their backs.

As indeed you do.

Then, as soon as you have told your kids, tell their teachers and the principal of their school. These are the people who have your children in their care most of the day. Alerted to what is going on, they can keep an antenna raised for any problems and will bring a deeper understanding to bear if problems surface. They are likely to have more experience with the effect of divorce on kids than you have.

When you do inform these school personnel, don't overinform them. Principals and teachers tend to be very good at being warm and endearing; it's an attribute of the profession, if not a professional necessity. The principal's office, with its cozy atmosphere and simmering coffeepot, can seem a perfect environment for letting your hair down and spilling the beans. It's not advisable. You don't need to give reasons, and doing so can come back to haunt you. All that's required is the information that you and your spouse are trying a separation, that it may affect your child's behavior to some extent, and would the school please be sure to send two sets of everything home in your child's backpack.

One more point: The thinking in general is that divorce is not great for children. Duh. One question is whether it is worse than living in a home dominated by a dysfunctional relationship. However that debate goes, it is worth noting that dealing with divorce in some ways can teach children some lessons about life's challenges and the need to confront them. Showing strength and support as a parent is therefore not just a way to help your kids get through the divorce; it may also show them something about assuming the mantle of adult responsibility—a foretaste of what is to come, one way or another.

The United Front, Part 2

That you are now and always will be a family is a legal fact, a social reality, and, except in cases of adoption, a matter of biological inevitability. That's the point that you need to make to your kids, not only when you sit down and tell them you're splitting up but in every bit of follow-up. Forever, actually.

One of the smartest moves I ever saw a divorced couple make involved a client of mine, one partner in a marriage that had produced three children, all in the preteenage cohort when the divorce took place. Once the papers were signed and the divorce was final, the whole family went on a trip together. Actually, it was a whiz-bang safari to some of the most famous game parks of eastern Africa, one of those once-in-a-lifetime experiences that probably all parents dream of sharing with their kids—and vice versa. Everything about the trip was focused through the family lens—except of course that there was no romance between the parents.

But the message was clear, and it was branded onto the brains of all the participants: This is us; we are a family, a unique and special configuration with a unique and special body of experience to our name, and whatever our living arrangements, the configuration does not change.

I can recall a similar experience in my own case. My family—mother, father, younger brother, and I—were all together on a family vacation in the summer when my parents sat us down and told my brother and me that they would divorce. As I mentioned, I was so caught up in my own self-importance—and had certainly intuited over time that their marriage was not perfect—that I took the news pretty well. When I look back on it now, I can well imagine the concerns both parents must have felt at the time, but their unshakably united front gave no clue of their own worries, and the very fact that we were together on vacation emphasized the reality of our family connection.

That united front never cracked. In fact, I remember that a few years later, when I was, as I considered myself, a terribly sophisticated college student in New York City, I got a phone call one day from both parents. Although each had by now repartnered, they had arranged a conference call to let me know that my kid brother had gotten himself a tattoo—and to solicit my insight and advice about an act that to them seemed unorthodox to the point of freakiness. Their worry was palpable. How could he do such a thing? Scarify his own body like that! Was he acting out? What did it mean? Did I think it was because of the divorce—in other words, had they caused this bizarre behavior? I was smiling to myself as I assured them that neither the divorce nor they themselves were the issue here. Rather, he had gotten the tattoo because he was fifteen. What they saw as bizarre behavior was, I assured them, a fashion statement in high schools all across the country. In fact, it was a very cool thing to do.

Yet in making this phone call together as a united front, my parents actually were assuring *me* that at whatever remove legally or geographically, we were still a family. I got the message and never forgot it. It makes all the difference in the world.

Family

With that one exception—teachers and principals—your next announcement of your impending divorce will be to the next people closest to you, presumably your parents, in-laws, siblings, or other family members.

How and what you tell your parents and your in-laws—and whether you tell them together or each of you tells your own parents—will depend entirely on the personal dynamics of your existing relationship with them. This can go any number of ways. Take the case of a woman I'll call Jenna. When her unfaithful husband, father of their two kids, confessed that he had also impregnated the woman he had sworn to Jenna he would stop seeing, she told him to get out. She also demanded that *he* break the news to *her* mother. Whether this was because she simply couldn't face doing so herself, or as punishment to him—her mother liked him enormously—I don't know. Nor do I know how the conversation between husband and mother-in-law went, although I would dearly love to. But he took his medicine and dealt with his mother-in-law face to face.

Because of course the crux of the matter is that announcing the divorce is in no way the end of things—not when children are involved. Jenna's mother and Jenna's ex-husband were forever inextricably linked through the two grandchildren. Yes, he was an adulterer and a lousy husband, but Jenna—and her mother—were still going to be connected to him for the rest of their respective lives. Ditto for any split-up involving children: Blood is thicker than water, and the attachment is forever. Future graduations, first communions, bar/bat mitzvahs, weddings, etc. are at stake, and any or all of them can sink under the weight of family animosities.

Maybe Jenna's insistence that her husband spill the beans had merit; perhaps she sensed that if she went "home to Mom," so to say, and did the spilling, she would tell too much and engender too much anger in her mother for relations ever to be civil again. Of course, when both of you tell the parents and in-laws, each of you can serve as a check on the other and as an encourager of sticking to the script you've decided on.

That script should aim for just enough information to persuade your folks that the split-up is the right thing to do and that you're both committed to it—without divulging details that will plunge them into depression or push them into bitterness. Remember that your parents feel about you as you feel about your children, and take it from there.

Friends

Your closest friends probably already know that your relationship is troubled. Whatever the circumstances, they have no doubt taken your side in what they regard as something of a war. In this war, they have probably already provided significant support to you and feel themselves well armed to see you through to final victory.

Let them know it's treaty time. And let them know why. Partisanship is fine, but from this point forward, you would like them to focus their partisanship on your family as a whole.

It cannot be said too often that what is best for you—what will most help you move on to the next phase of your life—is an amicable, cost-effective dissolution of the relationship. And nothing will make that tougher to achieve than a pitched battle between your friends and your soon-to-be-ex. When they run into him or her at the market, when your friends see your ex with a new love at the restaurant everybody goes to, they need to tamp it down, keep it civil, and remember that as friends to you and your children, they too need to move on.

At Work

Remember the scene in *Crazy, Stupid, Love* where the guy comes into Cal's (Steve Carell's character's) office and says, with a big smile, that when a coworker "heard you crying in the bathroom, we all thought it was cancer. But thank God, man! It's divorce."

"Yeah," answers Cal, "it's just my relationship."

Sobbing in the men's room is probably not the best way to alert coworkers that your marriage is over. And in fact, there are people at work who know little enough about your personal life now and don't need to know anything at all about the fact that it is changing. Certainly, you will want to alert any colleagues who have become friends—and any for whom a change in your marital status may be an essential piece of information.

That would be your boss, for starters, and the human resources department, if you work in a company big enough to have one.

Telling your boss is both a courtesy and a wise move. It is possible that as the divorce proceedings go forward, you may need to take off work to meet with a lawyer or a mediator or a custody consultant. Your personal schedule is likely to change as your living situation changes, and the way forward may be a bit bumpy until the situation stabilizes. A boss in whom you have confided is likely to be tolerant or even supportive of all this—at least up to a point.

Human resources will need to know because the change in your legal status may change your tax status, which means payroll will have to adjust its procedures, and/or your group health plan status. HR can take care of all that. Moreover, many companies offer various programs that can help you through some of the difficulties coming up as part of their benefits package—therapy covered under your health plan, a company support group of other divorced or divorcing employees, coping workshops, and other services. It couldn't hurt to check in to these programs.

But as with all the audiences you reach out to in this matter, the great difference between your divorce and your parents' is that you're in charge. You control whom you tell and what you say. It's a definite advantage over the past, and it's a powerful tool for helping you to deal successfully with your split-up and move forward in your life.

IN BRIEF

In the twenty-first century, as never before, the parties to a divorce write the script of how their relationship's dissolution is to be announced, explained, presented to others. That gives you both a responsibility to consider carefully what the script should say; above all, you should consider it together, as a united front—one story and one only.

1. In creating your script, you have almost limitless resources to draw on for assistance—experts in psychology, sociology, childcare; therapists; counselors of every sort. It makes sense to reach out for this assistance as needed.
2. In announcing your divorce to your children, it's essential to assure them you are and always will be a family, that this is between the two of you, and that both of you have their backs.
3. After telling your children, tell their teachers and the principal of their school.
4. In announcing the divorce to other family members, keep in mind that through your children, you will always be connected to these people.
5. Ask your friends to abandon (or at least keep to themselves) any bitterness they may feel toward your ex; that is the way they can best help you ensure a smooth process and advantageous resolution.
6. At work, let your immediate boss and your organization's human resources department know that you are in the process of getting divorced.

4

Separating

The day he moved out was terrible—
That evening she went through hell.
His absence wasn't a problem
But the corkscrew had gone as well.

—WENDY COPE, *"LOSS"*

Here's where it really gets real.

Separating is what divorce is all about, isn't it? It's what you intend: each of you going your separate way, linked together no longer. That is the human reality you're aiming for, but separation is also the core legal reality in the dissolution process, distinct from any physical distance you and spouse may or may not put between you. And the way you go about effecting this legal separation will determine the course of the dissolution process to come.

Chances are you've broken up before. Back in high school, you could say good-bye to the love of your life by having a good cry and handing back the various tokens of affection. Later, in college or graduate school, splitting up meant trying hard not to argue over which books or albums or CDs belonged to whom as you both exited the rental apartment and moved on. It was all pretty transient. No ties. No roots.

This is bigger, and it's tougher.

Here, you're dissolving not just a relationship but a family household—a social and economic unit with its own history, its own dynamics, its own shape and sound and style. It's a unit anchored in a community in which you formed part of a circle of other couples and were linked with a network of friends and neighbors.

You know all this. You have wrestled with the arguments and the wrenching emotions and have made the decision you know (or hope) is right. But given the central role this relationship has played in your life, no matter how bad it has become, and given the intensity of the feelings, pro and con, you have felt for your spouse or partner, the act of separating is nevertheless a little like cutting off a limb. It's a jolt that is likely to turn much in your life upside down and inside out, and you'll get it through it better if you're realistic about what's coming.

You'll also get through it better—both of you—if you vow to show each other consideration. Even—or especially—if consideration was lacking during the marriage, it will be de rigueur now. Indifference to or disdain for a partner's schedule, job, privacy, or personality quirks can be costly; inevitably, it will come back to bite you in the final agreement on money or custody or both. For everybody's sake, this is the time to do what you perhaps found so difficult during the marriage—communicate openly and regularly, respect each other's thoroughly irritating behavior, and, within reason, accommodate each other's foibles.

The Legal Thicket

Like just about everything having to do with divorce, the legal terms of separation—indeed the very definition of what constitutes separation—are jurisdictional and therefore vary by state. In your legal separation, you will want to protect yourself in terms of division of assets and debt liability, ensure an equitable custody and visitation arrangement, and get clarity on financial support—in effect, the same assurances you will seek in a final divorce settlement, but with the understanding that this is a separation and you are still legally joined. If that sounds easy, it often doesn't work out that way.

It was a lot easier back when our parents' generation separated; all they had to do was follow the norm. Based on well-worn assumptions about gender roles and on fairly tired social norms, the typical narrative said that the breadwinner—virtually always Dad in those days—would move out of the house, get himself what was routinely assumed to be a swinging bachelor pad with shag carpet and lots of brown and beige furniture, and sign a lot of checks for alimony and child support. On alternate weekends, he would zoom over to the house he had paid for and more or less honk his horn for the kids, whom he would then treat to two days of high-intensity fun events and lots of sugar-packed snacks and soft drinks while they sat in front of the TV, not to mention a string of complaints about how much of his hard-earned money he was paying "for your mother to just sit around." Revved up but exhausted, the kids would be deposited back home on Sunday night. Home, in turn, was the unquestioned precinct of Mom, to whom was assigned the full-time role of custody of the children and housekeeping—jobs considered her sacred duty and just what every woman wanted to do with her life. Although now, she inevitably did them for less and complained that she was simply not appreciated or getting enough help "from your father." The separation—and, more often than not, the divorce that followed—would rubber-stamp that paradigm and make it official.

If you've ever known any of the kids who experienced that kind of arrangement, you know that it wasn't a great way to grow up, and that both father-child and mother-child relationships suffered as a result.

Fortunately, those days are long gone. Today, within basic requirements for custody and care of children, no one is simply assigned a particular role. Both of you have the power to design your own roles and to create a separation arrangement that can meet both your needs—not just for protection of your rights and delineation of your responsibilities, but also for control over your destiny, for affordability, and for keeping your sanity and dignity intact while of course ensuring the best for your children.

In other words, you have choices, and each choice available to you will produce a different effect—possibly, a cascade of effects—depending on the jurisdiction and on your particular situation. For example, how does your state actually define "separation"? Is it enough to file a petition for divorce? Does separation mean you are no longer having sexual relations? Does it mean one of you has left the premises you shared as a couple? Suppose one of you wants to separate and other does not; how is separation defined in such a case?

What about money? In most states, signing a separation agreement draws a line; from the date of separation forward, everything each spouse or partner earns or creates belongs to him or her alone. What might that mean if the two of you decide to go to therapy together, not necessarily to reconcile but just to ease the separation process? Or suppose that after meeting together about custody, the two of you decide to have a glass of wine together, then another, and maybe a third. You grow sentimental, and you find that out of habit or through some other inexplicable force, you have fallen into bed together. Does the fact of your sexual intimacy hit the reset button on the date of separation—and is everything either one of you earned since the agreement now up for grabs in the property settlement?

Actually, the answer to that is yes, and it's pretty much exactly what happened to a client of mine. Separated for nearly four months, he and his ex had scheduled a joint meeting with their child's fifth-grade teacher to discuss ways to help the child through the divorce. This is precisely the kind of encounter that legally does *not* qualify as being-together time as a couple; that is, even with both spouses present, the time spent focused on the child is carved out as distinct from a "being-together activity." Being-together activities would include dating each other, or having sex, or seeing a therapist because you might reconcile, or anything else that smacks of the possibly getting back together or in any way "living together." But being together because you're doing something jointly on behalf of your child does not qualify as that sort of being-together activity.

The session with the teacher about easing the divorce for the kid was useful and encouraging, leaving both my client and his ex feeling rather warmly toward each other. So when the ex said she would love to see the new apartment he had rented and to check out the kids' rooms there, he was agreeable. Once there, it seemed natural to have a five o'clock glass of wine, as they always used to, and pretty soon, one thing led to another, and before you knew it, there they were—in bed.

Where the soon-to-be-ex-wife, as it turns out, used her smartphone to videotape the sexual encounter that took place there. Yes, Dear Reader, it had been a setup, and my client fell for it. The consequences? She was able to argue—successfully—that their sexual intimacy gave her a reasonable belief that the marriage was not irremediable and that they were still married. It meant that everything about the separation up to that point was wiped out; the clock had to be rewound and reset, and the four months of "separation" were recalculated as time spent being married. In a state like California, where the length of time of spousal support and the assessment of community property correlate proportionally to the length of time of the marriage, that proved to be very costly to my client.

And remember the family back in chapter 2 with the husband who moved out and onto a rented houseboat but came "home" every Sunday to have dinner with his kid and get his laundry done in the washer-dryer he had paid for? He and his wife never had sexual relations once they separated—in fact, there was a new woman in his life—but the Sunday dinners went on for years. When the couple finally got around to drawing up a financial settlement, the judge ruled that the Sunday routine gave reasonable belief that the two were *not* separated, which meant that everything the husband had earned in those years was considered community property jointly owned by husband and wife and to be split down the middle in the divorce.

It was a highly technical ruling. The husband's lawyer could and did argue that the Sunday visits represented time spent caring for the couple's child, time which, again, represents precisely the kind of togetherness in the name of child care that never "counts" as time together. To that judge, however, the regular Sunday routine—the afternoon with the kid, dinner for all three, and the wife doing the laundry—qualified more as "living together" than as "caring for the child," and it was that assessment that informed his ruling. And not all states are clear that once a couple is separated, the income earned is separate property. I know of one Utah-based pro skier who separated from her husband, proceeded to have her winningest season ever, and then saw the income from that season at risk of being considered joint property.

Nuances upon nuances, effects and aftereffects. Which is why I recommend that the first step in separating, before anyone has moved anywhere, is to consult a lawyer. From here on out, every decision you make is going to have consequences—some of them unintended—that will affect your future and the well-being of your children. Family law is the topography you must navigate in making those decisions, so now is the time to find the right lawyer to be your guide as you do the deciding.

We'll talk more about how to select the particular lawyer who is right for you in chapter 6. Suffice it to say here that you want an advocate for your interests and an expert who will inform you with sufficient information, insight, and advice to keep you in control of the process—starting now.

Most divorcing couples feel the same. This is the moment in the process when I and my colleagues in the family law field get the most phone calls asking for a meeting. Invariably, the question everyone asks is: "Should I move out?"

Separating Means Separating

Just as invariably, my answer is: "Yes—if you can." The reason is simple. Going from being two to being one is not easy. It takes some getting used to, and it requires some adjustments in habit and attitude. The sooner you can begin to know how that feels—what life will be like when the decree is finally granted—the better off you will be. It's important to be realistic about this.

Ending your marriage or partnership means no more warm body beside you at night—and no more quiet pillow talk. It means that when the kids are home with you, you are the sole evaluator of their behavior, the sole enforcer of rules, the sole adjudicator of disputes, the sole arbiter and judge of what is best for them or what they should do. Or, when the kids are with their other parent, it means a house that will seem eerily quiet and empty.

One of the things I never gave any thought to was my former partner's delightful habit of getting up early, going to Peet's, and bringing me a twenty-ounce latte in bed every morning. When we split, it was disappointing to realize: No more coffee! I suffered mightily through the first couple of weeks of getting two little boys up, dressed, fed, and out the door; obviously, I couldn't go out for coffee with all of that to do, and putting both boys in the car for a coffee run, there and back, seemed a Herculean effort not to be attempted without caffeine. Finally, a friend, tired of listening to me lament my misfortune, bought me a coffeemaker as a gift. What a revelation! Everybody is happier. But the point is that these are the things you don't think about, the adjustments to the small things that are really the fabric of life.

Maybe one of the things about your spouse you found unbearably annoying was the way he or she played fast and loose with the various sections of the newspaper, with no respect for logic or order. But at least he or she knew which article in the politics section you ought to read and what to do when you began your usual rant about Congress or the state legislature. You're on your own now;

there's no one there when you start fuming about today's editorial or the latest from Washington.

You'll want time to get used to all this as you are going through the process of dissolution, and having one of you move out means you can begin to understand what it will feel like to live alone—and to gain that understanding without your soon-to-be-ex in your face all the time. It beats going through the process "together" and then suddenly facing the cold, hard reality of being absolutely alone.

So having one of you move to another place, if possible, is certainly my recommendation, provided that three things are agreed upon: a schedule laying out exactly how you will manage custody of the children, another defining living arrangements vis-à-vis the jointly owned house in which one spouse continues to reside, and conditions of financial support.

One more thing: You have to really separate. I've split that infinitive precisely to emphasize the thoroughness, the seriousness, the sheer factualness of what moving out is all about. A case in point will illustrate, because the move-out was neither thorough, nor serious, nor particularly real, as it turned out, and the result was chaos.

When this particular couple decided to separate, they agreed that the husband would move out. The problem was that nobody quite knew where he had moved to. He seemed to flit in and out of his children's lives, showing up sporadically at his ex-wife's like one of those twinkling fireflies that illumine summer evenings in the eastern part of the United States. The metaphor is not inappropriate; it turns out Dad was sleeping on the trampoline in the backyard. In fact, his older son thought he saw him out there a couple of times. Needless to say, this "separation" played havoc with just about all aspects of the separation agreement and the ensuing divorce mediation.

Separating means separating, and moving out means entering into or establishing another household. That's the point: One household separates into two. Three legally defined agreements spell out just how it will work.

The first agreement, if you have children—if not, skip to agreement two—is the custody schedule, aimed at giving everybody, and above all, your children, a reliable schedule of time together. "Reliable" is the key word here: If Dad moves out but everybody knows that he will be back Tuesday, Wednesday, and Thursday mornings to make breakfast for the kids and take them to school, that establishes a routine and sets a pattern of normalcy—two essentials for reassuring your children that this divorce does not equal the end of the family. It means the kids know there will be time to gripe to their father; it means their father knows he will be part of the all-important discussion about what they're doing in school, which is the center of their lives. When it's your ex's turn with the kids and he's coming to the home, make yourself scarce. Don't hover; go to the gym or to Starbucks. It's your ex's time, and for custody to work, you need to get out of the way. But it all needs to be spelled out in an agreed-upon schedule that is clear to all. Clients often ask me what happens if they mutually agree not to adhere to the schedule. The breakfast police do not come to your home; you can certainly agree to whatever revisions are okay with you both. Keep in mind, though, that your original, filed custody agreement is a fallback and can be used by either of you if your agreement not to follow it becomes unworkable.

The second agreement defines ground rules for the use of the house from which one partner has moved. Just because you're still helping to pay the mortgage and still have a key to the front door does not entitle you to show up whenever you feel like it. That is disruptive to the lives of the spouse and children still living in the house, who need some guarantee of what the law calls "exclusive use and possession." Both partners should agree either on a schedule of times when the house is "open" to the departed spouse or on a procedure for making an appointment to visit the house at times other than those scheduled for custody visitations—or both, of course.

Finally, both of you—with the help of your lawyers—need to set forth exactly who pays for what during the separation. This can be a knotty issue—and a ticklish one. The rule of thumb is that the status quo lifestyle should be maintained as much as possible in the home in which the children reside—i.e., no big falling-off in the standard of comforts and conveniences to which they are accustomed. If you can afford to keep things as they were, you ought to. If separation means financial separation—i.e., my paycheck is all mine from here on out, and yours is all yours—the at-home spouse may find it difficult to maintain that status quo on a single income. If the departed spouse was the main breadwinner, he or she may find it difficult to try to maintain two establishments. It can all be costly as what was once a family treasury is stretched to its limits or beyond. That is why it is so important to run the numbers, see where you stand, and agree on how this separation is to be funded.

Again, I cannot stress too much how important communication and consideration are at this point. On all three agreements, being open in your discussions and respectful in your manner can save you money, time, and a significant amount of *angst*.

Your lawyer will refer to these three agreements as stipulations for interim custody, interim living arrangements, and interim support, although you can roll all of the agreements into one interim stipulation if you like. You will sign them and file them with the court, and they of course become legally enforceable.

But it is not always possible for one spouse to move out. As noted, it simply may not be affordable. Or, one or both of you may be afraid that if you move out, you give up your rights to the house and even your shot at fifty-fifty custody of your children. It's not true, but it can be a chilling thought. Fortunately, there are other ways to separate.

Same House, Separate Spaces

A 1989 movie, *The War of the Roses,* based on the book by Warren Adler, offered an acidly amusing, black-comedy version of what can happen when neither spouse in a dissolving marriage wants to move out of the house. With Michael Douglas and Kathleen Turner as the combative couple fighting—literally—over every material possession in the house, the result is that the two spouses pretty much destroy everything they're fighting about. Point taken, and it can and does happen that way. But it doesn't have to.

For one thing, you can take steps to get an unwilling spouse out of the house—short of actually accusing him or her of domestic violence. It is called a kick-out order, and it is sort of a combination restraining order and eviction notice. In most states, you can ask for such an order on your own, without having to confront your spouse in court, but you must allege that you're worried about possible abuse of yourself and/or the children.

This is a tough call. I had a client whose ex-wife was so desperate to get him out of the house that she beat herself up with a telephone handset in front of their child and then took photographs of her bruised face in order to have "evidence" of abuse. That's a long way to go both ethically and emotionally, but it certainly shows the level of desperation that can be reached when you try to separate in the same place.

The only possible preventive for such a dire circumstance is to set boundaries in the shared domain—establish borders, define time limits, create regulations for behavior, and articulate protocols for changing the rules if needed. Who gets the master bedroom? Who gets the master bathroom? Who is supposed to be with the children when, and where should the other one be during those times? You may need to establish schedules for control of the family computer, the TV remote, the sound system. You may want to devise rules about whether or not you can bring a date into the house, if one or both of you is seeing other people. What about weekends? Guests? Quiet times? Who feeds the dog, and does the feeder also walk the dog? All the details of living together that you once took for granted now have to be parceled out between you in order to avoid chaos and recriminations. Yes, you can set all this down in legal terms, sign the agreement, and file it with the court to ensure that it is enforceable, and it is advisable that you should do so.

Any way you slice it, separating while living under the same roof is difficult. But with a set of rules—and of course with ample doses of open communication and consideration for each other—it is eminently doable.

Nesting

Nesting is an arrangement that didn't even exist when our parents' generation was getting a divorce, or if it did, there wasn't a name for it; it's mostly a twenty-first-century invention. What it means is that the kids stay home and both parents move out, each one taking a turn visiting the nest and being at home with the children.

To save money, many couples share a single alternate residence, rotating in and out according to the custody schedule. For example, each spouse might do a week on—i.e., be in the nest with the kids—and a week off, then every other weekend on. Or it might be a Monday-Tuesday plus the weekend one week, then a Wednesday–Thursday plus the weekend the following week.

The hard part about this style of nesting is the parents' sharing of the single alternate space. Even if you're not there at the same time, it requires a particularly high level of consideration and respect for the other's privacy. For example, if you're dating, it might be best to do so at your date's home, not at the shared space your soon-to-be-ex-spouse will be returning to in a day or so when it's your turn to move in with the kids. You'll also need to look out for each other's personal items—books, papers, toiletries, used condoms. In a way, it's no different from when you were a couple and shared a space, except that you are in the process of uncoupling, so particular care should be taken.

If it's affordable, two alternate residences are obviously a lot more convenient and a lot more private. Another option is for one to find an alternate residence and the other to bunk with a friend or family member. Either way, nesting is a practical alternative. It's hard to prove convincingly that it succeeds, as is often claimed, in mitigating the disruptive impact of the separation on the children. There is something to the fact that the kids don't have to move. Backpacks, homework, favorite blanket, beloved stuffed animal, essential hair accessory all remain at the family residence.

How Nesting Works

Take the example of a typical family; let's pick a name out of the air and call them the Seavers.* The parents, Jason and Maggie, have split, and both have moved out, leaving their three kids, Mike, Carol, and Ben, in the home they grew up in. The need now is to codify how the coparenting will operate under this arrangement, and the solution is a schedule for sharing custody of the kids that gives both parents equal access to their children and equal time with them. This is what they worked out:

RE: Marriage of Seaver

Effective forthwith, the Seavers will begin exercising their custodial time pursuant to the following schedule:

I. Maggie will have the children, Mike, Carol, and Ben, in her custody and control on Mondays, Tuesdays, alternate Saturdays, and every Sunday beginning at 6:00 P.M.

II. Jason will have the children in his custody and control on Wednesdays, Thursdays, Fridays, alternate Saturdays, and every Sunday until 6:00 P.M.

III. During the time each parent has custody of the children, that parent may use the residence. Each will vacate the residence after dropping the children off at school at the end of his or her period of custody and control.

---

* With apologies to *Growing Pains,* the sitcom that ran on ABC television 1985–1992.

IV. Holidays

A. The parties will alternate Monday national holidays from Monday at 9:00 A.M. until return to school on Tuesday mornings. Jason will have Veterans Day, Presidents' Day, and Labor Day in even-numbered years and Martin Luther King, Jr.'s Birthday and Memorial Day in odd-numbered years. Maggie will have Veterans Day, Presidents' Day, and Labor Day in odd-numbered years and Martin Luther King, Jr.'s Birthday and Memorial Day in even-numbered years.

B. The parties will alternate Thanksgiving, with Jason having them from Wednesday after school until Friday morning in even-numbered years and Maggie having them from Wednesday after school until Friday morning in odd-numbered years.

C. Winter Break: The parties will alternate Christmas Eve from 3:00 P.M. on December 24 until noon on December 25 and will equally divide the rest of Winter Break. Maggie will have the first one-half of Winter Break in even-numbered years and the second half of Winter Break in odd-numbered years, and Jason will have the first one-half of Winter Break in odd-numbered years and the second half of Winter Break in even-numbered years.

D. Spring Break: The parties will equally split Spring Break and will alternate Easter Day. Maggie will have the half of Spring Break in which Easter occurs in even-numbered years; Jason will have the half of Spring Break in which Easter occurs in odd-numbered years.

A Coparenting Rehearsal

However you configure your separation, keep in mind that it is an important training ground for the coparenting that will characterize both your lives once the divorce has been finalized. In this as in everything, being considerate is the key strategy for success.

The other day, I was suddenly summoned to a meeting requiring an early flight from Los Angeles to San Francisco and therefore a 5:30 A.M. departure from my house. While my older son was with his father, my younger son was home with me, and there was no way his nanny could adjust her own schedule to arrive that early at my place. A couple of frantic calls to favorite babysitters also didn't work, so I called my son's father and asked if he could spend the night in my guest room and get Jack up and fed and off to preschool the next morning. It was an imposition, a deviation from the custody schedule agreed upon, and altogether out of order. But it was also something of an emergency. Fortunately, he was able to take it on, and he did, most graciously.

But I am painfully aware that this must qualify as an exception—an extreme measure the likes of which I can only resort to when there really is no other alternative. The "co" part of coparenting is always a work in progress—*co*operation, *co*nsideration, *co*mpromise—but the one absolute is that you both have your own lives now—your own circle of friends, your own schedule, your own commitments to other people and to yourself. The separateness that comes with separation is not to be tampered with; it has to be respected.

The essential way to think about it is to remember that the person from whom you have separated is no longer your backup. That automatic reserve in the fuel tank, the personal default recovery person you took for granted and counted on more than you ever realized—as babysitter, chauffeur, carpooler, gofer, delivery person, light-bulb changer, coffee-bringer, private Internet search engine, excuse-maker, liaison to your parents, and more—is not available anymore. This is precisely what being separated means.

You now need to create your own list of babysitters and carpoolers, to deal with your parents yourself, to run your own errands, and in general to find new ways to handle all those domestic, workaday, logistical circumstances you once addressed in tandem with your ex. There's a poster you see in a lot of corporate break rooms: "Clean up after yourself," the poster says. "Your mother isn't coming in today."

Neither is your ex. You're on your own. The period of separation is a good time to start rehearsing how that will work. It will probably feel difficult at first—for both of you—but I can assure you of this: It gets easier. In time, in fact, it all falls into place.

Doing It Right

After yet another fight—this one over the custody schedule—Matt retreated to the apartment over the garage, leaving the living room to Jane. The tiny apartment was a blessing, despite the frequent odor of diesel fumes from their old pickup truck down below, because the state of their finances meant that neither of them could afford to either rent or buy a new place until everything was settled. After Matt had been in the apartment for the usual cooling-off period, Jane called him on his cell phone. "Are you calm? We need to finish this talk."

"Agreed," said Matt.

"Why don't you come on back into the house?"

"Okay."

It was spring and quite warm in Montrose, an inland area of Los Angeles County far from the glamor of Hollywood and the mansions of Beverly Hills, and as usual, Matt was barefoot as he started down the staircase on the side of the garage. Ouch! Something sharp bit into the underside of his foot. Ouch! The other foot. Ouch! The next step down. And the next. And the next. It was too dark to see how to thread his way among the tacks Jane had scattered, with some care and with obvious purpose, on the steps. Matt tripped and fell, rattling his way to the bottom. He was bruised all over, and he was furious. He was still shouting when the cops arrived—in response to Jane's 911 call—and hauled him off. The local police prided themselves on their sensitivity to potential incidents of domestic violence.

As events proved, this is not a good way to start a separation. The satisfaction Jane derived from her infantile action was fleeting; Matt, whose fury had turned to a cold thirst for vengeance by the time he was released by the cops, retaliated with equally infantile "punishment," delaying every step of the proceedings and fighting over every penny. The incident thus blighted the entire process of dissolving the marriage, adversely affecting both spouses financially and poisoning every necessary interaction between them for years to come, thereby repeatedly damaging their children. For one cheap moment of drama, they had freighted their separation—and subsequent divorce—with unnecessary complications and an unsavory atmosphere.

It's a stupid as well as a destructive way to proceed because finding your way to a separation agreement, written or oral, with or without lawyers, is in my mind the really hard part about divorce. If you can manage it gracefully—with consideration, by communicating openly, and by showing respect for each other—you can save yourselves grief, time, and a great deal of money. The beneficiaries of those savings are your children, to be sure, but also yourselves and the separate futures on which you are about to embark.

IN BRIEF

In the twenty-first century, both parties have the power and the tools to create a separation agreement that can meet the needs of both of you. Done right, separation can serve as a rehearsal for civil, courteous coparenting in the future.

1. Consult a lawyer. Divorce means dissolving a legal reality; it starts with the act of separating.
2. Move out if you can.
3. Stipulate separate agreements or a single agreement covering interim custody—giving your kids a reliable routine of time with both parents; interim living arrangements—establishing rules for the use of the residence; and interim support—determining who pays for what.
4. If you are sharing the domain, create an agreement establishing boundaries and rules of behavior.
5. Specify precisely the schedule and rules of a nesting agreement.

5

Breaking Up Without Completely Losing It

You don't have to go through this alone. Nor should you.

No one would ever argue that divorce is anything less than a stressful experience at best. The emotional ups and downs can leave you reeling. The first Saturday night the kids spend over at your ex's place is downright tough; you're anxious about how the children will deal with it, and you're worried about yourself. An empty home can be an echo chamber of misgivings: Is this your life from now on? Will all the Saturday nights to come be this grim and lonely? Was this the wrong move after all?

No—to all three questions—but it may take time before you're convinced of that, before you feel again that you are the protagonist of a life story that really is turning the page to a new chapter.

Right now, you're a human being who feels hurt, sad, anxious, bereft, angry, resentful, frightened, stressed, all of the above, and more. The very fact that you are splitting up from the person with whom you have shared the most powerful intimacy—the person you assumed would be your soul mate and closest friend for life—is argument enough for reaching out to others. So it's not surprising that the first thing you look for is emotional support—comfort, caring, someone loving to hold your hand and tell you that everything will work out okay and, by the way, you still look hot.

The mistake is to assume that emotional support is the only kind of support you need. It isn't. However difficult your partnership had become, however alone you may have felt as part of a couple, and however much you may be looking forward to being free and on your own, cutting the ties of this relationship and untangling its intricacies can be a knotty process. It is a process that takes place in at least three spheres—legal, financial, and social. All three have their separate requirements and characteristics, and all three can stir those battering emotions. Even if you consider yourself the world's most rational and competent human being, the best organized, the most highly disciplined, it's still the case that there are a lot of decisions ahead, a lot of judgment calls to make, a lot of information to find, share, understand.

In such a situation, another pair—or pairs—of eyes and ears, another perspective on things, another fact from another person's experience to supplement and complement your own thinking can lead to better thinking, better judgment, and a better outcome.

And here's the good news: A generation's worth of expertise and experience in all aspects of this process—divorce, custody, financial support—is available to you. Thirty-plus years of legal decisions, reams of research on the impact of divorce on children and families, legal settlements addressing every possible permutation of family configuration and answering every conceivable form of human quirkiness are out there—an almost bottomless well of resources to draw on to help you think clearly, make the right judgments, and obtain the kind of settlement and achieve the kind of outcome you want. Take advantage of these.

Of course, helping you through all this is, to a great extent, your lawyer's job. But as we'll discuss further in the next chapter, one of the great differences between divorce a generation ago and divorce now is that today's generation doesn't have to—and is unwilling to—cede control over the process to an attorney. Your lawyer may and will advise; the decisions are yours. That is why it is wise to seek other sources of input and additional layers of support as you go through the process.

You already have one ready-made support group; it's called your family and friends, and you will need them now. You need their comfort and reassurance. They represent a universe in which you can be temporarily free of your worries and your hurt, where you don't have to watch what you say, where you know that everybody is on your side. That's the great upside of this ready-made support group: Family and friends are reliably partisan. They love you and want you to be happy and will jump through hoops to make that happen.

The downside of the family-and-friends support group is that they are reliably partisan. They love you and want you to be happy and will jump through hoops to make that happen. That often means they'll parrot back to you the resentments you have just expressed, agree with every argument you offer, second every goal you set, confirm your fears and fantasies. In truth, relentless partisanship may not at times be quite the help and support you need. Sometimes, taking sides isn't the point. And sometimes efforts to make you happy may obscure the picture or put off a reality you need to deal with.

Of course, you want and need the sheer comfort of family and friends. But you also need the kind of realistic objectivity that will empower you to get on with the matter at hand and resolve it in a way that is going to be best for you and your children. That is why looking outside the tight circle of your nearest and dearest is a good idea and one I highly recommend.

Helping You Think

My first recommendation is to find a professional therapist or counselor you can talk to. I know: Therapy is the standard American "fix-it" answer to everything. It has become so automatic a position that it strikes lots of people as just another cop-out. To others, going to counseling is an admission that you have a psychological or emotional problem, and that you're incapable of solving it on your own. Both reactions are somewhat facile, and neither is quite true.

We've already discussed the importance of counseling if there is a chance of saving your relationship. It is also important once you know you're going to be on your own. Some people are reticent to start from scratch, so you might inquire whether your joint counselor, if you liked him or her, would be willing to see you alone. Or, a referral and introduction from your joint counselor could be helpful.

The reason to seek counseling from a professional therapist is to give yourself an objective interlocutor—someone with no ax to grind—who can help you separate wheat from chaff as you ponder the many issues you're about to deal with. At the same time, this interlocutor is trained and seasoned in helping people in your very situation channel their raw emotion into concrete ways to achieve the best possible outcome for themselves and their children.

Of course, this is a time when you need to vent and be heard, and you probably don't need to pay someone just to listen. But why not vent to and be heard by someone with the expertise and experience to respond meaningfully and helpfully? That is the difference a professional can make. Just about every therapist or counselor or social worker is practiced in dealing with people going through failing relationships, ending them, and confronting issues of custody and support. They've heard myriad versions of these problems, and they've helped others work through them. They can suggest solutions that have worked for others and may work for you; they can offer ideas you may not have thought of. Even the most expensive therapist tends to be less expensive than a lawyer, so in addition to everything else, seeing a therapist is a cost-effective way of sorting through your own attitudes and thinking on these key issues—way cheaper than hashing it out in court.

Moreover, of course, therapists have been trained specifically to treat the stress and worries you're going through and to help you confront the anger, loneliness, fear, and all the other emotions roiling you at this time. In your therapist's office, you can lose it—burst into tears, explode in anger, hurl venomous obscenities, sob with self-pity, call your ex every name in the book because that is exactly what he or she deserves. In fact, it is far better to do any or all of that in front of your therapist rather than in a mediation session or in court or in a conference with the lawyers. It will do you no good whatsoever there, with your ex present; in fact, it might harm your case. But your therapist's office is a safe haven, a cone of silence; what happens within those four walls stays within those four walls—by law. So it is a good place to spew forth all the spleen and sorrow you need to release with all the drama you can muster—drama that in a legal setting would only raise the confrontational temperature and conceivably send a settlement back to square one.

And then of course, your therapist will help you deal with the sources of the sorrow and spleen and put to rest some of the demons of your personal drama.

I offer no specific suggestion as to what kind of therapist to see—apart from suggesting that it be someone with a license to practice and someone with whom you feel comfortable. Most of my clients have gone through some sort of counseling by the time they retain my services—either as part of trying to heal their relationships or of working out how to end them, or both. The range of fields of expertise they've taken advantage of runs the gamut from psychologist to psychiatrist to social worker to marriage and family counselor and more. True, my clients are in Southern California, a hotbed of therapies, therapists, and people accustomed to seeking professional counseling. But there are therapists the world over, and certainly in every town and city in every state. Check the yellow pages, ask at your local hospital or health center, or search the Internet.

There are also innumerable ways to pay for therapy and options that make it affordable pretty much across the board. A number of insurance plans continue to provide coverage for this important aspect of health. If yours doesn't, an Internet search will surface the local social service organizations that subsidize this kind of care or will link you to specific practitioners who offer affordable rates. If you have no Internet access, a phone call to the local hospital or health center should elicit answers.

Intermittently and irregularly, I go to a therapist. Doing what I do for a living is stressful and at times, it can get me down a bit. An unyielding opponent or parties who do not heed my advice can be frustrating and depressing. Being a coparent with the two separate fathers of my sons also has its pressures, and while I may be an expert in legal issues, the law doesn't cover everything going on in those relationships—not by a long shot. I think of the therapy the way people think about gym workouts or jogging or any defined exercise routine to which they're committed—as a way of maintaining my best self, a way of keeping my mind and emotions fit for the rigors of the somewhat unusual situation in which these men and I do our level best to do right by our children. It is extremely helpful to know that such help is available and can be relied on.

Helping You Through It

I just ran an Internet search on "divorce support." In less than a quarter of a second, my preferred search engine returned 81.4 million links. That was global, so I thought I'd try something more restricted. I picked a midsized state, searched "divorce support Kentucky," and in less than half a second got 2.3 million links. That doesn't mean there are more than two million divorce support groups in Kentucky, but it does mean that it won't be hard to find a link to one near you just about wherever in the state you live.

These days, in fact, the Internet is your portal into a treasure trove of what are known as divorce "resources"—everything from Divorce Source Radio to the annual Divorce Expo, with keynote speakers, seminars, and a marketplace where the newly alone can shop for financial services, self-improvement products, spas and personal trainers, singles resorts, meet-up groups, and other products and services aimed at helping them either succeed alone or get together with someone else.

It is all too easy to chuckle over the in-your-face bluntness of such initiatives, but there's little question that the people who have started them—and the people who are surfing the links right now—are on to something. Call it the cluster effect: People in a certain boat want to go where other people in the same boat are also going. In the case of dissolving the central relationship of their lives, people may feel an isolating sense of shame or failure. It's not a subject they are comfortable discussing with the happily married or successfully coupled among their friends and family, so they are understandably eager to reach out to others who have done it before or are in the process of doing it now. Maybe, they figure, they can learn an easier way to get through it or a better way to handle it or some tips on how to feel less lousy about everything. Maybe someone else's experience can shed light on their own, if they can get someone else to share that experience. It's what so many of my clients have said to me at the end of the process: "If only I had known at the beginning what I know now."

It's an extremely good idea to try to know it early on—and to try to learn from those who have gone through it or are going through it at the same time you are. And it may not be necessary for you to run a global or even a statewide search to find the right support group for you. There may be one in your neighborhood or in the wider community. Odds are that you are not the only parent of your children's friends who is going through this. Nor are you the only member of your book club, the only person in your workplace, the sole dog owner at the dog park—you get the picture—who is splitting from your partner or spouse and would love some company. Ask around. When you drop your kids at school, ask the other parents. *Ask* your fellow book club members, your colleagues at work, the other dog walkers.

If that doesn't work, put up a sign: "Looking for a divorce support group. Please call this number." Post it wherever people will see it—the library, the community bulletin board outside the supermarket, houses of worship, the gas station, the post office. Chances are good you'll get responses.

If not, or if the group you find does not seem amenable, start your own. The marketing term for this is an "affinity group"—a fancy way of saying people sharing a similar experience. Again, post a sign where it will be seen—how about the courthouse where the family law judges exercise their jurisdiction? Do you want a support group composed on the principle of "the more the merrier," a group inviting anyone and everyone who may be dissolving a relationship? Or do you want to circumscribe the terms of your affinity group a bit more, defining it in terms of shared identity or a particular issue or emphasizing a particular theme? For example, maybe you want to limit your group to people over forty, or to men only, or to working mothers, or to people who want to talk about custody issues and nothing else. If that's what you're looking for, articulate the particular kind of affinity you want in your description of the group.

Some years ago, I found myself with seven clients who shared two things in common: They were all young men with young children and they were all seeking custody of their children—all going through the same thing and confronting similar issues as they contended with that particularly vexing issue. I brought them together in a group and turned over the firm's conference room to them one night a week. Their discussions made them, among other things, better clients; in hashing out the issues and their concerns together, and by bouncing ideas off one another's minds and experiences, they were able to clarify their thinking, and that gave me more options and a stronger foundation to make their cases for them.

Their group sessions helped each of them. Each was undergoing an experience that was unusual in the community he lived in; each was, in a sense, an anomaly within his surroundings. The conference room sessions gave them acceptance, comfort, camaraderie, and sympathy as well as the practical benefits of legal solidarity. The seven also quickly became a network, providing babysitting for one another, going on joint excursions with their kids, and exchanging mutual aid when it came to various household functions. They became and have remained friends—well into second marriages for some and ongoing single fatherhood for others. A shared need prompted the bonding. But it was the unfolding discovery that they were not alone and the realization that each had something valuable to offer that got them through the experience of divorce and their fight for custody. The clear result, for all seven men, was a better outcome in court than they might otherwise have obtained.

The Flip Side

Of course, there is always the chance of an unwanted accompaniment to all this support—namely, bad advice or a skewed perspective or a really bad idea. The only protection from this is to be careful, which is easier said than done given the typically vulnerable condition of many people reaching out to others for help. In a sense, that vulnerability makes you an easy mark, even if—perhaps especially if—the other person really is trying to help. I cannot count the number of occasions on which I have been second-guessed by a client reiterating to me what he or she was told by "a woman at a cocktail party." Going beyond the fact that this relationship likely formed when both parties were inebriated, nine out of ten times, the woman was not a family law practitioner. So I do not care what she had to say.

Therefore, as you would in any other endeavor in which you are seeking information or counsel, assess your source, don't believe everything you hear or read, and take what people say with a grain of salt.

To assess your source, you need to go to it—directly. Maybe it's the lawyer in me, but hearsay—second-, third-, or fourth-hand information—just doesn't cut it. If your yoga instructor's cousin's second wife reportedly went through the same thing you're going through, get her number and ask her about it yourself. Then you'll be able to discern just how close the similarities are and to probe for details that may pertain to your own situation.

For heaven's sake, don't assume that because you found it on the Internet, it's accurate, true, or trustworthy. I am not even referring to the fact that the Web is a well-known gathering place for every kind of fringe lunacy and every disappointed rejectee with an ax to grind. I mean it rather in the sense that if a search engine finds it, and if it has a solid-looking logo, and if it carries a ponderous-sounding name, it must be an unimpeachable source. It ain't necessarily so. It may well be an unimpeachable source, but it may also be a quickly hatched marketing scheme for attracting "hits." Few things are easier these days than putting together a logo and fancy name.

When friends, acquaintances, and coworkers rush to tell you what they think or what they've heard, wariness is warranted. Whispered confidences, even from the most well-intentioned soul mate, are no more profound because they are whispered—or because they come from a soul mate. Somehow, you'll need to filter out the feverish piffle, and the best way to do that is simply to keep your eye on the prize, which is to get through this process with as little confrontation as possible and to emerge from it with your mind, spirit, wallet, dignity, and children safe, sound, and whole.

The process of dissolving a relationship has a way of undermining trust. Yet where advice and counsel and the experience of others are concerned, this is a time when it's particularly important that your trust antenna remain sensitive. The help of others is a good thing; it can be important to achieving the outcome you seek and to keeping you whole as you go through the process. But you'll need good judgment about where, how, and from whom that help is forthcoming.

IN BRIEF

Divorce requires thinking and deciding about legal, financial, and social issues. Don't hesitate to seek the support of those who can help.

1. Your lawyer will educate you in the law and how it applies to your situation. This is invaluable support, but remember that you must control the process.
2. Family and friends offer essential comfort and encouragement, but their partisanship should not obstruct the need for objectivity.
3. A therapist who can respond meaningfully and helpfully to your concerns and your emotional turmoil is invaluable.
4. The world is full of divorce "resources"—most of them accessible online—and it can also be helpful to join or start a support group of people going through the same thing you're going through.

6

Lawyering Up

Everything in this book is about you taking control of the dissolution of your marriage or partnership. Control is the great difference between the split-ups couples had to settle for a generation ago and the kind of divorce that is possible today. Yet as liberating as it is to be able to exercise control, it also imposes a high level of responsibility and demands no small amount of effort. Yes, you have the chance to play an active role in getting the settlement you seek and the outcome you want. But as with any activism, it will take work.

Pro persona representation—pro per, as we call it, which is acting as your own lawyer—is a viable option if the issues are simple. There are several Web sites available that enable litigants to represent themselves. For example, LegalZoom has an excellent three-step divorce program. If your divorce is more complicated, however, you may need an attorney.

I have represented a number of celebrities. These are often the folks who would just as soon have their assistants do it for them. It only takes one telephone call or meeting for me to make very clear that such an approach will not yield them the best results. Nor is it the manner in which I practice my profession. If you are going to be the master of your own destiny, you really have to show up.

Being master of your own destiny actually keeps going after you've hired a lawyer. For one thing, your lawyer needs your help. Nobody knows your opponent as well as you do. Second, essential as the attorney's role is in taking you through the process, it is still up to you to set the ground rules. Ground rules mean, first, what you as a partner and parent want to achieve for yourself and your kids, defined in terms of realistic expectations for a lawyer to pursue. It's up to you to lay those out articulately and clearly. Ground rules also mean that when you have decided to fight tooth and nail to keep the Tiffany sterling silver picture frame that holds the wedding photo of the marriage you are trying to dissolve, your lawyer will stop you. That is not a battle you should be paying a lawyer to wage—it is not a battle worth waging—and a good lawyer will so advise you.

When our parents divorced, they looked for a lawyer who could be a combination of pit bull, therapist, and maybe even golf partner, wingman, or date to the club social. No more. In today's no-fault environment, inspiring fear in a courtroom is of little value and less efficacy; the aggressive snarling of the killer litigator is out of place in this generation of dissolution. Even the no-compromise issues, like a move-away custody case, must be handled delicately and with grace. Meanwhile, if you've followed the recommendations in chapter 5, you have your own therapist by now—or some equivalent kind of counseling—and don't need to spend billable attorney hours getting therapeutic counseling from somebody who went to law school. As for friendship: no. You're hiring a professional for a business transaction that you hope will be completed with dispatch; no one wants the dissolution process to last long enough to qualify you and your lawyer for eternal friendship.

Similarly, when our parents hired a lawyer to handle their divorce, they turned the whole thing over to him—it was usually a "him"—with no questions asked and no stipulations imposed. That leave-it-to-Daddy attitude is out of touch today. You're probably not comfortable ceding control of anything to anyone—from your children's education to your health to your financial investments. Why would you relinquish control of the legal proceedings that will shape your family's future?

You won't, of course. It means that not just in choosing who will represent you, but also throughout the process, you will want to stay on top of the situation—partly out of vigilance to make sure your lawyer isn't keeping things from you or going off in unheard-of directions, partly because of those ground rules: You set them, and you owe it to your lawyer to monitor them. It's pretty simple really: If you're not willing to take control, you have little ground for complaint if things don't turn out right for you. Besides, control is one of the most powerful tools there is for achieving an amicable and cost-effective dissolution.

So what are you looking for when you sign up a lawyer to represent you as you end your marriage or partnership? A problem-solver, an advocate, an expert advisor on the law and on your rights and responsibilities, a strategist, a negotiator, and a litigator. That is the package of skills required; among the pool of qualified lawyers available for you to choose from, there will be undoubtedly be different levels of experience and success. You will therefore need to spend time and mental muscle doing some research and sifting through your choices. Go with your gut on this, and know your audience.

The Short List

Advice is rarely in short supply when people know you and your spouse are splitting. Friends flock to you with recommendations as to the lawyer you must choose or the one you must stay away from, both sets of recommendations being heavily larded with tales of huge settlements achieved or total disaster suffered by a friend of a friend of a friend. It's usually easy enough to go to the source—that is, to the friend of a friend of a friend—and ask him or her what in fact happened. How close was the settlement to what the person wanted? How long did it take to get to it? And does the person think it was because of the lawyer that the settlement turned out so well—or badly—and happened in such good time? How did the person's attorney handle him or her? How did the attorney handle the other side? A practitioner who is well liked by peers is always a plus. Still, even as you drill down for information and assessments, keep in mind that every case is different, every divorce is individual, and that what you want when the process is over may be very different from what others were seeking, whether they were perceived to have won or lost.

It may be better to solicit referrals—although preferably not from parents or best friends. Remember: They are not objective, and they're probably angry, and anger is not a good starting point for a business transaction. Instead, ask your banker, your accountant, your financial advisor, your therapist—professionals who in the normal course of doing business may naturally interact with lawyers, who have your best interests at heart, but who have no skin in the game themselves.

It is also possible to go "cold calling" online or in the local yellow pages. Lawyers and law firms are listed as a matter of course in telephone directories, and they also buy advertising space in which they elaborate further on their skills and practices. You can also apply to your state's or even a specific city's bar association as well as to the American Bar Association (www.americanbar.org) to find listings of lawyers near you. And you can check the ratings of lawyers you're tempted to put on your short list in such third-party directories as Martindale-Hubbell (www.martindale.com) or The Best Lawyers in America (www.bestlawyers.com).

But be aware of this important fact as you surf the Internet or the reference section of your local library or your phone book: Family law as a distinct practice is limited primarily to large cities in the most populous states. Miami, Los Angeles, New York, and (oddly, given its size) San Francisco have sizable family law bars, but in much of the rest of the country, family lawyers are general practitioners who handle other kinds of civil litigation as well; their profiles are likely to read "traditional client representation and litigation." This means that they are equipped to bring a range of different kinds of lawsuits but may not be completely conversant with every recent development in family law practice. Not to worry. They will be completely conversant with the judges who preside over family law cases and, precisely because they litigate a diversity of cases, they will be well experienced in representing clients at the bar.

There is a professional association for family law practitioners. It is the American Academy of Matrimonial Lawyers (www.aaml.org); it is a highly respected membership organization, and it is a fine place to find information and news about family law as well as about family lawyers.

All this checking and counterchecking of referrals should help you whittle the names down to a short list of local possibilities.

With the reference work assuring you that the lawyers on your list are at least experienced in dissolving marriages or partnership relationships, and with the personal recommendations of that friend of a friend of a friend or of your banker or broker or therapist, you're ready to make a few calls.

The Call

The purpose of the call is to get an appointment to meet with the lawyer in his or her office. Certainly, it is possible to consult on a preliminary basis over the phone, but I highly recommend an in-person consultation in which both you and the lawyer can judge your chemistry and comfort levels as well as how good you both are at asking and answering questions. With many lawyers, the consultation is free, but a good many others put a price on it. Partly, they do so as a matter of course—time is money, and lawyers' hours are always billable—and partly, it's a way of filtering out the nonserious. Don't be put off by it; just be aware that there may be a fee.

In many law firms—again, in mine, for example—you will be routed first to a gatekeeper before an actual lawyer gets on the line. In my case, it's my secretary, who runs a brief but fairly substantive screening process. She will take down basic information like your name, your spouse's name, how long you've been married, how many kids you have, where you are filing your case, and the like. The screening process runs a quick check of our database to make sure, for example, that your spouse didn't phone us a year ago and come in for a meeting in which confidential information was relayed; that would mean I couldn't represent you. Remember the famous episode of *The Sopranos* in which Tony's putative new neighbor, a slimy lawyer if ever there was one, advised him to make appointments with all the top divorce lawyers in North Jersey so Carmela wouldn't be able to find legal representation? It worked, too; and in a later episode, she freaked out at this further evidence of Tony's controlling ways. We watch out for that sort of thing in this initial screening process.

You'll want to ask some questions, too. First, you'll want to know if this lawyer even does preliminary consultations; some do not. Then, you'll need to find out if hiring him or her is in your financial ballpark—not just the fee for the consultation, but the retainer you'll be asked to pay if you go ahead and hire the lawyer and the hourly rate that will be drawn down from that retainer. You'll want to know the standard retainer fee, the terms—for example, is the fee refundable if you reconcile or under other circumstances?—and whether the fee will be paid by you, your spouse, or the two of you out of a joint retainer account. How does the billing work, what increments of an hour are used to set the rates, and do you see a detailed billing statement every month? Finally, you'll need to be sure the lawyer has room in his or her schedule to give your case the attention it warrants. If you're calling in May and the lawyer has a full docket of cases that will tie her up until November, that's probably no good. On the other hand, if she's wrapping up her current caseload and will be taking new cases in a couple of weeks, that would probably work. But keep in mind that this is someone you're engaging to change your life in a substantive way. Your schedules and agendas really do need to mesh.

If it all adds up, schedule an appointment.

The Consultation

You have ahead of you a difficult, possibly long, certainly life-changing process to go through. Is this the person you want piloting the process and representing your interests in a negotiation? That's the question you need answered in this face-to-face meeting.

To do so, you must first articulate in your own mind what is important to you—the expectations you have, the outcomes you're hoping for—so that you can ask the questions which draw out the lawyer's reaction.

Yes, some of it is going to be chemistry. Does the lawyer put you at your ease? Are you comfortable talking with him or her and specifically, are you comfortable asking questions? Do the two of you click?

You can find out a lot about whether or not you click as you seek hard answers to some specific questions. For example, one key fact to elicit is the lawyer's settlement rate versus his or her litigation rate. In other words, what percentage of this lawyer's cases end up before a judge and what percentage get settled through negotiation?

How does the lawyer feel about collaborative law, in which the parties basically give up the threat of litigation and agree to work out a settlement through any of various alternative dispute resolution processes? If the lawyer does mediation, how does it typically work—with a retired judge or with a mediator? With the lawyers present or just the couple?

In answering your questions, is the lawyer perhaps condescending or dismissive? Alternatively, do you find her or him too intimate, pushing for friendship when what you want is a professional who will do the job?

Does he or she strike you as well organized, as someone who won't waste time? That's essential when they're on the clock and you're paying by the hour. Will the lawyer himself or herself be handling things, or will matters be handed off to a lower-billing associate? In my office, as is standard, there are usually at least two attorneys assigned to each case. While I will oversee my cases, attend depositions, and make court appearances, some of the preparation work, discovery, and day-to-day client contact is handled by an associate who bills at a lower rate.

And perhaps above all, is the lawyer listening to you? Are his or her answers true responses to what you have to say, or do they seem practiced boilerplate that have been repeated a million times?

You have the right to ask personal questions—whether the lawyer is or has ever been married, whether he or she has been divorced, whether he or she is a parent. I always speak a little about my personal situation—that my parents were divorced, that I have been divorced, that I have two children from two different dads, neither of whom I was married to and with whom I share custody and coparent. It's not easy, I'm the first to admit, but we have figured out ways to make it work. I do this not to sell myself but to let the prospective client know that I probably have a good idea of what he or she is going through and am likely to recognize the concerns expressed.

Of course, a lawyer needn't have been through a divorce or shared custody to be capable of recognizing your concerns; you should be looking not for an equivalent experience on the part of the lawyer, but for a sense of common understanding of your circumstances and your feelings.

Taking Control

The Harriet Buhai Center for Family Law is a social service project cosponsored by the Black Women Lawyers of Los Angeles, the Los Angeles County Bar Association, and the Women Lawyers Association of Los Angeles. Its mission is to protect victims of domestic violence by providing free family law assistance and legal education to those unable to afford it, thereby enabling them to exercise their right of meaningful access to the courts. I volunteer at the Center, and my work there has demonstrated that divorce is the great equalizer. Regardless of the number of zeros behind a client's net worth, all feel a similar fear, anxiety, and heartbreak regarding the ending of their partnership. Like my wealthy, high-profile clients, the low-income clients we help at the Center must participate in the process and take the helm of their own cases.

Except in a few cases, we don't represent the Center's clients in court; rather, the assistance we provide is to teach clients, for many of whom English is a second language, how to fill out the required paperwork and how to go into court and represent themselves. This is of course more cost-effective, but it is also more productive and more beneficial. Simply put, understanding the process—knowing their rights and recognizing what's possible and what's to be expected—empowers these clients. They already know what their case is; learning about the law and how to navigate the system equips them to make their case. And if they have to go back to court later to modify a custody or support arrangement, they're ahead of the game. Been there, done that, know the ropes, don't have to hand the future of their families over to someone else.

The same is true when you have the best lawyer you can find and are paying that lawyer handsomely to pilot you through the dissolution of your marriage. The better you understand the process your lawyer is going to take you through, the better you can make that process work on your behalf. No lawyer is as invested as you are in the outcome; it makes no sense simply to turn the process over and wait for the results.

Believe me, it's also much more helpful to the lawyer if you are actively involved and energetically engaged in the process. Nothing helps a lawyer help his or her client more than that client's ready and regular participation in every step of the divorce proceedings. My constant request to my clients is to give me all the information you can. Supply me with lists. Pester me with names and dates and times. Overwhelm me with data via e-mail, fax, and text—although preferably, make sure it is organized and identified. The more actively engaged a client is, the better the job the attorney can do on that client's behalf—for less money, in less time, with a better shot at achieving the kind of settlement the client wants.

There are few things you can do for yourself that will be more important than finding a lawyer you are comfortable working with—and then staying on top of the process every step of the way.

IN BRIEF

In seeking a lawyer, you are looking for an advocate, an expert advisor on the law and on your rights and responsibilities, a strategist, a negotiator, and a litigator. But remember: No lawyer is as invested as you are in the outcome of your case, so it is necessary to become and stay involved in the process; that is also the best help you provide to your lawyer.

1. To find a pool of lawyers from whom to choose, solicit referrals from other professionals you know or deal with—an accountant, banker, business leader. Check out bar association listings as well, and don't neglect Internet research.
2. In a preliminary fact-finding consultation, determine the lawyer's fees, terms, and schedule availability.
3. An in-person meeting is worthwhile, even if you have to pay for it, to explore the lawyer's record of achieving settlements via mediation/negotiation vs. via court proceedings, to get a feel for the lawyer's manner, and to see if there is chemistry and a sense of comfort between you.

7

Custody

Dad hates Mom. Mom hates Dad. It simply makes you want to be so sad.

—KURT COBAIN

This is the tough one.

First, it's tough on the emotional level. No one has ever asked a parent to be objective about his or her children, and no one expects you to be objective as you confront the fact that ending your relationship with their other parent will have consequences on your kids' lives. Subjectivity, however, can be a force for good where custody issues are concerned—that is, if the subjectivity translates into being at all times on the side of your children and acting in their best interests. What you want to watch out for is the kind of subjectivity that spirals down into anxiety or tips over into anger toward your ex, neither of which will do your children or you any good at all.

Which brings us to why custody is so tough on the practical as well as the emotional level. On the one hand, you and your spouse or partner are at odds and are splitting. On the other hand, on the issue of your children's custody, you are trying to find agreement and act as one. Your aim, whether you admit this to yourself or not, is to remain a family even after you have broken the central relationship that formed the family in the first place. To put it charitably, a certain amount of tension is inherent to that situation.

That is why it is so important that you confront one very central fact of your life going forward—namely, that through your children, you are inextricably bonded to the spouse you're splitting from. Apart or together, you both have the responsibility as well as the right to ride the ebbs and flows of the parent-child relationship. So until your kids reach legal majority, you and your ex will need to deal with each other in some way, shape, or form on every issue affecting them—their schooling, where and how they spend vacations, why and when and how they're disciplined, their health, if and where they go to college and how it's paid for, where and with whom they spend Thanksgiving and all other relevant holidays year after year after year after year.

You and your ex are also likely to run into each other at a range of rites of passage. You'll both attend such coming-of-age fetes as first communions, bar/bat mitzvahs, *quinceañeras;* you'll both have seats of honor at graduations; and presumably, you'll both attend your children's weddings. In fact, chances are you will have to plan and perhaps pay for such celebrations jointly. You are likely to be cograndparents one of these days. That you share this joint interest for the rest of your lives is something to keep in mind as you think about the custody agreement you will draw up and then have to live with. If you can infuse those arrangements with consideration fueled by civil communication, both of you, not to mention your children, will be better off.

Fortunately, today's style of divorce offers numerous ways to do that. A generation or so ago, children of divorce still typically lived with their stay-at-home mothers and saw their fathers on alternate weekends—and maybe for dinner one or two nights a week. And the truth is that the children of those divorces generally did not have a good experience growing up. I was an exception; although I am the child of that generation's style of divorce, my experience was about as good as it can get. That experience has always informed my legal practice, and I have to say I think it equips me particularly well to guide today's divorcing parents toward a better experience for their kids.

But remember back in chapter 4 when I said that even if you had never shown each other consideration during your marriage, the moment of separation was the time to start? That goes doubly when it comes to custody. Keeping in mind that as equal parents, you're in this custody arrangement together for your lifetimes, and acting accordingly, can make all the difference in the world to your children.

Custody Defined

First, let's distinguish between legal custody and physical custody. The former refers to the authority to make decisions about out-of-state travel, religion, health, academics, welfare, and the activities in which your children participate. The latter is the actual hands-on time a parent spends with the child or children. Both legal and physical custody may be awarded jointly to both parties or to just one of you. But as a matter of right, no matter who you are, or the size of your wallet, or however smart or foolish you may be, you have an equal claim to custody of your child or children. (The exception is a parent shown to be unfit or incompetent by reason of condition—i.e., mental disturbance or some other complete inability to deliver care—or behavior. That is the only "disqualifier" for parenthood the law recognizes. Believe me: No less than once a month does a prospective or current client call me with his or her own diagnosis of the spouse as bipolar, manic-depressive, schizophrenic, or psychopathic. Unless one is institutionalized, the state is unlikely to declare your spouse unfit, so let it go. Court-ordered counseling, rehabilitation, monitored visits, etc. are far more likely. Judges want children to experience both of their parents, "crazy" or not. But unfitness is beyond the scope of this book.)

In other words, you can have not a penny in your pocket and be the biggest jerk in the history of the world, and you still have the right to custody. Or, you can be divorcing someone with not a penny in his or her pocket who is also the biggest jerk in the history of the world, and there is nothing you can do about it. He or she, by virtue of being the other parent of your children, has just as much *right* to custody as you do. I like the way the Keanu Reeves character put it in the movie *Parenthood*: "You know, Mrs. Buckman, you need a license to buy a dog, to drive a car—hell, you even need a license to catch a fish. But they'll let any butt-reaming asshole be a father." And I'm afraid the same is true for being a mother. That's the reality; get used to it.

And in practice, in fact, joint legal custody is today the norm, so both of you are almost certain to have to share equally in making the basic decisions about your children's welfare and how they spend their time.

Where physical custody is concerned, joint custody is also quite common, but it is not uncommon for one parent to be granted primary custodial care, and there are still cases where one parent has sole physical custody, with the noncustodial parent awarded only visitation.

Not surprisingly, it is not always all that easy to know where one form of custody ends and the other begins, or to make the two forms mesh seamlessly. The result easily becomes another point of stress in the tension of the joint custody situation. Officially, the sharing of legal custody means you both have the right to determine the activities your kids sign up for—and are therefore both responsible for those determinations. Typically, however, one parent or the other signs the kids up for karate, soccer, ballet, and the zillion other extracurricular activities kids get involved in. That means that the *other* parent either has to spend part of his or her custodial time taking the kids to their activity, or the kids will miss the activity. Not so great. Try telling your child that he can't play in the all-star game because you have planned for him to attend Aunt Edna's ninetieth birthday celebration that day. Expect a major tantrum followed by an epic sulk. And you may have to go back to the drawing board with your ex.

That is why the core issue in physical custody is figuring out the schedule—the amount and arrangement of custodial time "awarded" to each parent. In most courts today, the presumptive starting point is a fifty-fifty split, something that wasn't even on the radar a generation ago.

But fifty-fifty is *just* the starting point. It, and everything else having to do with custody, are negotiable, and everything negotiated in a custody arrangement is modifiable. So it should be, because conditions and circumstances change. Employment status can change, finances can change, marital status can change, children's circumstances as they grow up can change (the sweet gap-toothed six-year-old you had when you first split is now sixteen and a half, constantly asking to borrow the car, was found with a fake ID and a six-pack of Heineken last month, and definitely needs to be spending more time at Dad's). Even people's minds can change. New situations may require new arrangements and a return trip to court—or preferably, consultations with each other—for new negotiations, new decisions, and a new custody schedule. For better or worse, what you and your spouse agree to now as your custody plan is not incised in marble; you have the power to introduce changes to it if and when you feel change is needed.

With that in mind, how should you start to create a custody arrangement and establish a coparenting schedule?

Figuring Out the Custody Schedule

First, it's important to understand that two core values must be accommodated in such a schedule and incorporated into the agreement drawn up. One core value is the recognition, affirmed by the courts, that both parents need to be present in the lives of their children. Again, this was not always the case. In an era when the social norm was the working father and stay-at-home mother, it was simply assumed that children were "better off," as the phrase went, remaining with the full-time mother at home while the working father footed the bills and saw his children more as a visitor than as a parent—the chairman of the board sweeping in for a few intense moments before being swept out again. That model has long since fallen by the wayside. Today's social norm, buttressed by reams of sociological and psychological studies, embodies the idea that each parent plays a distinct role in a child's development, that those roles complement each other, and that both are essential. The vast majority of people have two parents; having both participate in the lives of their children, if willing and able, is seen as better for the children, and by the way, it is better for the parents, too.

The second core value to be accommodated in a custody schedule is that the shuttling back and forth between these two essential presences in their lives can be disruptive to the children. It is by definition unsettling to go from one home to another; it is time-consuming; it can be confusing.

In fact, this is one reason why specific standards about proximity are written into a separation agreement. Even at a minimum of disruption, kids of divorce can spend a lot of time in cars. A client of mine recently felt lucky to find a wonderful house to move into just a couple of towns away after he separated. But what is a piece-of-cake distance as the crow flies is a nightmare in Los Angeles traffic, so my client spends a lot of time tuning in to the latest traffic reports and worrying about whether or not he is going to get his daughter to school on time; to say the least, it detracts from their "quality time" together. And it's why in Los Angeles as in many jurisdictions, anything more than about thirty miles, which can easily represent an hour in the car, is the outside limit a child can be expected to travel between parents without mutual agreement or a court order.

Compounding the potential disruption that travel between the two homes can cause are the logistics surrounding all those pieces of paraphernalia attached to kids, paraphernalia that changes frequently but seems to expand with age. Baby gear is actually relatively easy to consolidate, and it's something you as a parent control. It's when kids start to get their own stuff that the problem becomes an ordeal, especially because they tend to scatter their stuff hither and yon. Making sure they have the right items with them can be an organizational muddle—the right shoes, the American Girl doll of the moment, the correct stuffed animals, the essential cool hoodie or de rigueur sports team jersey, etc., not to mention the various electronic devices kids plug themselves into and/or need for homework. Yet these items give children a sense of home; they are totems of stability, uniform emblems kids rely on to reassure themselves of the constancy of family life. Paying attention to them is therefore a critical requirement for both parents as they work out a custody plan. Don't just think you can buy two of everything. iPad minis are expensive, and wait until the first time both of them end up at Mom's.

Informed by these core values—the need for both of you to be engaged in your children's lives and the equal need to minimize the disruption this might cause and establish a stable routine—your aim in drawing up a custody schedule is to maintain the status quo. That is what is best for the kids, and it is also what the court is going to want. So step one is to figure out the status quo, which is something you have almost surely taken for granted. I recommend that you begin to keep a schedule of the time each of you spends with the children. When you do, I think you'll be surprised at the pattern that emerges. The truth is that most of us think we spend far more time with our kids than we really do, so figuring out what is real provides a good reality check.

Do this before you separate if you can, but keep it up during the separation. Chart the frequency and amount of the time each of you spends with the kids: how often the departed spouse comes to visit or the kids go to the other parent's house and the nature of those visits or stays. *Had kids for sleepover . . . Ex took kids out to dinner . . . Kids and ex visited his parents . . .* etc. And monitor how the children respond to it and the impact on their lives. Then you can begin to create a workable schedule. If it happens that what works best for your kids is also what's convenient for you, that's the best possible solution, but the best interests of the kids come first.

This isn't to say that "fairness" should not be a consideration in drawing up a custody schedule; it should be. To the extent possible, the obligations—of both work and other responsibilities—and indeed the preferences of both parents should be accommodated. But again, the first priority is fairness to the children, and that is certainly how the courts see things.

Fairness does not include the proposition that a nonworking parent is entitled to more custodial time than a working parent. It is a dubious proposition to begin with: Not working doesn't necessarily mean the parent is spending more time carrying out the custodial task. I know a number of divorced parents who spend more time with their personal trainers and their lunch companions than with their children; in those cases, it's the nanny who is carrying out the custodial care. In any event, the law will not penalize a working parent; equal rights mean equal rights.

This cuts the other way, too. That is, just because you don't have a job doesn't mean that you're automatically "hired" to assume the bulk of custodial care. This is an issue that comes up a lot over what is known as the right of first refusal, which is written into most of the judgments I get involved with. Right of first refusal simply means that if it's your custodial time and you suddenly have to be out of town overnight, your ex gets first crack—the right of first refusal—at taking over care of the kids that night. Only if your ex can't or won't take the kids, for whatever reason, do you hire a sitter or arrange for alternate care. Yet in my experience a lot of parents—and I have to say, fathers in particular—get annoyed or worse when their ex-wives say no to this. There's still that sense that it's the mother's job to be available to her children—and in this case to the convenience of their ex-husbands—at all times. "Pretend she's dead," I tell these dads. "Don't expect her to pick up the slack when you have something else to do."

One final important note about drawing up a coparenting schedule: Some people assume that the more time they can get with the children, the more money they will be awarded in support. Or, from the vantage of the higher-earning parent, the fear is that the less time with their children they are awarded in a custody schedule, the more support they will have to pay. But it really doesn't work that way, and it is in no way worth worrying over or trying to negotiate. The financial difference is minuscule—not nearly enough to fight or even fuss over. And the fact is that you spend money when your kids are with you, and money is a different issue to be settled under a different rubric, as the next chapter will make clear.

The custody schedule of course needs to be appropriate to the age or development level of the children involved, and the schedule almost surely will change over time as your children grow older. A typical schedule when children are younger and therefore cannot be away from either parent for too long and have fewer regularly scheduled activities is what's known as a two-two-three. A sample of the two-two-three is the kids spending Monday and Tuesday with Mom, Wednesday and Thursday with Dad, and then Friday through Sunday with Mom. Then it flips: Monday and Tuesday with Dad, Wednesday and Thursday with Mom, and the weekend with Dad. And so on.

The two-two-three often morphs into the two-two-five when the kids are older and have their own schedule of soccer practice, ballet class, playdates, and other after-school "obligations." A sample of the two-two-five would be spending Monday and Tuesday with the mother, Wednesday and Thursday with the father, then alternating the "backs" of the week—i.e., Friday through Sunday with Mom one week and with Dad the next week.

Another typical schedule alternates entire weeks, so that each parent has a week "on" and a week "off" with the children. Or the kids stay with one parent Monday through Thursday and with the other Friday through Sunday, and they reverse the pattern every six months. That's a schedule that's becoming less common—parents don't like not having their kids over the weekend—but it works well for some, and it does change every half-year. And in some cases, the old traditional schedule from generations ago still works, especially with very young children: The weekdays are spent with one parent at the main home, and Saturday morning to Sunday night with the other parent, who also may visit the child or children one or two evenings during the week. As the children get a little older and start school, the definition of the weekend expands; it begins Friday after school and ends Monday morning when the kids are dropped off at school again.

Here are some typical custody schedules. Again, I've taken the liberty of drawing on families familiar to many of us from television sitcoms—the Huxtables of *The Cosby Show,* the Winslows of *Family Matters,* and the Arnolds of *The Wonder Years.* I mean c'mon, did you ever consider what would happen if any of those perfect TV families split?

July 2013

HUXTABLE FAMILY CUSTODY
2 - 2 - 5
Minor Children: Theo, Vanessa & Ruby

	Sunday	Monday	Tuesday	Wednesday	Thursday	Friday	Saturday
Jun 30 - Jul 6	Jun 30	Jul 1	2	3	4	5	6
		CLAIRE		CLIFF		CLAIRE	
Jul 7 - 13	7	8	9	10	11	12	13
	CLAIRE			CLIFF			
Jul 14 - 20	14	15	16	17	18	19	20
		CLAIRE		CLIFF		CLAIRE	
Jul 21 - 27	21	22	23	24	25	26	27
	CLAIRE			CLIFF			
Jul 28 - Aug 3	28	29	30	31	Aug 1	2	3
		CLAIRE		CLIFF		CLAIRE	

July 2013

HUXTABLE ALTERNATE CUSTODY SCHEDULE
2 - 2 - 3

	Sunday	Monday	Tuesday	Wednesday	Thursday	Friday	Saturday
Jun 30 - Jul 6	Jun 30	Jul 1	2	3	4	5	6
		CLAIRE		CLIFF		CLAIRE	
Jul 7 - 13	7	8	9	10	11	12	13
		CLIFF		CLAIRE		CLIFF	
Jul 14 - 20	14	15	16	17	18	19	20
		CLAIRE		CLIFF		CLAIRE	
Jul 21 - 27	21	22	23	24	25	26	27
		CLIFF		CLAIRE		CLIFF	
Jul 28 - Aug 3	28	29	30	31	Aug 1	2	3
		CLAIRE		CLIFF		CLAIRE	

May 2013

WINSLOW FAMILY CUSTODY SCHEDULE

Week on/Week off -- Monday 3 p.m. to Monday 8 a.m.

Minor Children : Eddie, Laura & Judy

	Sunday	Monday	Tuesday	Wednesday	Thursday	Friday	Saturday
Apr 28 - May 4	Apr 28	29 CARL	30	May 1	2	3	4
May 5 - 11	5	6 HARRIETTE	7	8	9	10	11
May 12 - 18	12	13 CARL	14	15	16	17	18
May 19 - 25	19	20 HARRIETTE	21	22	23	24	25
May 26 - Jun 1	26	27 CARL	28	29	30	31	Jun 1

November 2012

ARNOLD FAMILY CUSTODY SCHEDULE

Alternate Weekends & Wednesday Overnight

Karen, Wayne & Kevin with Norma at all times not set forth below.

	Sunday	Monday	Tuesday	Wednesday	Thursday	Friday	Saturday
Oct 28 - Nov 3	Oct 28	29	30	31	Nov 1 NORMA	2	3
Nov 4 - 10	4	5	6	7 JACK 3 p.m. to 9 a.m.	8	9 JACK	10
Nov 11 - 17	11	12	13	14 JACK 3 p.m. to 9 a.m.	15	16	17
Nov 18 - 24	18	19	20	21 JACK	22 JACK	23 JACK	24 JACK
Nov 25 - Dec 1	25 JACK	26 JACK	27	28 JACK 3 p.m. to 9 a.m.	29	30	Dec 1

Temporary Parenting Plan

There may be no such thing as a typical custody arrangement; the point is to create a plan that works for your particular situation. Here's an example of a temporary parenting plan for a couple, the Keatons*, who have two small children, Alex and Mallory. If it looks and sounds complicated, everybody nevertheless grew accustomed to it; eventually, it just became the norm for this family.

---

* Based on the family portrayed in *Family Ties,* the sitcom that aired on NBC from September 22, 1982 until May 14, 1989.

1 Laura A. Wasser, Esq. (SBN173740)
WASSER, COOPERMAN & CARTER, P.C.
2 2029 Century Park East, Suite 1200
Los Angeles, California 90067-2957
3 Telephone No.: (310) 277-7117
4 Facsimile No.: (310) 553-1793
5 Attorneys for Petitioner
6
7
8 SUPERIOR COURT OF THE STATE OF CALIFORNIA
9 FOR THE COUNTY OF LOS ANGELES
10

11 In re the Marriage of	)	CASE NO. ____________
	)	
12 Petitioner: ELYSE KEATON	)	[Assigned to Dept. ____,
	)	Hon. ____________]
13 and	)	
	)	STIPULATION AND ORDER RE
14 Respondent: STEVEN KEATON	)	TEMPORARY PARENTING PLAN
15	)	
	)	
16	)	

17 IT IS HEREBY STIPULATED by and between Petitioner, ELYSE KEATON, individually,
18 and by and through her attorneys of record, Wasser, Cooperman & Carter, P.C. by Laura A. Wasser,
19 Esq., and Respondent, STEVEN KEATON, individually, and by and through his attorneys of
20 record, ____________________, by ______________, Esq. as follows:
21 1. The parties shall commence participation in a child custody evaluation effective
22 immediately. Each party shall pay for one half of the evaluation without prejudice as to character or
23 future right of reimbursement.
24 2. The parties are both temporarily living in the family residence, which is Petitioner's
25 separate property. During the time period when Respondent is looking for an appropriate residence,
26 the parties shall share custody of the minor children, ALEX KEATON, born November 15, 2007,
27 age 5, and MALLORY KEATON, born May 23, 2010, age 2, as follows:
28 ///

- 1 -

MARRIAGE OF KEATON — STIPULATION AND ORDER RE TEMPORARY PARENTING PLAN
L.A.S.C. CASE NO. ____________ — Stip re Temp Parenting Plan CC Eval.wpd

1 3. Respondent shall have custody of the children on Tuesday and Thursday mornings
2 form the time the children wake up until the time Respondent leaves for work in the morning
3 (approximately 8:00 a.m.).
4 4. Respondent shall pick ALEX up at school at 4:30 p.m. on Tuesday and Wednesdays
5 and alternate Thursdays. On Tuesdays and Wednesdays Respondent shall have custody of ALEX and
6 MALLORY from 4:30 p.m. until the time the children go to sleep (7:30 p.m.). On the alternate
7 Thursdays when Respondent picks ALEX up he shall deliver ALEX to his piano lessons.
8 5. Petitioner shall pick ALEX up at school at 4:30 p.m. on Monday and Friday and
9 alternate Thursdays. On Mondays, Fridays and alternate Thursdays Petitioner shall have custody of
10 ALEX and MALLORY from 4:30 p.m. until the time the children go to sleep (7:30 p.m.). On
11 Mondays she shall deliver ALEX to his soccer lessons. On the alternate Thursdays when Petitioner
12 picks ALEX up she shall deliver ALEX to his piano lessons.
13 6. The parties shall alternate weekend days from Saturday when the children wake up
14 until Sunday when the children wake up and Sunday when the children wake up until Monday when
15 the children wake up, commencing with Respondent having custody on Saturday, October 20th and
16 Petitioner having Sunday, October 21, 2012 and alternating Saturdays and Sundays thereafter (e.g.
17 Petitioner has October 27 and Respondent has October 28).
18 7. MALLORY participates in toddler group at ________________ on Tuesdays from
19 9:45 a.m. until 11:30 a.m. and at _____________ on Fridays from 12:30 a.m. until 2:30 a.m. The
20 parties shall alternate attendance at the toddler programs commencing Friday, October 19, 2012 when
21 Petitioner shall attend the ___________ program. Respondent shall attend the _______ program.
22 8. On Friday October 26, 2012, Petitioner shall attend the ______________ program on
23 Tuesday October 23, 2012 and Respondent shall attend the ______________ program on Tuesday,
24 October 30, 2012.
25 9. Regardless of the schedule set forth above, the parties shall share custody of
26 MALLORY and ALEX on Halloween.
27 ///
28 ///

- 2 -

MARRIAGE OF KEATON STIPULATION AND ORDER RE TEMPORARY PARENTING PLAN
L.A.S.C. CASE NO. __________

Stip re Temp Parenting Plan CC Eval.wpd

1 10. The parties shall both attend ALEX's birthday party celebration on Saturday,
2 November 2, 2012 at 4:00 p.m. at __________. After the birthday party, the parties shall both help
3 ALEX open his birthday presents at the residence.
4 11. Petitioner shall take the children to school and to their respective daily activities and
5 with the exceptions of the times assigned to Respondent above, pick them up therefrom.
6 12. During the times designated as one parent's custodial time the non-custodial parent
7 shall make him/herself scarce despite the fact that the parties are both living in the family residence.
8 13. This Stipulation and Order is being agreed to without prejudice to either party's claims
9 or contentions.
10 **APPROVED AS TO FORM AND CONTENT:**
11 DATED: __________________ ______________________________
ELYSE KEATON, Petitioner
12
13 DATED: __________________ ______________________________
STEVEN KEATON, Respondent
14
APPROVED AS TO FORM ONLY.
15
DATED: __________________ WASSER, COOPERMAN & CARTER
16 Professional Corporation
17
By: ______________________________
18 LAURA A. WASSER
Attorneys for Petitioner
19
20 DATED: __________________ ______________________________
21
By: ______________________________
22
Attorneys for Respondent
23
24 **ORDER**
25 The above Stipulation having been read and good cause appearing therefor, IT IS SO
26 ORDERED.
27 DATED: __________________ ______________________________
JUDGE OF THE SUPERIOR COURT
28

- 3 -

MARRIAGE OF KEATON
L.A.S.C. CASE NO. __________
STIPULATION AND ORDER RE TEMPORARY PARENTING PLAN AND CHILD CUSTODY EVALUATION
Stip re Temp Parenting Plan CC Eval.wpd

It's a Schedule, Not a Battleground

Once you and your spouse have agreed on a custody plan and your lawyers have filed it in court, you of course must abide by it. Historically, this is where the trouble comes in.

Occasional deviations from the plan for the most part can't be helped. Things come up; nobody is totally in charge of his or her own schedule, and sudden emergencies or sudden opportunities will prompt both of you to ask for an exception to the schedule to be made. Sometimes when kids are sick, they have a preference about where they want to be—or sometimes the parent does. My son once needed to be returned early from his father's simply because he had thrown up on every clean set of sheets in the house. In need of both clean laundry and emotional recovery for himself, my ex asked for an exception to the schedule and brought Luke home to throw up on some of my bedding. You will need to practice the same flexibility in adjusting to your ex's exceptions as you would want your ex to extend to you. After all, he or she will become your first and best babysitting option, and mutual consideration and accommodation help keep that option open.

Flexibility is also important when it comes to make-up time. When your ex calls on Monday and says something has come up and he can't take the kids this weekend but would like to make up the time with them the following weekend instead, you're probably inclined to be flexible and say yes. It's when he calls at midnight on Thursday or at 6:00 A.M. Friday and says something has come up and he can't take the kids this weekend that you may need to stretch your flexibility muscles a bit more. Of course, flexibility can be stretched too far, and only you know when your own limit has been reached.

Many of my clients are in the entertainment industry and therefore spend big chunks of time away from home for concert tours, location shoots, or press junkets. Making up custodial time is so difficult to track that it almost isn't an issue. But the ability to bend the custody schedule overall is so essential that we write into the custody agreement a paragraph committing the parties to "exercise flexibility."

Doing so takes some organizing, for whenever the call from your ex comes, you need to be ready to deal with these deviations from the norm. Let's say your ex leaves a message at your office that there is a medical emergency and she has to perform surgery on one of her patients, so it's up to you to take your son to his dentist appointment. It will be inconvenient but not outrageously so for you to adjust your own schedule to meet this eventuality; the problem is that you have absolutely no idea who your son's dentist is, where the dentist's office is located, or what kind of dental insurance plan your son has. That's bad planning. In coparenting, you both need the same information at your fingertips: dentist, doctor, insurance cards, babysitters, teachers' names, school principal, school nurse, soccer practice schedule, ballet class, karate lessons, best friend's parents' names and phone numbers, and the like.

But having equal access to such information cannot become an excuse for playing fast and loose with the schedule. The odd emergency is one thing; missing your turn on the schedule time after time is not. Few things send a clearer message to your children that you don't care about them than your failure to show up when you're supposed to.

Yes, some parents turn custody into just another battlefield in their ongoing war with each other. Many are not even aware they're doing it; they believe they are acting in the best interests of the child. They're not, and I'm afraid I see this kind of behavior all too often.

I see kids becoming the rope in a tug-of-war or, even worse perhaps, used as messengers of vitriol. "Daddy says I shouldn't call you Mommy, I should call you Sarah," one client was told by her child. "And he says this isn't my home. *His* house is my home."

That was her cue to pick up her child in her arms and say, "Daddy is so funny sometimes, isn't he? Let's go see what's new in the garden . . ." She didn't. She called her lawyer, then e-mailed her ex, accusing him of willfully damaging their son psychologically and of doing so to alienate him from his mother. And the ex replied in kind: "It is impossible to respond to your insanity. . . . I don't know if you actually believe your lies, or you just don't care and will do anything it takes. Either is sick. . . ."

Their one-on-one exchanges when the boy was dropped off at the other's house were equally ugly but more shrill for being in person. Naturally, those few moments were the only time they could be in each other's company and thus represented their only chance to spew the venom that had built up inside. Did they think their three-year-old wouldn't sense the battle between them? Did they suppose he wouldn't be harmed by it? Ask his psychiatrist twenty years from now.

The sad thing is that these parents hang on to these accusations in the hope that they will get justice in court. Yes, claims of fault do matter when it comes to questions of custody, but the truth is that judges are pretty good at distinguishing between internecine spousal battles and questions of parental fitness, and they tend to have little interest in the former. Your spouse is obnoxious? Annoying? Spiteful? Trying to use the court to get back at you? Judges are prepared to believe that all of the above may be true, but they are loath to spend even a second determining whether or not your particular complaints are true.

A wise judge once expressed it to me this way: "Mother Teresa rarely marries the evil Rasputin," he said, a reminder that it does take two to tango and that the couple in question had walked willingly into each other's arms. The fact is that the two of you procreated—and here you are. Blaming each other simply reinforces the truth that two wrongs do not make a right, and it leaves judges with the impression that while the two of you may indeed deserve each other, your children deserve better.

"Mommy, if you want me to hate her, I will," says the eight-year-old in Chris Columbus's 1998 movie, *Stepmom,* about the woman his father is dating. But judges are not moved by complaints leveled against your ex's new significant other. I've frequently received and rejected—requests from clients to write into the custody agreement a provision that the kids should not be "subjected to," in the usual phrase, "that man" or "the other woman." That just doesn't cut it. What your ex does in his or her new life is his or her own business, and so long as your children are not endangered, there's nothing you can do about an ex-spouse's choice of partners. The ex-wife of one client of mine was appalled that he was now dating a porn star and that their kids were occasionally in the porn star's presence. Her lawyer hauled a stack of DVDs containing the new girlfriend's movies into court, but the judge was having none of it. "This woman's choice of career is not on trial," she ruled drily. "It is not illegal, and I have seen no evidence that she is practicing her trade in the presence of the children." There was clearly no detriment to the children and no fault on the part of my client—a very happy man.

Sometimes, in fact, claims of fault can actually backfire. The divorced wife of a client of mine was so horrified to discover that her husband had logged on to a gay porn Web site that she decided it somehow constituted child molestation. She went to court to accuse him of sexually violating his own children. It is a very ugly allegation and one that walks a very fine line of proof—i.e., at what age should parents stop their kids from climbing into their bed or showering with them? The trial dragged on for three difficult weeks, an experience my client found mortifying and frightening in the extreme; he feared he might lose his children. In the end, the court found no evidence whatsoever of molestation. What it did find was that the ex-wife was guilty of having alienated the children from their father. Whatever her underlying motivations—leftover mistrust from the divorce perhaps, or distress at an ex-husband she now found deviant—the court ruled that her behavior was depriving her children of a healthy relationship with their father, and it was she who paid the legal price, losing her status as primary custodial parent.

Extreme though that example is, it speaks volumes about how trying to block or undermine your spouse's relationship with the children can come back to haunt you. And it is (or ought to be) yet another object lesson in the fatuity and real danger of allowing your feelings about your ex to contaminate your joint custody arrangement.

For one thing, like the three-year-old boy who became the arena for his parents' battles, children sense it when there is bitterness between the two most important people in their lives, and they are affected by it in numerous adverse ways. A client I'll call Peter came home from work to what I will always consider the worst message in the world on his answering machine. It was his ex-wife, ranting, raving, calling him every name in the book, lambasting him in a profanity-laced tirade that ended with her declaration that absolutely everyone hated his guts. Just before she slammed the phone down, a little voice cried out on the tape: "I don't hate you, Daddy!"

She had delivered the entire performance in front of their seven-year-old son.

Six years later, that boy, exhausted by his mother's rage against his father, petitioned the court to be removed from her care. He's a strapping teenager now and living with his father, but only time will tell what the long-term harm of his mother's behavior might be. She herself never saw it that way; she imagined herself a tigress fighting for her young, not a woman so irresponsible as to subordinate the interests of her child to her anger against her ex-husband.

Again, this is an extreme example. The vast majority of parents are worlds away from such behavior. I present this case only as a cautionary tale: Self-control is one of the first casualties of anger; losing it puts you at risk of both injuring your children and, at the extreme, of losing them. Be warned.

Joint Custody Means Shared Parenting

How can you avoid the effect of these heated emotions? The emotions themselves probably can't be extinguished, but the behavior needs to be managed. So here is one of the essential principles of divorce in the twenty-first century—namely, that one of you has to be consistently a rational, normal, solid human being no matter how much of an asshole the other is. If both of you were consistently rational, normal, solid human beings, that would be ideal. But at a minimum, one of you must be, and since you are reading this book, you are elected. Children really only need just one parent to be a noncreep; one is enough for them to be all right, to stay mentally and emotionally and developmentally sound.

This seems like a tough row to hoe. Parents love blaming each other for mismanaging their children's upbringing. But I promise that if you don't succumb to the blame game, your kid will turn out fine. Or not. The truth is of course that the perfect couple who remain married forever and do everything right can end up with children who are feckless, flighty, and immature, while the most screwed-up wackos who romp through a series of relationships and ride a roller coaster of irresponsibility can produce exemplars of productivity and conscientious citizenship. Go figure.

The truth is that you can only be in charge of you. You cannot station your grandmother in your ex's house to make sure the place meets your standards of cleanliness and morality. You cannot dispatch the behavior police to oversee every activity your ex and your kids get up to when it is your ex's custodial time. And no judge on earth is going to reduce your ex's custodial time for using profanity in the presence of your young children in the car when he or she has been dangerously cut off by someone driving while texting. In my experience as both a parent and lawyer to parents, I have observed that it is actually a lot less stressful to just blow off your ex-spouse's nonsense. Answer it, and you can spiral into real anger; dismiss it—or replace it with rational behavior—and you and your children can all move on.

Still, how do you manage the nitty-gritty of sharing parenting with an ex—even when you have mastered the art of not being sucked into what you regard as his or her wackiness, irrationality, or self-indulgent fixations?

One way is to not compete with your ex. I call it the chest-beater syndrome: Now that you are split from your spouse, you are going to be Tarzan, possessed of capabilities far beyond those of ordinary humans, capabilities that enable you to be the best, the smartest, the most clued-in, most vigilant parent in the world—sensitive to every nuance of your children's behavior, able to tap the temperature of their emotions at any moment, and current with the latest study, the most recent development, the most up-to-date technology of parenting.

But parenting is not a competitive sport, and the truth is that regardless of whether animal prints are in or out this season, you wouldn't be acting like Tarzan if you were not going through a divorce. It is in fact not necessary to swing through the trees and perform feats of superhuman strength in order to be a good parent. Setting impossible standards for yourself just undermines your confidence; it doesn't do a thing for your kids. Instead, be the best parent you can be when your children are with you—without going for a knockout performance every time your ex drops them off.

By the same token, don't try to minimize your kids' time with your ex, shaving off a minute here or an hour there, or insisting that your time with the kids match exactly your ex's time with the kids down to the nanosecond. Put away the stopwatch, be present, and put the time to good use. After all, the hours or days when your kids are with your ex are a time of built-in, free childcare, and the solitude can be stimulating. I always find it so; I am psyched when my kids walk out the door to be with their other parent, and I am always thrilled when they walk back in the door.

Finally, don't fight your ex over holidays or special days that are meaningful to you both—the kids' birthdays, Thanksgiving, other key observances in your lives. Think about it: If you insist on having the kids with you exclusively this birthday or Christmas, it means you will not have them at all next birthday or Christmas. Wouldn't it make more sense for them to be with each of you for part of the day? Or, even better, spend the time together. Kids love this; they love having both parents in the same place on these special days. My kids do (you should see our posse on Halloween!). And it doesn't surprise me, because I did too when I was a kid. After my parents' divorce, we would invariably have Thanksgiving at the home of my mother and stepfather. On the guest list were my brother and me, my father and his wife and her kids, and my stepfather's kids with their mother, my stepfather's ex-wife. We still go to my mother's for Thanksgiving, but now there's a whole new generation to deal with, and the number of people just keeps multiplying.

Just as you don't compete for *time* with your kids, don't compete over how the time is filled. You and your spouse are equal but separate parents now, just as you are equal but separate individuals. That they are the children of distinctive and perhaps very different individuals, with distinctive and perhaps very different values, habits, tastes, opinions, likes, and dislikes is a fact of life—and is probably not a bad lesson for kids to learn. You can't twist yourself into knots and pretend to be someone you're not when the kids are with you.

That goes for discipline as well. It is ideal to be on the same page, but failing that, you do the best you can with the cards you've been dealt. Your castle, your rules—as the saying goes. The kids do things differently over at Dad's house? Too bad. Right now they are in Mom's house, and they will abide by the principles of conduct Mom establishes; this too is a fact of life they will encounter again in their experience.

Don't Sweat the Small Stuff

Again, child custody arrangements are infinitely modifiable. But on the other hand, if you go to court over and over, repeatedly seeking modifications that adjudicate disputes between you and your ex, judges tend to become irritated, which is understandable. They expect that two adults should be able to come to some sort of sustainable working agreement, rather than appealing to King Solomon to cut the baby in half on every issue.

That is why it is so important to differentiate between profound disputes over fundamental principles and annoyances over matters which, when you take a breath and think about it, really don't carry cosmic significance. The latter you can bring up in a discussion, if you and your ex deal in amicable discussion, or you might just grit your teeth and let it pass. For the former—the profound disputes over fundamental principles—you will need to thrash out your differences, preferably in a discussion or meeting, through mediation and/or with counseling help if that doesn't work, or in court as a last resort.

Maybe the profound differences over fundamentals were what drove the two of you apart in the first place. No matter. You need some kind of resolution now that your children are at stake, and the very first step is to get onto the same page on things like disciplining your kids, nutrition, their education, religion—if any—and the basics of how you want them to conduct themselves in the world. Disparity on these fundamentals, creating a fundamental inconsistency in the way you do your parenting, can engender the kind of stressful confusion that is truly harmful to children. Mediation may be the best way to sort through the disparity until you find your way to a workable compromise; it is much less expensive than paying attorneys' fees and going to court. But a court order may indeed be necessary to reach a solution weighted to the interests of the children.

A client of mine had begun potty-training her daughter, only to find out that when the little girl was at Daddy's house, the potty wasn't even on the radar screen. Consistency is of course essential in potty-training, and potty-training is central to any child's development, so this constituted a serious and very profound disparity that had to be solved. The solution was achieved without going to court and indeed without rancor, but this was by no means an issue that could be skirted or dismissed; both parents had to be on the same page.

Even when both of you agree on the basics, however, there are still bound to be disagreements, debates, even disputes. The trick is to keep them from spilling over into the kind of discord that makes you want to drag each other into court, which can be so costly in time, money, and goodwill. So when you perceive that your ex has lapsed on anything less consequential than the fundamentals, a little plasticity and a dollop of tolerance are a good idea.

A case in point helps illustrate the difference. It concerns what is known in my business as the Disneyland parent. No rules prevail at all in this parent's household. Kids are not reminded, much less pressed, to do their homework; they drink sugary sodas and eat junk food; they stay up til all hours; and nobody checks to see whether they ever shower or change their clothes. This is life with the "fun" parent, but when the fun parent keeps the fun going during midweek custody, it means trouble. Kids who arrive at school late, tired, wired from Pop-Tarts, not particularly pleasing hygienically, and unprepared for their academic work warrant a quick trip to the principal's office and a stern phone call to the parents. If your ex is a Disneyland parent on school nights, a correction is required, and if it takes a trip to court to effect the correction, so be it.

But for Disneyland on weekends, indulgence may be a better prescription. I regularly hear complaints from clients, mostly from women clients, that their ex-husbands never make the kids brush their teeth and that the fathers' weekends with the children should therefore be curtailed. Well, I firmly believe children should brush their teeth, and I believe their fathers as well as their mothers should insist upon it, but I also believe it is more important that the children spend time with their other parent than that they attend to their teeth. In due course, if maternal discipline doesn't work, other pressures are likely to get them to brush their teeth as regularly as their mothers would like. In the meantime, it's worth asking if this justifies a battle with your ex and an appeal to the legal system—my guess is the judge would laugh the offended parent out of court—or is rather something all parties might just learn to live with.

There are other paths to dispute resolution besides mediators, lawyers, judges, or letting the whole thing drop. Your own therapist, if you have one, or the therapist the two of you consulted before splitting, or a child therapist may help you both bridge the gap—or give you another way to approach the issue. Coparenting specialists are particularly well suited to the task. Typically certified in psychology or social work, these specialists can cut to the chase, offer examples of how others have dealt with the same or a similar problem, outline the potential effects on your children of various approaches to resolution, and help you communicate. In fact, these days courts frequently order a couple to deal with a coparenting specialist—an indication of the efficacy of these counselors.

I have a client who is a committed vegan, as was her former partner until their separation. She has since modified her restriction of animal products, which means that when the couple's children are with her, animal-based foods are available. For her former partner, this is a serious issue; she feels very strongly that their kids will benefit from the vegan way of eating they were introduced to as babies. Deep beliefs make for thorny negotiations, and it took a coparenting specialist to put the emphasis where it properly belonged—not just on lowering the emotional heat and resolving this one problem, but on providing the estranged couple practical ways to stay in communication and in agreement. When they are in my client's custody the children adhere to a less stringent, vegetarian diet.

Technological advances can help very much in ensuring a smoother way of communicating. Even *The New York Times* has taken note. In a November 23, 2012 article by Pamela Paul entitled "Kramer.com vs. Kramer.com," the paper of record said that technology is providing divorced parents useful alternatives to hearing the voice or seeing the face of their ex. Texting and e-mailing are wonderful options for coordinating with and notifying your coparent about everyday issues.

Apropos, there is a Web site that helps couples do that, and I want to give it my unsolicited and unqualified endorsement. It is www.ourfamilywizard.com, and it is, first and foremost, a superb way for a divorcing couple to communicate with each other about the custody schedule and all custodial issues. You are both required to open an account, but the price is reasonable and in my view well worth it. The site lets you establish a calendar you both can access, track shared expenses, leave messages for each other, store medical and school data that needs to be shared, and more. It is also a portal to all sorts of resources and information, and of course you can get it as a smartphone app so you can log in at any time. The communications between you are private but also represent a good evidentiary reflection of what is happening between you. It has become so useful in so many courts that a number of judges across the country now order the parties in a custody case to sign up. I recommend it as a very helpful tool in the often hard work of establishing a custody plan, sticking to it, and flagging—and often resolving—issues that arise between you. And anything that can help you keep your eyes on the prize—namely, on your kids' happiness and well-being—is worth your attention.

IN BRIEF

It's essential to keep in mind always that through your children, you are inextricably bonded to the spouse you're splitting from. Until your kids reach legal majority, you both have the responsibility and the rights of parenthood, so you will need to deal with each other regularly, especially as changing circumstances—yours or those of your growing children—require reconfigurations of your child custody arrangements.

1. To create a sensible custody schedule, track the current status quo of time each of you spends with the children.
2. Be flexible about inevitable deviations from schedule, but remember that reliability of a routine is important for children.
3. Stay rational; if your ex acts foolishly, try not to respond in kind.
4. Pick your battles; focus on what's really important. Don't sweat the small stuff.

8

Spousal Support

Divorcing couples are right to think that ending their marriage will affect their financial situations. But all too often, they are wrong—or at least unclear—about just what the effect will be.

If you are the higher-earning spouse, male or female, and have been the major or sole provider of the household lifestyle, don't for a moment think that you're going to enjoy a sudden, massive infusion of cash into your bank account when the marriage ends.

By the same token, if you are a stay-at-home parent and expect you will continue to operate after your marriage on the kind of budget you have grown accustomed to during it, you are probably equally unrealistic. You're not going to be left out in the cold; the higher earner is typically required to continue to support the household lifestyle, just not in the same house. But supporting two households out of the same single income that used to support one is likely to mean somewhat reduced circumstances in both.

So when it comes to financial issues—the subject of this chapter and the next two—you both need to start by getting real. Certainly, where spousal financial support is concerned, that means getting your expectations in line with how the courts and the economy will affect what you can expect to provide or receive.

Essential to achieving a reasonable, sensible, workable support agreement is an understanding of precisely what spousal support is and what it is not. For one thing, spousal support is by no means the same thing as child support, which we'll discuss further in the next chapter. Child support is a legal requirement over which the courts retain jurisdiction until the child has reached legal majority. You can't negotiate away the court's jurisdiction on child support; when it comes to spousal support, however, you can negotiate a limit or even an end to the court's jurisdiction over your agreement.

Also, note that spousal support applies only in the case of marriages, civil unions, or registered domestic partnerships—if the latter have been duly codified before the proper authorities. For same-sex couples or anyone else in such domestic partnerships, "duly codified" means that their union has been properly licensed and the license properly filed. Such couples should check with their local municipal clerk's office to be sure—that is, if they want the protection of spousal support in case they ever split.

Cohabiting couples, by contrast, are not subject to the jurisdiction of the courts in this matter. They are, of course, required to provide financial support for any children of their union, but financial payments from one spouse to the other are not a matter for the courts. Certainly, cohabiting couples may draw up their own agreements for alimony-like payments, but such agreements are litigated in civil court only if breached—palimony cases.

The purpose of spousal support payments is to prevent any unfair economic consequences that may result from the end of the marriage or to compensate for such unfairness. That is why spousal support is also known as maintenance and as alimony, the latter deriving from a Latin verb meaning "to feed" or "to sustain." Specifically, spousal support is meant to help the lower-earning spouse or the spouse who served as caretaker of the household and/or the children—usually one and the same person—transition through the divorce process until she or he has become self-supporting.

We all know the classic cases that illustrate the justice of this:

Item: One spouse goes to work to support the couple while the other spouse finishes law school or medical school or other professional or job training, thus deferring or restraining his or her own career ambitions for the benefit of a long-term economic benefit, which the ending of the marriage then wipes away.

Item: One spouse agrees to be the stay-at-home parent until the couple's children are all in school, a process that takes a decade. This hiatus from the workforce effectively diminishes the stay-at-home spouse's economic value and makes it tougher for her or him to reenter the workforce without supplemental education or training; even with such training, the chances of this spouse finding remunerative employment are lowered, along with earning power and longevity of working career.

Item: After thirty-five years as spouse, companion, career support, homemaker, and parent, the nonearning or lower-earning partner is almost completely incapable of entering the economy in any meaningful way or in any capacity that might provide even basic financial needs, much less support the person to the standards to which he or she has become accustomed during the marriage. In any economic era, but particularly in one as bruised as the current global reality, this spouse is almost surely locked out of any economic activity at all, so the end of the marriage could mean a drastic reduction in circumstances at a time when the spouse has few powers to reverse those circumstances.

A generation ago, of course, it would have been obvious on its face that in all these examples, the spouse not in the workforce or deferring entry into the workforce or serving as the full-time homemaker was the female half of the couple. Breadwinner-husband/stay-at-home-wife constituted the expected configuration and was the traditional and familiar situation.

But that is no longer the case. Dual-earner couples are today the norm and the majority. In many cases, the wife is the higher-earning spouse. And the courts, which have wide latitude when it comes to determining both the amount and duration of spousal support, are uneasy with the old gender roles. Moreover, judges do not want their rulings on alimony to be perceived as either a reward or a punishment for one spouse or the other. What is good for the goose is indeed good for the gander.

Once again, demographics and evolving family law have pared away outmoded shibboleths and brought the issue of spousal support down to its basics. For the spouse receiving it, it's about money to live on while you're rethinking and probably reshaping your life. For the spouse providing it, it's one of the responsibilities you undertook when you entered into the legally recognized and therefore legally binding union you are now ending. It's not meant to keep the lower-earning spouse in the lap of luxury while the higher-earning spouse bunks in a refrigerator box under a freeway overpass to pay for that luxury, and except in cases where the marriage has lasted a long time—the rule-of-thumb minimum definition for "long" is ten years—it is ideally and for the most part not something that goes on forever. Still, it does suck for the person paying. This goes back to what I said at the beginning of the book about contractual obligations you didn't necessarily think about while walking down the aisle.

To Have and to Hold

Here's where the rubber of those dewy-eyed wedding vows really hits the road of obligation. Continuing to support a spouse after the marriage is over—when you've lost that loving feeling and may not be able to stand the sight of each other—really is a question of justice. As a couple, you each contributed to the marriage and to the household you have formed. You each had your separate roles. You may each have made sacrifices for the benefit of the union you have formed. Deferring or forfeiting a role in the workforce, providing financial support during the earning spouse's professional training, or taking on the task of primary parent or homemaker all constitute contributions to the union the two of you have formed, while putting off your own ambitions also constitutes a sacrifice. Although different in kind from the paycheck the earning spouse brings home, these are contributions that can in some ways be measured in financial terms, while their value also goes beyond the financial. The aim of spousal support is simply to balance both spouses' contributions to their union, as well as the sacrifices one or both have made for the benefit of the marriage, with the needs both will have when the marriage has ended.

One client of mine coming out of a same-sex relationship aptly pointed out that his young ex really had contributed nothing to their union. "I worked my butt off while he spent, traveled, enjoyed fine wine, food, and clothing. We have no children, and if anything, he precluded me from working more because he so often demanded my attention. Now I have to pay support to dissolve our domestic partnership." I replied as I often do to clients in similar situations: "You married him, darling."

That's why support has to be paid. It may serve as a temporary rehabilitative bridge helping a spouse transition from one stage of life to another, as a reimbursement for sacrifices made, as a virtually permanent support obligation, or as a combination of these functions, as the judge's discretion dictates.

And that discretion is far-reaching and profound, as judges take into consideration a wide range of factors to determine in what way and how much each party should contribute to maintaining, as far as possible, the standard of living established during the marriage. Judges will consider:

- The marketable skills of each spouse and whether there's really a market for the skills. If there is a market but the skills are lacking, what it will take and how much it will cost to get the needed skills. If there are skills but no market, what it will take to get new marketable skills.
- The extent to which the supported party lost out by not working during the marriage but contributing in other ways to the household or to the supporting spouse's career preparation and success—and how much that contribution is worth.
- The financial needs of each, how long the marriage lasted, how much the paying spouse can afford.
- The financial resources of each—e.g., all assets and income, earned and unearned, active and passive, from paychecks, perquisites, investments, trust funds, etc.
- The age and health of both parties.

- Any history of domestic violence—on the grounds that no one should finance his or her own abuse.
- The "balance of hardships" between the two parties.
- The goal of ensuring that the supported spouse becomes self-supporting in "a reasonable amount of time."

To this fairly standard list, family law in most states adds "any other factors" the court deems pertinent, with no limit on any factors the court might consider "just and equitable." Broad discretion indeed.

The court also has wide discretion—again, no limit—in determining how long the support should last. Justice has demands here as well. Deferring a career is not just a matter of putting off entry into the workforce; it also handicaps the ability to enter the workforce later—or at all. So the obligation to maintain that spouse rightly needs to go on for a while. On the other hand, unless we're talking about a marriage of such longevity that the nonearning spouse hasn't a prayer of ever finding gainful employment, the obligation should not go on indefinitely. I once had a client whose ex-wife tried to start up one "innovative" enterprise after another. All fell flat, and the years went by, with my client dutifully paying the agreed-upon spousal support. The judge finally delivered an ultimatum to the ex-wife: *Six more months of support.* He could not legally order her to get a job, but that was the gist of his message. Burger flipper, call center rep, coffee shop cashier, supermodel, whatever: It was time for her to stop playing and get serious. She did.

Only a handful of states set guidelines for how long spousal support should be forthcoming, but one fairly general rule of thumb is that it should last half as long as the marriage did—up until the so-called "ten-year rule." Courts tend to maintain their jurisdiction over support issues for marriages of that or greater length; a judge is unlikely to order a spouse who has been the primary parent and homemaker for three or four decades to go out and get herself a career. This ultimately is to prevent people from becoming the state's responsibility and going on welfare.

So the end of a marriage that lasted nine years and ten months, for example, would typically see the higher-earning spouse paying spousal support for just under five years, presumably a sufficient amount of time for the non- or lower-earning spouse to get his or her act together and find a way to make a living. A marriage of two years commits the higher-earning spouse to make payments for a year, and so on.

Of course, if the nonearning spouse in either of those marriages were a stay-at-home mother with an infant at her breast, a judge might well refuse to set a termination date for the support on the grounds that caring for an infant is likely to delay the woman's ability to plunge into the job market. On the other hand, if the non-earning spouse is a forty-year-old mother of school-age children who has a law degree she just has to dust off, a judge might decide that spousal support is necessary only for as long as it takes her to do the dusting. The judge will expect that this woman will or should be back on her financial feet well before the time equivalent to half the length of her marriage has gone by.

Spousal support does end if and when a receiving spouse remarries or, in some states, even moves in with someone in a cohabiting relationship. Death also puts an end to spousal support—that is, the death of the receiving spouse. Various provisions in the support agreement can actually provide a receiving spouse a hedge against the termination of support through the death of the higher-earning paying spouse. The agreement might require the paying spouse to take out a life insurance policy naming the receiving spouse as beneficiary, or it might demand a portion of the death benefits from a pension or annuity plan, or it might even commit the deceased's estate to continue making maintenance payments until the death of the receiving spouse parts the couple once and for all.

Waiting for Support

The Harriet Buhai Center for Family Law in Los Angeles, where I volunteer my services, provides free legal assistance to women—mostly—who then go on to represent themselves in the judicial system. In other words, the lawyers like me who do pro bono work at the Center don't go into court with our clients; instead, we empower them to go into court on their own, helping them understand the process and supporting them with documentation and information about procedures. A number of them are in danger of domestic violence, which can give new meaning—profoundly difficult meaning—to every step of the divorce process.

A client I'll call Angela typifies what I mean. She was desperate to get her two kids and herself out of the apartment she and her husband shared because he often drank too much, and when he did, he became violent. He had already taken a couple of swings at Angela, and she was now terrified he could hurt the children. So Angela packed up her kids and herself and moved them all into her car.

Angela had a good job managing a grocery store, but her income only covered living expenses; she had no savings she could put down as the two-months'-rent security payment required for a new apartment. Meanwhile, the husband she was desperate to avoid made minimum wage in his day job as a mechanic but pulled in substantial cash in payment and tips working by night as a valet parker at a swanky West Hollywood restaurant. It is hard to prove claims about cash payments at any time, but when you are acting pro per—that is, representing yourself in court—it's even harder. Angela knew her husband kept a significant stash of cash somewhere in the apartment she had run from, but she was too afraid to go look for it. She believed she and the children were entitled to some of it; what she wanted was a court order for her husband to pay some support, a divorce, and the chance at a new life. That's what the Buhai Center was helping her with, but like every Californian seeking to dissolve a marriage, Angela had to wait a considerable while for a court date. She worried too that once the date was set, her husband might not even show up.

Meanwhile, she was raising her kids in a car.

One warm summer evening, Angela spotted her husband leaving the apartment building to head for his valet parking job. He was carrying an overstuffed plastic shopping bag, held close to his body under his arm, and he walked with his head down, looking around furtively to see if anyone noticed him. Angela stayed in the shadows and followed him as he ducked into the alley at the end of the block. She watched him push some garbage cans aside and hide the plastic package, then slide the garbage cans back in place to obscure the spot. When her husband had left the alley, she waited til she was sure he would not come back; then she

waited some more. Finally, she pulled back the garbage cans and saw the package stuffed into a concrete hole behind them. She pulled it out, slid the cans back into place, and took the package back home to the car.

It was the cash stash, secreted in the alley because, as she would later learn, her husband had gotten a tip that the police were planning to search several apartments in the building looking for drugs. Angela's husband was no drug dealer, but he worried that the presence of the cash would be grounds for the police to think otherwise. So he had decided to hide the money for a day or two until things calmed down.

By the time he went back for it, his wife had used it to rent an apartment some miles away. At the same time, she sought the Center's assistance in obtaining a temporary restraining order against her husband; because of the allegations of domestic violence, the order was quickly granted. Angela's husband never knew who had taken the money and never bothered her again. And she was able to give herself and her kids a fresh start in life—paid for, albeit unwittingly, by their father.

Nevertheless, next time you get angry about your spousal support situation, just remind yourself that at least you and your kids aren't living in the car.

Taxes

Spousal support is considered taxable income by both the state and the federal governments, which means that the receiving spouse must declare it as income and the paying spouse may deduct it for income tax purposes.

That goes for all marriages, of course, including same-sex marriages in those jurisdictions where such marriages are legal. But same-sex couples in states that do not yet recognize same-sex marriage need to look into exactly what their state law directs about this matter. In California, for example, which, inexplicably, has yet to legalize marriage equality, many same-sex couples are legally joined in domestic partnerships, and state law regards them as full spouses in every way. It means that the paying spouse in a dissolving domestic partnership in California can take a deduction at the state level for the support paid—but not necessarily at the federal level. This "split decision" causes family lawyers like me to think up various stratagems and play all sorts of legalistic games to protect clients on either side of a domestic partnership.

Take the case of a couple I'll call Tyler and Daniel. They had been registered domestic partners in California for more than a decade when they decided to split. As the higher-earning partner, Tyler had accepted that he would be paying alimony, which he could deduct from his taxes at the state level. But he would still have to pay federal gift taxes on the amount, and at the going rate, that would mean he would almost be doubling his support—which Tyler did not find acceptable. His only out would be to pay a lower lump-sum payment up front or a smaller monthly support payment—neither of which was acceptable to Daniel. So the case went to court, where the judge ordered a somewhat complicated deal in which Tyler "won" the lower federal tax liability but indemnified Daniel for the loss, while the court decided to retain jurisdiction over the matter—not the neat, clean, simple ending both men had hoped for, but a solution in any event.

It seems silly to have to go through such twists and turns to get a fair ending, but until marriage equality is universal, if you're part of a same-sex couple in a state that doesn't recognize same-sex marriage, please find out what the potential tax impact will be for both the paying and receiving spouse as you end your relationship.

For the receiving spouse in a marriage, however, the need to pay taxes on spousal support also means that you need to add that liability to the estimate of how much support money you are going to need. Coming up with such an estimate is your first and most important task as you start thinking about spousal support.

Get Ready for Paperwork

The guideline for a court assessing the amount of spousal support to award is that it should be sufficient to support the receiving spouse as far as possible in the lifestyle to which he or she became accustomed during the marriage. Income available for support includes perquisites—company car, expense account meals, corporate credit card—and is capped at the highest earnings achieved during the marriage. If the paying spouse makes $100,00 a year while married and then earns $150,000 after separation, the marital lifestyle–spousal support should not go above the $100,000 mark. The guideline was established in another era of family law and probably could use some updating, but as a standard to shoot for, it actually works pretty well, even in this post-global-financial-meltdown era.

To measure that lifestyle in financial terms, it is necessary to know what you spend to have it and keep it—day in, day out, week after week, month after month. Expenditures for shelter, food and drink, clothing, utilities, insurance, and transportation probably leap to mind as the major items you pretty much cannot live without in this day and age. You probably know your monthly bill for mortgage or rent, your average monthly bill for power, heat, and air-conditioning, and what you pay to put gas in the car and/or commute to your job each week, but do you really know what you spend on eating, drinking, and clothing yourself? Do you remember the amounts in those semiannual or quarterly bills for homeowners' insurance and car insurance? And then there are all the other things we tend not to think about so much because we pay for them with cash or a credit card.

So the way to get hold of what you really spend is to write it down. All of it. Every expense, every day, cash or credit, for a month. Your lawyer can probably help you organize how to do this; my firm, for example, provides very detailed expense sheets that track the sorts of costs that are so much a part of the fabric of life in Southern California that people tend to forget about them—like valet parking. The equivalent in northern Maine would probably be fuel for the snowblower.

Once you commit to writing everything down—from the smallest expense to the largest—you will find things you simply don't think of as you go about your business: the manicure, pet food, gifts you buy for friends or relatives, charitable contributions, the gardening bill, eating out, magazines and newspapers, the service contract on your computer, the tips for all and sundry during the holidays. What about the bills you pay on a recurring basis online—health insurance, memberships, cable TV? Or the bills you've authorized your bank to pay via electronic funds transfer—contribution to your 401(k), fuel delivery, loan payment? Write down your habitual savings as well; many courts will provide for a savings component as a part of marital lifestyle.

MONTHLY EXPENSES/NEEDS OF

(1) Rent/Mortgage Payments *(residence)*
a. 1st Mortgage $______
b. 2nd Mortgage $______
c. Rent $______
Total $______

(2) Real Property Taxes *(residence)*
Total $______

(3) Real Property Insurance *(residence)*
Total $______

(4) Maintenance *(residence)*
a. Repairs $______
b. Gardener $______
c. Pool Service $______
d. Maid/Housekeeper $______
e. ______ $______
Total $______

(5) Food & Household Supplies
a. Food at Home $______
b. Food Eaten Out $______
c. School/Work Lunches $______
d. Household Supplies $______
Total $______

(6) Utilities & Telephone
a. Gas $______
b. Water & Power $______
c. Telephone $______
Total $______

(7) Laundry & Dry Cleaning
a. Laundry $______
b. Dry Cleaning $______
Total $______

(8) Clothing & Shoes
a. Client $______
b. Children $______
Total $______

(9) Medical

	Client	Children
a. Doctor	$______	$______
b. Optometrist	$______	$______
c. Dentist	$______	$______
d. Prescript.	$______	$______
e. Psychiast.	$______	$______
Totals	$______	$______

(10) Insurance

	Client	Children
a. Life	$______	$______
b. Health	$______	$______
c. Accident	$______	$______
d. Disability	$______	$______
Totals	$______	$______

(11) Child Care
a. Babysitter $______
b. Allowances $______
c. Clubs $______
d. Summer Camp $______
Total $______

(12) Payment of Child/Spousal Support
(For This/Previous Marriage)
a. Spousal $______
b. Child $______
Total $______

(13) School
a. Children $______
b. Client $______
c. Tuition, Lessons & Tutors $______
d. Supplies $______
Total $______

(14) Incidentals
a. Cigarettes $______
b. Cosmetics $______
c. Hair/Nail Care $______
d. Subscriptions $______
e. Social/Business Dues $______
f. Pets $______
g. Charities $______
h. Gifts $______
i. Cable Television $______
j. Vacation(s) $______
Total $______

(15) Entertainment
Total $______

(16) Auto Expenses
a. Car Payments $______
b. Insurance $______
c. Gas and Oil $______
d. Repairs $______
e. License $______
f. Car Washes $______
g. Parking $______
h. Auto Club $______
Total $______

(17) Other
a. Church/Temple $______
b. ______ $______
c. ______ $______
d. ______ $______
e. ______ $______
f. ______ $______
Total $______

TOTAL MONTHLY EXPENSES/NEEDS: $______

Add in the expenses for things that happen once or twice a year, like vacations or getting your car detailed, and the things you know are coming up pretty soon that you will have to pay for, like kids' braces or your mother's sixty-fifth birthday.

Force yourself to record the impulse buys or the quick-trip replacements: shampoo, batteries, the notebook you're using to keep track of your expenses, the cute pen to write stuff down in the notebook.

Sum up the total, average it out on a monthly basis, factor in whatever percentage of taxes you'll be responsible for as the receiving spouse, and the result is an approximate monthly nut. Your lawyer can help you here too, and we are often aided by software in doing so. In California, we rely on DissoMaster. In New Jersey, it's CIS. New York, Arizona, Pennsylvania use EzSupport. Divorce Financials offers a program that lets you "compute required spousal support payments based on the custodial parent's after-tax budget requirement" for all fifty states, according to its Web site. They all work in similar fashion. The lawyers plug in the numbers for each party's income or wages, plus passive income from any investments, plus deductions for property taxes and mortgage interest, plus any other support payments—e.g., for children from yet another marriage—and the program spits out a number. Then you and your lawyer can agree on what you should try to achieve in negotiation.

And in a spousal support agreement, virtually everything is negotiable—the amount of support, the length of the term, even the manner of payout. Everything is a bargaining chip. For example, in a longer-term settlement, the amount of support awarded tends to go down over time, so you potentially have the option to offer a shorter term for a larger amount, or vice versa. Or, suppose you have agreement on the term of the support—say, three years. You look ahead and check your assets and ready cash and decide to offer a lump-sum payment up front instead of consigning yourself to writing out a check once a month. The lump sum would likely be less than the total you'd be paying over thirty-six months, which is your upside, but the downside risk, of course, might be that your ex takes the money and remarries in six months, or that you might lose your job and be stuck with little or no reserve. It might nevertheless be worth the risk, depending on your income and your desire to cut the cord and not have to deal with your ex even by writing a check each month. In any event, it's another factor to toss into the negotiating mix.

What's more, everything is *infinitely* negotiable. You can revisit the terms of a support agreement without limit.

Which doesn't mean it's easy.

The receiving spouse is entitled to support at a level which enables her or him to continue to live the lifestyle to which he or she became accustomed during the marriage. This does raise questions as to some of the perks. I recently had a case in which the wife of a Hollywood producer was insisting that she be entitled to fly privately on the movie studio's plane. Clearly, the studio was not keen on this idea, as it was a perk reserved for her husband. The judge ruled that her producer ex had to pay her enough in spousal support to enable her to fly close to the manner to which she had become accustomed—namely, first class on commercial flights—but that she had no claim on the private jet because she was no longer Mrs. Producer. This came as a rude awakening to her, as did her future inability to attend the Oscars and Golden Globes, or to make choice restaurant reservations at the last minute.

For Love or Money

Spousal support is a difficult subject. At issue are love—or its loss—and money, which, along with their closely aligned cohort, power, also very often present in the equation, are among the most volatile flash points in human relations. Emotions are running high as you negotiate, and not-always-pretty personal dynamics are at play. It's why people hire lawyers.

Express your resentments and frustrations to *them;* it's what lawyers are there for, and it's what we're paid for. And we're used to getting an earful. "I supported him throughout our relationship. Why is he living in comfort in the house *I* paid for," one client recently began, "with *my* children, enjoying a lifestyle in which nothing has changed, while I'm stuck in a cramped one-bedroom apartment with rented furniture and an empty refrigerator?" It's a good question. And you don't have to be the woman's lawyer to understand the slow burn of her anger.

But the answer to her question is that she married him. Together, they created a household. He and she agreed that she would pursue a career while he maintained the home and assumed the role of agreeable companion or host at a range of events and obligations that bolstered her career. Both parties to the marriage were to benefit over the long term from this division of labor. That was the deal—spoken or unspoken, articulated or assumed—and now that the marriage was over and the ex-husband was in effect either fired from his role or quit and therefore was no longer in line for the promised future benefits, she owed him. A court was ordering her to compensate him for the loss and to support him while he found another path to future benefits. That she was maybe morally bound as well might be a matter of dispute or at least discussion; that she was legally bound was not. End of story. But not, of course, the end of her frustration.

It's tough enough to continue to pay through the nose to support someone you're no longer living with if that ex is the parent of your children, your onetime great love, your pal and inspiration when you were both young and eager. But if you're sending checks to the ex-wife who took up with the tennis instructor and is now living with him in your house and paying, through your spousal support, for the instructor's monthly teeth-whitening, that really is valid grounds for off-the-charts frustration.

By the same token, the ex may feel that he or she has been bailed on just when things were finally starting to pay off in your career. Stuck with the house, with a leaky roof, worn-down furniture, and all of the kids, he or she now has less money to pay for everything, while you sail off into the sunset, relatively responsibility-free, to begin your new life. He or she is likely bitching to his or her attorney about how the support "is not enough."

Either way, the main reason to keep your frustrations between you and your lawyer, resisting the temptation to make your gripes a cause célèbre in the negotiations, is financial. Your grievances and your worries are no doubt legitimate, but the subject of the negotiation is money, and the aim is to agree on how much and for how long. Period. Burdening those two issues—amount and duration—with the anger, resentment, regret, disappointment, etc. that you are feeling only serves to drag out the negotiations, make them tougher, and thereby put money in the lawyers' wallets. It isn't worth it.

In other words, and this is another of those essential principles of divorce in the twenty-first century, it is cheaper to pay your ex than to pay your lawyer. Believe me. The relatively few extra dollars you will pay to satisfy a demand you really don't want to satisfy will be as nothing compared to the bill you will get for the hours of time you spend complaining to me, arguing your case, and cataloging your grievances. I understand your frustration; every lawyer understands a client's frustration. And I assure you that we sympathize. But the real aim here is to close this chapter of your life and turn to a fresh page, and the way to do that is to leave your anger in your psychiatrist's office and let your lawyer effect a compromise, get an agreement, and get you out.

It's easy to forget this or certainly to rationalize it away when you are in the throes of a dissolving marriage. Psychology has a lot to say about the use of money as a lever of power, a weapon, a surrogate for other issues in a relationship. Remind yourself that spousal support is owed and will be paid, tell your lawyer your needs vis-à-vis that support, and then, as much as possible, let him or her do the job. It's the law. Live with it. This is *your* family, and these are *your* obligations.

Your lawyer will also step back into the process if and when payments are not forthcoming. If you're the paying spouse and you lose your job or take a beating in the market or for whatever reason are unable to satisfy the court's payment order, your first call should be to your ex to see if you can work out some interim arrangement until you get back on your feet. This is hardly the time you want to start paying lawyer's fees all over again. Instead, if you can work out a reasonable solution with your ex and put it in writing, you'll both have a measure of protection—your ex against losing out on basic operating money, you against getting stuck for support arrears.

Support arrears is a circumstance you want most earnestly to avoid. Your ex may seek compensation for arrears by asking the court to garnish your wages or salary or bank account or even your tax refund. Support is a debt that cannot be discharged through a declaration of bankruptcy, and it never goes away. Deadbeat spouses, like deadbeat parents, are always hunted, and courts are notoriously unsympathetic to claims of poverty. An editor client of mine, whose income, after a number of rich years, plummeted virtually overnight, was thrown out of court when he asked the judge to revisit his support agreement. "You're paying a lawyer," the judge observed, and that was enough to invalidate his claim of penury. Another guy I know, who had the sense to relinquish the lawyer and act pro se in court, fared equally badly. "You clearly have enough to put food in your belly and gas in your car," the judge said, "in which case you have enough to pay something toward your ex-wife—as required by law. I'm a taxpayer; I don't want to be responsible for her. She was your wife."

So even if times are tough, try to remember that there is a time limit to your spousal support obligation, and remind yourself that it pays in more ways than one to settle this monthly bill on a high-priority basis.

And if you are the receiving spouse, a little empathy is in order. Consider that even though it is the law and you have both signed the agreement, it is very likely embittering to write a check to someone to whom you are no longer married. For you, spousal support represents an opportunity to make the necessary changes of transition—moving to a new house, perhaps, or even to a new town, putting the kids in a different school, striking out on your own to meet new people. Time has been given to you, in a very real sense, to think about how you will start over. More than time, you really have been given the luxury to ponder how you will ensure a livelihood for yourself now that you are no longer somebody's spouse.

So your ex may write the monthly check to you with teeth gritted and may seal it with venom, and every time you receive it, you may grow even more furious that it isn't for a bigger amount. But whatever the feelings it arouses, the check is making it possible for you to take this time to consider how to get back on your feet. It's why I strongly recommend that you try to feel some appreciation for the check and for the check-writer—and that you find a way to demonstrate that appreciation.

And if you can't feel it, it's a really, really good idea to demonstrate it anyway.

IN BRIEF

Spousal support is aimed at preventing or compensating for any unfair economic consequences that result from the end of the marriage. The assumption is that both of you contributed to and/or made sacrifices for the unit you became as a couple, and that both now have different financial needs; spousal support considers the former in determining what each is due for the latter.

1. All aspects of spousal support are negotiable, including the length of the court's jurisdiction over the matter.
2. Support is taxable for the receiving party, tax-deductible for the paying spouse.

3. The rule of thumb is that support should, to the greatest extent possible, maintain the receiving spouse in the manner to which he or she became accustomed during the marriage.
4. To determine the amount, determine current cost of living; be sure to track every daily expense as well as major expenses and liabilities.
5. It is cheaper to pay your ex than your lawyer—really.

9

Child Support

Again, this is about money. It is not about visitation or contact, nor is it about physical custody, emotional support, or spiritual comfort. It is about paying for the food, shelter, clothing, and educational needs of your child or children, something which both parents are obligated to do by law. Child support in the United States is in fact a matter of federal law, the statute requiring that each state legislature establish guidelines for determining child support expenses and review the guidelines at least every four years.

Child support is remitted by one parent to another, and payments must continue until the child reaches legal majority—eighteen in virtually all of the fifty states—or has graduated from high school, whichever occurs *later.* Payments also cease if a child marries or becomes an emancipated minor. An emancipated minor is a person under the age of eighteen who has been removed from the control of his or her parents—and the parents freed of responsibility for the kid—by court order. The reasons are usually that the minor has married, or has obtained a degree from MIT at the age of fourteen and has job offers from every tech company on both coasts, or is an entertainer with an agent and an entourage and no need of parental financial support, or for some other reason that the court agrees makes it in the "best interest" of the child to gain emancipation. It's quite rare, but it's an exception to be acknowledged.

Almost no one anywhere on earth disputes the need for child support nor that it is a parental responsibility to provide it. The quibbles come, not surprisingly, over the amount of support and how it is spent. An ex-husband does not begrudge the $5,000 per month he pays for his child's food, clothing, and shelter—until he sees the kid in a hand-me-down raincoat and shoes a size too small while his ex-wife sports Hermès scarves and wields the latest Balenciaga handbag.

How Much?

What is surprising to many people is that the amount of child support tends to be a lower number than that of spousal support. The main reason for this is that child support is always nontaxable, and it is of course cheaper to pay in after-tax dollars than in before-tax dollars.

People are also often surprised to find that the amount of child support may not be evenly distributed among multiple children. If you are ordered to pay $9,000 in child support and you have three kids, you're probably not supporting each kid at $3,000 apiece. Rather, chances are that the youngest child has been awarded a level of support higher than that of his or her two older siblings, the reasoning being that younger kids simply cost more. That is, their support will be required for a longer time; even after the older kids reach majority, younger ones still require the collective infrastructure the older ones once enjoyed, along with their individual needs for clothing, education, health, and the like.

Some state guidelines designate specific expenses to be paid as part of child support and earmark others to be split between the parents. In some states, for example, both parents are responsible for their children's medical insurance, while in others—California, to take one example—the paying spouse generally buys the medical insurance and both parents share the uninsured medical expenses.

Higher education is another variable item that sometimes comes up when child support is discussed, although it is not officially an issue once majority is reached or the child has graduated from high school. No court will order payment for higher education, and I don't recommend even discussing it as a matter of child support. The issue, however, is that some colleges and universities simply assume that both parents will be footing the tuition bill, and they routinely consider a paying spouse's income in assessing need for financial aid. Moreover, clients know this is an expense that looms before them, and they think they need to get it settled *now.* In such cases, I might suggest, if the money is available, that a portion of the monthly child support, by agreement, go into a college fund—a 529 plan or some other vehicle of both parties' choice. Or, if there is a dispute over the property division, I will recommend that instead of paying the lawyers to fight over it, the couple just agree to put it toward the kids' college fund. It is easier to give money to your children than to your ex—or certainly to your ex's lawyer.

But while this may mean it makes sense to look into the financial assistance instructions of any colleges or universities your kids may be considering, the main lesson is to check the rules and regulations and guidelines in your state about which expenses constitute child support in your state and which do not. Remember of course that where state guidelines are concerned, they may be changed in four years—if the legislature does its job.

Determining a Dollar Figure

Child support guidelines in most states are expressed as percentages of earnings. These percentages are calculated based on data for the statistically derived earnings of the higher-earning spouses in statistically devised families and on the reasonable needs of their children. Those needs include housing, food, clothing, transportation, entertainment, health care, and miscellaneous items. They're the starting point for determining your child support needs, but since there is really no such thing as a statistical human, they are only the starting point.

The situation gets a bit more complicated when the family consists of high earners. If the state guidelines are followed, the percentage-of-earnings figure for the child support award is likely to be inappropriate—excessive in relation to the kids' actual needs and therefore not "reasonable." So high earners can opt out of the guidelines and let the courts determine a support award based on such factors as the lifestyle of the children, the standard of living in the home, and the actual income as arrived at by lawyers compiling financial information during the discovery process, as we'll discuss in greater detail in chapter 11.

But for most families, the first step, just as it was for spousal support, is to start tracking the actual outlay of expenditures—in this case, for each child in the family. Begin by assessing a percentage of the shelter and food costs each kid represents, then zero in on what you actually pay to clothe each and keep him or her in school supplies or other necessities. If you are the custodial parent and you work at a full-time job (a forty-hour week), most states require that your ex pay half the bill for childcare; check to see if that is the case in your state. Of course, if you are the custodial parent and you hire a babysitter for a night out with your buddies, that's on your dime.

Also as with spousal support, the best way to do this expense tracking is to write down every child-related expenditure every day. That's the most solid assurance you can give yourself that you are really capturing how much gets spent and on what. The things you don't think about unless you're shelling out for them right at the moment are key: haircuts, birthday gifts your kids give to their friends, field trips, karate class, after-school frozen yogurt, tutors, books, iPad apps, cell phone covers, Halloween costumes. The number of items paid for in the course of a day and the total cost of everything over a week or a month are bound to surprise you. And when your ex makes grumbling noises of incredulity at the money being spent on the children, you can just show him or her the recorded evidence.

In addition to basic support, there is something called support add-ons. These are the special items over and above core needs that parents agree their children should have: summer camp, for example, or private school, or the class trip to Washington, D.C., or tutoring, therapy, braces, and extracurricular activities. Who must pay for these add-ons and how much is a matter of discussion and negotiation, but I firmly believe that both of you should be glad to pay some portion. Neither of you—and certainly not the lower-earning spouse—wants to cede control over your children's lives, and paying your half of these costs is a good way to maintain control. It's also an important message to send; I know I have made certain my own children are clear that they are supported by both their parents.

What I do advise is that as much as possible, each of you pay the costs directly—for private school, camp, the tutor, ballet lessons, ceramic classes, whatever. You may have to ask for separate bills or spend a bit of time exchanging accounting information with each other—or with each other's lawyers, business managers, or accountants—but if you can manage, it is in some sense a "cleaner" way of dealing with your joint responsibility to support your children.

Some parents object to the paying spouse doing his or her own direct payment; they find it paternalistic, or an instance of Big Brother telling them how to bring up their children. *Don't question my motives,* runs their argument, *and don't tell me how to spend the support money the law demands you provide.* And in a sense, the law backs them up: In most states, there is neither any restriction in law on how the receiving spouse spends the support money nor any accountability for how it is spent. Fewer than a dozen of the fifty states allow courts to demand an accounting from custodial parents, but nobody tells you how to spend it. So this is an issue you will need to settle between you.

Changes

Like spousal support, child support is infinitely modifiable. That's fortunate, because kids' lives and needs change pretty frequently, and so therefore do the costs of raising them. It seems to me that every time I turn around, my older son has grown into the next larger shoe size; keeping him in sneakers is becoming prohibitively expensive.

So suppose you both decide that your child should go to boarding school. Naturally, each of you will pay half the tuition and board, as well as other school-related costs. But the paying parent will probably seek a modification in the amount of the support award now that the child is no longer living with the custodial parent. The custodial parent, in turn, will likely argue that since the kid will return home for various vacations, it is still a custodial responsibility to provide room and board. True. The child needs a room to come home to and food and other necessities of life while there. But the court will likely decide that the stark reduction in time spent at the custodial parent's home warrants an equally steep reduction in the child support award the paying parent is required to provide.

Pawns?

Perhaps not surprisingly, the money issue can frequently exacerbate an already disputatious divorce. In any event, it offers a particularly convenient channel for feelings of anger, resentment, vindictiveness, and the like. I have seen child support payments used as weapons often enough to know that even love for their children does not moderate those feelings in some people, nor temper their behavior. And the amount of money involved has little bearing on the behavior, either.

In a recent case involving an extremely wealthy couple, my client, the husband, agreed that his ex-wife would be the primary custodial parent and that the kids would continue to live mainly with her—and the menagerie of three dogs, two cats, and two very cute bunny rabbits—in the home they had grown up in. The point of contention was the amount of child support she was asking for; we considered it excessive, made an extremely generous counteroffer, and when that was refused, went to court.

As noted, there is a special formula, which tends to be highly detailed, for determining the amount of support appropriate for children of high earners. This was duly applied, and the judge came up with a number that was actually less than what our side, the father, had offered—and far less than what the mother had demanded. The day after the judgment was handed down, she drove over to her ex's mansion and deposited at his gate one small bunny—along with a note stating that she was so beggared by the court's decision that she could no longer afford to maintain the animal.

I honestly didn't know whether to laugh or cry when I heard about this. I wasn't sure—am still not sure—if it is laughable or pathetic. It is certainly absurd, in the true sense of the word, but my blood runs a little cold wondering what the poverty-stricken mother told her children—and how they might be affected in the long run. Fortunately, in their case the father is as sensible as he is generous. The bunny is happily residing with him Bel Air, so the cardinal rule of divorce—that at least one party must remain rational—still prevails. But the lesson is clear: Child support is about money to provide material goods and services to your children, so try to keep your feelings about your ex out of it.

"You Take the House"

After twenty-seven years of marriage, three grown children, and a shared home that was a magnet for all the kids of the neighborhood and the site of legendary Memorial Day parties, Paul told Tricia that he had fallen in love with the new paralegal at the firm—twenty-two years his junior—and intended to marry her. Laden with guilt, he assured Tricia he would be generous, and he was—almost to a fault. But the one thing Tricia wanted most of all was the house, and that was the one thing Paul refused to give up. There was a simple reason for that; Ashley, his new love, had been part of the office contingent attending last year's Memorial Day party and had just simply loved the place, with its stone fireplace, solid wooden beams, tall windows, gracious lawn and gardens. And what Ashley wanted, Paul was determined to give her.

Tricia's lawyer made sure he paid through the nose to be able to do so, and she persuaded Tricia that it really made sense for her to make a fresh start somewhere else. "You'll find living in a condo liberating," the lawyer said to her. "I promise."

But Tricia had loved her house with a fervor that perhaps only deep familiarity can bring. She knew its quirks, had purchased all the furniture, art, and *objets* in the house lovingly through the years—a preoccupation in which Paul had no interest and took no part—had raised three children here, had welcomed friends, had created a nest of comfort and convenience for her husband. The house was *hers*.

And so, on her last night, she determined that she would at least go out in style. She ordered a huge platter of delicacies from the finest seafood store in town—shrimp, crabmeat, mussels from Prince Edward Island, plus tubs of cocktail sauce, rémoulade sauce, and lots of caviar—and brought home a chilled bottle of her favorite champagne to wash it down.

She placed the feast before her on the table in the dining room, hung with portraits of her children, but Tricia found she had less of an appetite than she had thought. Even when she had finished the bottle of champagne, the platter seemed still heaped with shellfish. Tricia rose from the dining table and, carrying the platter with her, slowly and deliberately visited each room of the house to say good-bye—the living room with cozy fireplace and the tall windows curtained in heavy gold fabric, the den where she and Paul used to work on jigsaw puzzles together, the master bedroom and kids' bedrooms with their many windows that always made the house so bright and cheery, the kitchen where she had taken such care over meals without number for so many years.

The next day, Tricia drove away from the house just as Paul and Ashley were driving up. Ashley especially couldn't wait to take possession of the house, and for a while, it seemed to be the paradise she had hoped for.

They noticed the smell after a week or so and at first thought it was nothing. Paul had grown up in the countryside and concluded that a mouse had died inside the walls. "The corpse will just dry up," he told Ashley, "and the smell will disappear." But he was concerned. In all the years he had lived in this house, nothing like this had ever happened.

And the smell didn't disappear. After a month, they called in exterminators, who left behind a harsh odor of disinfectant; when it faded, the original decaying, stale, fishy smell was still there. Over the next few months of stench, Ashley hired experts who recommended a series of home remedies: baking soda in the carpet, charcoal briquettes in the basement, vinegar spray in the air. Paul bought a set of ozone generators, summoned a mold remediation specialist—who found no mold but charged him to remediate anyway—and wondered why Ashley couldn't learn to live with it. They were sniping at each other all the time now. She couldn't understand why he couldn't fix it; he couldn't understand why she kept whining. Paradise had turned into a disaster, and relations between them were deteriorating fast. In time, weary from the discomfort and hoarse from yelling at his new wife, Paul decided his only option was to sell, but the real estate agent assured him he would get nothing for this house once it went onto the market, and nothing is about what their only offer consisted of.

As they drove away from the house the morning of the closing, the new owner pulled in. Tricia's key still worked. She set down her things—the movers would arrive later—grabbed a can of Lysol and a long, narrow brush out of her purse, then pulled the ladder out of the utility room and dragged it into the living room. She set the ladder in front of one of the windows, climbed up, pulled apart the curtain rod holding the heavy gold curtains, shook and then brushed out of it the bits of decomposing shellfish and blobs of caviar and remoulade she had stuffed into it so long ago, spritzed Lysol down each end of the curtain rod, then closed it and set it back in its brackets. Then she went around the house and did the same thing to all the other curtain rods in all the other rooms.

She had brought another bottle of chilled champagne with her. She opened it, poured a glass, took a first satisfying sip, then

curled up in her favorite chair and telephoned her closest friend. "I'm back home," Tricia said.

Admit it: Isn't there something wonderfully satisfying about this story?

IN BRIEF

Federal law holds both parents responsible for paying for the food, clothing, and educational needs of their children. The law requires each state legislature to establish guidelines for determining child support expenses and to review the guidelines at least every four years. It is important to understand your state's guidelines.

1. Child support payments are nontaxable.
2. To begin determining the amount of child support, track your actual outlay for all child-related expenditures.
3. Child support is always modifiable.
4. Be mindful of add-ons; they add up.

10

Dividing Up Assets and Liabilities

There's a fairly straightforward way to understand the difference between community property, which governs how assets and liabilities are to be divided in nine states—Arizona, California, Idaho, Louisiana, Nevada, New Mexico, Texas, Washington, and Wisconsin (and is an option in Alaska)—and equitable distribution, which is the norm everywhere else.

Under the community property formula, the spouses are regarded as equal co-owners of everything earned or acquired during the marriage—all assets, all income, and all debts or liabilities, everything except gifts and inheritances.* This is the case even if just one of the spouses did the acquiring, or earned the income, or incurred the debts, and even if just one is listed as owner of the property or asset. In ending the marriage, therefore, the split is also equal. It's fifty-fifty, each spouse being entitled to half of everything co-owned. In California, for better or worse, the rule is pretty hard and fast, and the courts are fairly inflexible on the subject.

---

* Fairly obviously determined: A gift might be the first-edition book your best friend bought, wrapped, and gave to you for your birthday. An inheritance is the silver tea service your Aunt Tilly bequeathed to you in her will—along with the admonition to keep it well polished.

In equitable distribution states, by contrast, a fifty-fifty split is not the goal. Instead, the goal is a fair division of everything earned or acquired during the marriage—except, again, gifts and inheritances—and a range of factors may be taken into consideration in assessing what's fair: how long the marriage lasted, how old and how healthy or fit each spouse is, the individual earning potential of each spouse, the standard of living the two experienced as a couple, the contributions each made to homemaking and/or childcare during the marriage. The final division of assets and liabilities under equitable distribution may in fact end up being fifty-fifty, but the point is that there is flexibility—nothing hard and fast—about getting to that outcome.

In practice, of course, wherever you live, you and your spouse are free to negotiate the division of your assets and liabilities your way. The first thing to do, therefore, is to determine precisely what constitutes your marital property—the assets earned or acquired and the debts incurred during the marriage. This is sometimes easier to do if you look at what you had coming into the marriage and carve those assets out of the equation. The second thing to do is then to figure out a division of assets and debts that makes sense. By "making sense," I mean a division that will neither unduly impoverish nor grossly enrich either one of you, and one that will leave both of you with what you need to move on in your lives. In other words, divide it up so that each of you ends up with pretty much an equal amount of economic value.

Joint Property, Separate Property

Start by understanding that what you bring into the marriage you also take out of the marriage. If you bought your own home before the marriage, and your spouse then moved in with you, that house remains yours—*unless,* in a spurt of loving generosity, you decided to put your spouse's name on the deed along with yours, or unless the mortgage was paid off or serious renovations were made with money that belongs to you both. Bottom line? You may want to make sure neither happens. You also own separately any gift or inheritance willed specifically to you during the time of your marriage. And in most states, you own everything you earn or acquire after the date of separation, which is why date of separation can be so important.

Just about everything else belongs to the two of you—or actually, to the unit the two of you represented while married, also known as the "community." That's why it is so important to figure out precisely what comprises "everything else."

For example, what about gifts that were given to both of you? Like at your wedding? My father always had a practice of writing the wedding-gift check to only the party he knew well. If it was deposited into a joint account, that was their choice.

A wise person once said that the less you have, the easier divorce is. But however much you have, you need to inventory it. One of the first things you'll need to inventory is money.

As we'll show in greater detail in the next chapter, it is very difficult to hide money. It takes a great deal of planning, over a long period of time, and a fair amount of effort to stash any kind of cash or financial instrument in a way that its presence is concealed. Even then, it is unlikely to stay concealed. Money that has been spent does not show up, but money sitting in a bank account or in a real estate investment trust or in an exchange-traded fund or even in a Section 529 plan somewhere will show up when a lawyer asks for records. So if your spouse has withdrawn $200,000 from his own special savings account that you didn't even know he had, you will learn about it. And you or your lawyer will want to know exactly where it went, because his own special savings account was actually marital or community property.

Of course, more than money is involved. Your joint assets as a couple may start with your house and your time-share condo at the beach, but real estate is only the beginning. All of your non–real estate property is also at stake—from your investment portfolio and your spouse's 401(k) to the art on the wall and the boat in the garage, to the furniture in the living room and the appliances in the kitchen, to the frequent flyer miles toted up by the spouse who travels for work. Frequent flyer mileage, in fact, is a big-ticket item and by well-established law a community property asset. Don't forget about it.

And don't forget the dog, either. Or the cat, parrot, gerbil, boa constrictor, or other pet. Just as the art, the boat, and the kitchen appliances are goods, pets are chattel. They are community property. A judge will award the pet to one or the other of you; to avoid this, you can come up with a joint custody agreement or make the pet another asset to be bargained for.

The standard way to divide your joint property is to make a list, and the recommended way to do that is for the two of you to walk through your home, together, bearing notepads, separately colored stickers, or tape. Logic will help decide ownership, but value is equally a consideration so that the split is as fair and as even as possible. You will need to value items not by the price you paid for them but by the price the item could command if it were being sold tomorrow at an estate auction—or more likely, a garage sale. The five-thousand-dollar sofa you bought for the living room ten years ago is likely to go for under a thousand at a sale, despite the care lavished upon it all this time. So note on the sticker tag the value of each item and which of you claims it, and when you put it all together in a list, you'll be able to see if there is a fairness gap or value gap. Then you can mix and match items on the list to equalize the outcome.

A Mobile App for Dividing Property

It's not just for lawyers anymore! Yes, attorneys have DissoMaster, Propertizer, Executioner (not what it sounds), and more. Now clients too can access computerized divorce help on a computer or tablet. iSplit is the first of these programs; more are sure to follow. iSplit lets the user drag and drop assets and debts representing ten different categories so you can see how various configurations of property division look on the screen. Keep on changing the configuration, shifting furniture, bank accounts, appliances from one spouse to the other to see what happens. As a way to get negotiations going, this kind of interaction, available at the click of a mouse, can be very useful indeed. I love this app!

Creative Types

Not all assets are as easy—or as logical to assign ownership to—as blenders and bathtub accessories, microwaves and iPad minis. Intellectual assets, which figure heavily in my practice, are particularly thorny to figure out. The law says that anything you create during your marriage is joint property; anything you create after the date of separation is not. So when a big-time movie star announces he is putting future film projects on hold just as his high-profile marriage unravels, may we deduce that his reasons for doing so are not strictly to focus on his family problems?

The song a musician composed and recorded years ago during her marriage is to be released on a compilation album next month, long after the marriage has become a memory. Does the ex-husband take home a portion of the proceeds?

A novelist works for years on his book. Progress is slowed as he marries, fathers two children, and divorces his wife. Finally, his novel is published, becomes a bestseller, and the rights are sold to a hotshot Hollywood producer for zillions of dollars. Who owns the property and enjoys the windfall?

The answers are: Yes for the big-time movie star suddenly deferring his future film projects as his marriage unravels; he or she is not about to share the earnings from those projects with the spouse walking out the door.

Yes for the ex-husband of the musician; he is entitled to his share of the earnings from the song composed while he was married to her.

As for the novelist and his ex-wife, the answer is that both get something. Specifically, the ex will be entitled to a percentage of the value the created work realizes that is equal to the proportion of the work that was created during the marriage.

It's why both parties to a divorce hire lawyers. For although the formula is simple—what was created during the marriage is joint property—figuring out exactly what fits the definition of "created" isn't so easy. Once it has been figured out, it is also not so easy to administer the resulting accounting. Suppose, for example, that you are entitled to a percentage of a royalty on your ex's book, which, although still in print, is hardly the hit it was when it first came out. So the amount of the royalty is itself dwindling over time, and in addition, the size of the royalty owed to your ex diminishes over time as certain sales targets are passed. It means that the amount of money you're actually entitled to from this one work must be routinely adjusted before its quarterly payout to you. Since many creative people—and not-so-creative people as well—find this sort of detailed bookkeeping unfathomable at best and tedious at worst, it is often left to business managers, accountants, and financial controllers. An awful lot of ex-spouses find it far simpler to take a lump-sum payment rather than dive into what strikes them as an administrative quagmire. And their lawyers are likely to breathe a sigh of relief when they do so.

Big Ticket

Perhaps counterintuitively, it is the large assets that often provide rich opportunities for working out a fair division of property. A house is everybody's biggest asset and typically a couple's most significant investment, and it can be sold, rented out, or held on to as part of a property settlement. Who gets what share of the sale proceeds or rental income and how and over what time period the payout is implemented are just a few of the variables. As I write this, the housing market is showing the first stirrings of upward movement after its collapse in 2006—finally—but many houses around the country still cannot be sold for any kind of profit. If that is the case for a divorcing couple, one possibility is for the custodial parent and children to remain in the house *as tenants* while the other spouse moves out. Your marriage may be over, but your joint ownership of this asset continues, and the community that you represent as joint owners has become the landlord of the house. So each partner, acting jointly as landlord, pays his or her half of the mortgage, insurance, and property taxes, while the custodial parent living in the house pays rent for maintenance and is responsible for the utility bills.

Or suppose you bought a business during your marriage—say, a pizza parlor (not surprisingly, since I am the mother of two young boys, the first business that comes to mind). You both paid for it, and you both take profits from it, but only one spouse is actively involved in running the place. While no great shakes at flipping dough, this spouse is a marvel at managing a business—as evidenced in the steady profits the pizza parlor returns. When the two of you divorce, the spouse not running the place should think long and hard about what makes the most sense financially vis-à-vis this jointly owned enterprise. Should you take the money through a buyout and be done with it? Or is there merit in holding on to your half-ownership and, since your spouse knows how to run the place successfully, keeping him or her on as the salaried manager? You won't know the answer until you get the business appraised, see its value, and consider the ramifications of both options, but the questions are worth asking.

Debt

Debts are also jointly owned. Lily learned that Adam was cheating on her, and her instant reaction was to max out every credit card the couple had. Since spite was her aim, this was a winning move:

Credit card debt certainly qualifies as community property, so Lily had nicely created a liability for which Adam would be responsible—or which she could trade off for something she wanted in return in the final settlement.

Adam, in turn, had a lawsuit judgment hanging over his head from a run-in with a restaurant chef whose bouillabaisse he was sure had given him food poisoning. Adam is a hothead, one reason Lily was divorcing him. But the punitive damages he owed to the chef, while not megabucks, nevertheless represented a debt for which Lily would be responsible should the intemperate Adam skip town or fail to make payment.

There's a deal in there: One liability can cancel out the other. Or, the higher-earning spouse might offer to assume both liabilities in return for keeping the car, or maybe for a slightly bigger cut of the proceeds from the sale of the house, or maybe even for more time with the kids.

Interestingly, division of property is often the least contentious aspect of dissolving a marriage relationship. The wars that go on over property are typically less brutal than the wars over support or custody. Maybe it's because people perceive property as just things. Support and custody concern your children and your ability to get along on your own and seem far more electrically charged with emotion.

Whatever the underlying reason, it does seem that even the bitterest of ex-spouses can accept that assets and liabilities should be divided between them. Such acceptance is a good basis on which both can work to divide their property as fairly as they can, with outcomes as equal as possible.

IN BRIEF

The ideal division of assets and liabilities neither unduly impoverishes nor unduly enriches either party; rather, it leaves both with what you need to move on in your lives. In effect, each ends up a fairly equal amount of economic value, if with different amounts of money or property.

1. What you bring into the marriage as yours you take out of the marriage as yours.
2. Generally, everything you earn or acquire after the date of separation is yours.
3. Everything else belongs to the "community" and is subject to negotiation in determining the division of assets and liabilities.

11

Discovering Discovery

A client I'll call Blair was the stay-at-home wife of a highly successful corporate executive—call him Doug—who spent a great deal of time traveling on business. Doug's frequent, prolonged absences may have been one reason their marriage was unraveling, but Blair found another when she noticed a charge on the couple's AmEx bill for $2,799, paid at what she knew to be a very fashionable women's clothing store in New York.

Blair hadn't been to New York in years, but Doug had been there precisely when the purchase was made. So Blair phoned AmEx customer service, identified herself as the joint holder of the account and the wife of the purchaser, and asked the agent to "remind" her what the transaction in New York was all about. It was for a single item, she was told: a Chanel clutch bag. Certainly a classic in the world of fashion accessories, but not exactly Doug's sort of thing, and he clearly hadn't bought it for his wife.

That evening, while Doug was showering, Blair scrolled through the backlog of calls on his phone and found a whole lot of calls to and from someone named Chanelle. A coincidence, despite the variation in spelling? Blair tapped "Call Back," and a woman answered. Blair introduced herself and asked the woman if she knew Doug.

"Yes, I do," said the woman.

"May I ask how you know him?"

"I am a professional call girl," Chanelle explained. "I have had a relationship with Doug for more than a year."

Blair took a moment to let this sink in. Then: "Do you by any chance have a record of the times you met?" she asked.

"Oh yes," said Chanelle. "I have all of it. I keep it all on the iPad he bought me." She paused. "I use the Mint app, so I can sync with my iPhone and my laptop as well."

It was certainly gratifying to know that Chanelle's record-keeping could be accessed so easily and on so many devices. It also prompted Blair to put forth a proposal. "If I buy you an airline ticket and put you up at the Four Seasons Hotel, would you be willing to come out here to California and tell me all about it?"

"Business class?" Chanelle asked.

It would be, and Chanelle did, and the result for Blair was a detailed record of thousand-dollar-a-day assignations; lavish evenings at the legendary Petrossian restaurant, where Chanelle and Doug shared their appreciation of fine caviar; and of course the almost eponymous Chanel clutch for Chanelle. In all, Doug's misappropriation of community property, which he did not deny, amounted to some $200,000, for half of which he of course had to indemnify Blair in the final divorce settlement.

The point of this story is not the divorce, however, but the fact that it took Blair a total of about six minutes to find out exactly what her husband was up to on all those out-of-town business trips. It is yet another reminder, if one were needed, that it is virtually impossible to hide anything you do in this age of e-mailing, Instagram, GPS-equipped smartphones, and all the rest of it. Ask David Petraeus, Eliot Spitzer, Anthony Weiner, and a host of other once-powerful figures. And especially where financial matters are concerned, when it comes to dissolving a marriage, any dissembling at all is strictly against the law—on penalty of perjury. You need to disclose fully and factually, which is precisely what the discovery process is all about.

The Purpose of Discovery

As its name makes clear, the discovery process is about bringing to light information, situations, and truths that might otherwise remain out of sight. Money is the primary if not the sole focus here. As Deep Throat hinted to Bob Woodward during *The Washington Post*'s Watergate investigation, following the money is essential; it will almost always take you to other underlying or latent realities.

But discovery is not just an exercise in sleuthing. It has a very practical purpose—namely, to enable you to make the case for the settlement you will ask for, and to provide you with the hard evidence that supports your case. I have been in situations where it was clear that one party really had no coherent facts to back up the claims made. In a recent case, for example, the opposing counsel insisted that since my client admittedly had an estate valued at $10 million, the departing wife was entitled to $5 million, not the $2.5 million we were proposing. It was an easy matter for me to demonstrate that my client had $5 million at the time of his marriage; he earned another $5 million during the marriage. His soon-to-be-ex therefore was entitled to $2.5 million, half of the community property earned during the marriage. All anybody had to do was look at the record. The documentation was as clear as Chanelle's, and it told a straight story. Knock off a few zeros; the application is the same. As my CPA friends like to remind me, numbers don't lie.

A straight story is what you want your lawyer to have when he or she goes into court to make a legal argument on your behalf. Discovery is the process in which you put that story together. What is learned in discovery will shape the story the lawyer tells to make your case and articulate the legal argument on your behalf.

So the cardinal rule for the discovery process is to put it all out there. Don't hold any information back from your lawyer or, by extension, from the spouse you're splitting from. Not the extra credit card you got for your own exclusive use and which you think is not really anybody's business but yours, not the cash you pay for Botox treatments you would prefer to keep to yourself, not the minuscule income you received last year for a short story you sold to a literary review absolutely no one has ever heard of.

For one thing, it's a solid bet that anything you conceal will come out anyway. In this digital environment, it's bound to; in fact, the longer something is concealed, the better its chances of going viral. That represents a considerable difference from a generation ago, when it was not unknown for parties in a divorce to indulge in creative accounting or the artful disposition of cash to avoid putting all of their financial cards on the table.

Perhaps as a result of those disinclinations to reveal the *whole* truth, family law has developed compelling rules of procedure for eliciting a broad range of information. When you fill out and sign one of the several form interrogatories we'll discuss in a moment, you're effectively under oath. As I don't have to tell you, dissembling when under oath is a very bad idea and can have extremely costly consequences.

There's a famous case of a woman who separated from her husband, bought a lottery ticket, and won a pile of money. The winnings definitely qualified as her own property, since she had purchased the ticket well after the date of separation, but inexplicably, she did not disclose the gain. Of course, the word got out, and the judge, while conceding that the lottery prize money was indisputably hers, nevertheless ordered her to pay half of it to her ex-husband in the final settlement—as a penalty for her failure to disclose.

One more thing: The public today is vastly more financially sophisticated than were our parents and grandparents. Dual-earner families, financial broadcasting 24/7 on television and the radio, and more people than ever before participating in such financial activities as stock market investing, mortgages, student loans—as well as in foreclosures and bankruptcies—mean that just about everybody is pretty familiar with how money works. It also means that people keep track of their finances in a way they probably did not a generation ago.

All of this—the broader knowledge about financial matters, the procedures for disclosure, and the fact that no reason or excuse for nondisclosure can beat out the technology of revelation—also means that trust really can be the engine of divorce in the twenty-first century. Trust, it turns out, is the most cost-effective route to disengaging from your spouse, and full disclosure is its essence. When Doug owned up to his affair with Chanelle, it made it easier for Blair to believe he was owning up to everything else as well, that he wasn't trying to hide things. That, in turn, made her less inclined to try to soak him for every penny no matter how long it took or what it cost either one of them—both financially and in terms of any civil feelings the two might ever have for each other.

Whatever information you have, put it out there. It will cost you less and can gain you much more than you suppose.

Disclosures

Most states mandate the exchange of financial information between the two parties, but specific procedures for what needs to be disclosed, how, and when differ from state to state. Some states require a preliminary declaration of disclosure—in California, such a declaration must be provided within sixty days of petitioning for dissolution—and then a final disclosure at the time of settlement. Some states waive the final disclosure altogether. As part of the research you began way back in chapter 1, it is easy enough to familiarize yourself with all these procedures for your particular state.

Helping you put together the information required for the exchange are form interrogatories—questionnaires you fill out that tell lawyers and the court everything the state thinks the lawyers and the court need to know to come to a fair settlement. These also differ in form and format from state to state. (You can probably find and even download samples of your state's form interrogatories online.) California's family law form interrogatory has twenty-one questions, all of which can be answered in anywhere from a few words to pages of facts and figures. Florida's form is in outline form and asks for six basic categories of information. The state of Washington's interrogatory has nine pages of questions in tabular form. Nevertheless, they're all asking for more or less the same thing—namely, the full details of both parties' assets, liabilities, income, and expenses.

FL-140

ATTORNEY OR PARTY WITHOUT ATTORNEY *(Name, State Bar number, and address)*:

TELEPHONE NO.: FAX NO.:
E-MAIL ADDRESS:
ATTORNEY FOR *(Name)*:

SUPERIOR COURT OF CALIFORNIA, COUNTY OF
STREET ADDRESS:
MAILING ADDRESS:
CITY AND ZIP CODE:
BRANCH NAME:

PETITIONER:
RESPONDENT:
OTHER PARENT/PARTY:

DECLARATION OF DISCLOSURE
☐ Petitioner's ☐ Preliminary
☐ Respondent's ☐ Final

CASE NUMBER:

DO NOT FILE DECLARATIONS OF DISCLOSURE OR FINANCIAL ATTACHMENTS WITH THE COURT

In a dissolution, legal separation, or nullity action, both a preliminary and a final declaration of disclosure must be served on the other party with certain exceptions. Neither disclosure is filed with the court. Instead, a declaration stating that service of disclosure documents was completed or waived must be filed with the court (see form FL-141).

- *In summary dissolution cases, each spouse or domestic partner must exchange preliminary disclosures as described in* Summary Dissolution Information *(form FL-810). Final disclosures are not required (see Family Code section 2109).*
- *In a default judgment case that is not a stipulated judgment or a judgment based on a marital settlement agreement, only the petitioner is required to complete and serve a preliminary declaration of disclosure. A final disclosure is not required of either party (see Family Code section 2110).*
- *Service of preliminary declarations of disclosure may not be waived by an agreement between the parties.*
- *Parties who agree to waive final declarations of disclosure must file their written agreement with the court (see form FL-144).*

The petitioner must serve a preliminary declaration of disclosure at the same time as the Petition or within 60 days of filing the Petition. The respondent must serve a preliminary declaration of disclosure at the same time as the Response or within 60 days of filing the Response. The time periods may be extended by written agreement of the parties or by court order (see Family Code section 2104(f)).

Attached are the following:

1. ☐ A completed *Schedule of Assets and Debts* (form FL-142) or ☐ A *Property Declaration* (form FL-160) for *(specify)*:
   ☐ Community and Quasi-Community Property ☐ Separate Property.
2. ☐ A completed *Income and Expense Declaration* (form FL-150).
3. ☐ All tax returns filed by the party in the two years before the date that the party served the disclosure documents.
4. ☐ A statement of all material facts and information regarding valuation of all assets that are community property or in which the community has an interest *(not a form)*.
5. ☐ A statement of all material facts and information regarding obligations for which the community is liable *(not a form)*.
6. ☐ An accurate and complete written disclosure of any investment opportunity, business opportunity, or other income-producing opportunity presented since the date of separation that results from any investment, significant business, or other income-producing opportunity from the date of marriage to the date of separation (*not a form*).

I declare under penalty of perjury under the laws of the State of California that the foregoing is true and correct.

Date:

(TYPE OR PRINT NAME) ▶ SIGNATURE

Page 1 of 1

Form Adopted for Mandatory Use
Judicial Council of California
FL-140 [Rev. July 1, 2013]

Martin Dean's ESSENTIAL FORMS™

DECLARATION OF DISCLOSURE
(Family Law)

Family Code, §§ 2102, 2104, 2105, 2106, 2112
www.courts.ca.gov

THIS FORM SHOULD NOT BE FILED WITH THE COURT FL-142

ATTORNEY OR PARTY WITHOUT ATTORNEY *(Name and Address)*: TELEPHONE NO.:

ATTORNEY FOR *(Name)*:

SUPERIOR COURT OF CALIFORNIA, COUNTY OF

PETITIONER:

RESPONDENT:

SCHEDULE OF ASSETS AND DEBTS
☐ **Petitioner's** ☐ **Respondent's**

CASE NUMBER:

- INSTRUCTIONS -

List all your known community and separate assets or debts. Include assets even if they are in the possession of another person, including your spouse. If you contend an asset or debt is separate, put P (for Petitioner) or R (for Respondent) in the first column (separate property) to indicate to whom you contend it belongs.

All values should be as of the date of signing the declaration unless you specify a different valuation date with the description. For additional space, use a continuation sheet numbered to show which item is being continued.

ITEM NO.	ASSETS DESCRIPTION	SEP. PROP	DATE ACQUIRED	CURRENT GROSS FAIR MARKET VALUE	AMOUNT OF MONEY OWED OR ENCUMBRANCE
1.	REAL ESTATE *(Give street addresses and attach copies of deeds with legal descriptions and latest lender's statement.)*			$	$
2.	HOUSEHOLD FURNITURE, FURNISHINGS, APPLIANCES *(Identify.)*				
3.	JEWELRY, ANTIQUES, ART, COIN COLLECTIONS, etc. *(Identify.)*				

Page 1 of 4

Form Approved for Optional Use
Judicial Council of California
FL-142 [Rev. January 1, 2005]

SCHEDULE OF ASSETS AND DEBTS
(Family Law)

Code of Civil Procedure, §§ 2030(c), 2033.5
www.courtinfo.ca.gov

Martin Dean's ESSENTIAL FORMS™

ITEM NO.	ASSETS DESCRIPTION	SEP. PROP	DATE ACQUIRED	CURRENT GROSS FAIR MARKET VALUE	AMOUNT OF MONEY OWED OR ENCUMBRANCE
				$	$
4.	VEHICLES, BOATS, TRAILERS *(Describe and attach copy of title document.)*				
5.	SAVINGS ACCOUNTS *(Account name, account number, bank, and branch. Attach copy of latest statement.)*				
6.	CHECKING ACCOUNTS *(Account name and number, bank, and branch. Attach copy of latest statement.)*				
7.	CREDIT UNION, OTHER DEPOSIT ACCOUNTS *(Account name and number, bank, and branch. Attach copy of latest statement.)*				
8.	CASH *(Give location.)*				
9.	TAX REFUND				
10.	LIFE INSURANCE WITH CASH SURRENDER OR LOAN VALUE *(Attach copy of declaration page for each policy.)*				

FL-142 [Rev. January 1, 2005]

Martin Dean's ESSENTIAL FORMS™

SCHEDULE OF ASSETS AND DEBTS
(Family Law)

Page 2 of 4

ITEM NO.	ASSETS DESCRIPTION	SEP. PROP	DATE ACQUIRED	CURRENT GROSS FAIR MARKET VALUE	AMOUNT OF MONEY OWED OR ENCUMBRANCE
11.	STOCKS, BONDS, SECURED NOTES, MUTUAL FUNDS *(Give certificate number and attach copy of the certificate or copy of latest statement.)*			$	$
12.	RETIREMENT AND PENSIONS *(Attach copy of latest summary plan documents and latest benefit statement.)*				
13.	PROFIT-SHARING, ANNUITIES, IRAS, DEFERRED COMPENSATION *(Attach copy of latest statement.)*				
14.	ACCOUNTS RECEIVABLE AND UNSECURED NOTES *(Attach copy of each.)*				
15.	PARTNERSHIPS AND OTHER BUSINESS INTERESTS *(Attach copy of most current K-1 form and Schedule C.)*				
16.	OTHER ASSETS				
17.	TOTAL ASSETS FROM CONTINUATION SHEET				
18.	TOTAL ASSETS			$	$

FL-142 [Rev. January 1, 2005]

SCHEDULE OF ASSETS AND DEBTS
(Family Law)

Page 3 of 4

Martin Dean's ESSENTIAL FORMS™

ITEM NO.	DEBTS-SHOW TO WHOM OWED	SEP. PROP	TOTAL OWING	DATE INCURRED
			$	
19.	STUDENT LOANS *(Give details.)*			
20.	TAXES *(Give details.)*			
21.	SUPPORT ARREARAGES *(Attach copies of orders and statements.)*			
22.	LOANS - UNSECURED *(Give bank name and loan number and attach copy of latest statement.)*			
23.	CREDIT CARDS *(Give creditor's name and address and the account number. Attach copy of latest statement.)*			
24.	OTHER DEBTS *(Specify.)*:			
25.	TOTAL DEBTS FROM CONTINUATION SHEET			
26.	TOTAL DEBTS		$	

27. ☐ *(Specify number)* : ________ pages are attached as continuation sheets.

I declare under penalty of perjury under the laws of the State of California that the foregoing is true and correct.

Date:

_______________________________ ▶ _______________________________

(TYPE OR PRINT NAME) (SIGNATURE OF DECLARANT)

FL-142 [Rev. January 1, 2005]

SCHEDULE OF ASSETS AND DEBTS
(Family Law)

Page 4 of 4

Martin Dean's ESSENTIAL FORMS™

FL-150

ATTORNEY OR PARTY WITHOUT ATTORNEY *(Name, State Bar number, and address)*: TELEPHONE NO.: E-MAIL ADDRESS *(Optional)*: ATTORNEY FOR *(Name)*:	*FOR COURT USE ONLY*
SUPERIOR COURT OF CALIFORNIA, COUNTY OF STREET ADDRESS: MAILING ADDRESS: CITY AND ZIP CODE: BRANCH NAME:	
PETITIONER/PLAINTIFF: RESPONDENT/DEFENDANT: OTHER PARENT/CLAIMANT:	
INCOME AND EXPENSE DECLARATION	CASE NUMBER:

1. **Employment** *(Give information on your current job or, if you're unemployed, your most recent job.)*

Attach copies of your pay stubs for last two months (black out social security numbers).

a. Employer:
b. Employer's address:
c. Employer's phone number:
d. Occupation:
e. Date job started:
f. If unemployed, date job ended:
g. I work about hours per week.
h. I get paid $ gross (before taxes) ☐ per month ☐ per week ☐ per hour.

(If you have more than one job, attach an 8 1/2-by-11-inch sheet of paper and list the same information as above for your other jobs. Write "Question 1 - Other Jobs" at the top.)

2. **Age and education**
   a. My age is *(specify)*:
   b. I have completed high school or the equivalent: ☐ Yes ☐ No If no, highest grade completed *(specify)*:
   c. Number of years of college completed *(specify)*: ☐ Degree(s) obtained *(specify)*:
   d. Number of years of graduate school completed *(specify)*: ☐ Degree(s) obtained *(specify)*:
   e. I have: ☐ professional/occupational license(s) *(specify)*:
   ☐ vocational training *(specify)*:
3. **Tax information**
   a. ☐ I last filed taxes for tax year *(specify year)*:
   b. My tax filing status is ☐ single ☐ head of household ☐ married, filing separately
   ☐ married, filing jointly with *(specify name)*:
   c. I file state tax returns in ☐ California ☐ other *(specify state)*:
   d. I claim the following number of exemptions (including myself) on my taxes *(specify)*:
4. **Other party's income.** I estimate the gross monthly income (before taxes) of the other party in this case at *(specify)*: $
   This estimate is based on *(explain)*:

(If you need more space to answer any questions on this form, attach an 8 1/2-by-11-inch sheet of paper and write the question number before your answer.) Number of pages attached: ________

I declare under penalty of perjury under the laws of the State of California that the information contained on all pages of this form and any attachments is true and correct.

Date:

____________________________________ ▶ ____________________________________
(TYPE OR PRINT NAME) (SIGNATURE OF DECLARANT)

Page 1 of 4

Form Adopted for Mandatory Use
Judicial Council of California
FL-150 [Rev. January 1, 2007]

Martin Dean's ESSENTIAL FORMS™

INCOME AND EXPENSE DECLARATION

Family Code, §§ 2030-2032, 2100-2113, 3552, 3620-3634, 4050-4076, 4300-4339
www.courtinfo.ca.gov

FL-150

PETITIONER/PLAINTIFF: RESPONDENT/DEFENDANT: OTHER PARENT/CLAIMANT:	CASE NUMBER:

Attach copies of your pay stubs for the last two months and proof of any other income. Take a copy of your latest federal tax return to the court hearing. ***(Black out your social security number on the pay stub and tax return.)***

	Last month	Average monthly
5. **Income** *(For average monthly, add up all the income you received in each category in the last 12 months and divide the total by 12.)*		
a. Salary or wages (gross, before taxes)	$	
b. Overtime (gross, before taxes)	$	
c. Commissions or bonuses	$	
d. Public assistance (for example: TANF, SSI, GA/GR) ☐ currently receiving	$	
e. Spousal support ☐ from this marriage ☐ from a different marriage	$	
f. Partner support ☐ from this domestic partnership ☐ from a different domestic partnership	$	
g. Pension/retirement fund payments	$	
h. Social security retirement (not SSI)	$	
i. Disability: ☐ Social security (not SSI) ☐ State disability (SDI) ☐ Private insurance.	$	
j. Unemployment compensation	$	
k. Workers' compensation	$	
l. Other (military BAQ, royalty payments, etc.) *(specify)* :	$	
6. **Investment income** *(Attach a schedule showing gross receipts less cash expenses for each piece of property.)*		
a. Dividends/interest	$	
b. Rental property income	$	
c. Trust income	$	
d. Other *(specify)* :	$	
7. **Income from self-employment, after business expenses for all businesses**	$	

I am the ☐ owner/sole proprietor ☐ business partner ☐ other *(specify)* :
Number of years in this business *(specify)* :
Name of business *(specify)* :
Type of business *(specify)* :
Attach a profit and loss statement for the last two years or a Schedule C from your last federal tax return. Black out your social security number. If you have more than one business, provide the information above for each of your businesses.

8. ☐ **Additional income.** I received one-time money (lottery winnings, inheritance, etc.) in the last 12 months *(specify source and amount)* :

9. ☐ **Change in income.** My financial situation has changed significantly over the last 12 months because *(specify)* :

10. **Deductions**	Last month
a. Required union dues	$
b. Required retirement payments (not social security, FICA, 401(k), or IRA)	$
c. Medical, hospital, dental, and other health insurance premiums *(total monthly amount)*	$
d. Child support that I pay for children from other relationships	$
e. Spousal support that I pay by court order from a different marriage	$
f. Partner support that I pay by court order from a different domestic partnership	$
g. Necessary job-related expenses not reimbursed by my employer *(attach explanation labeled "Question 10g")*	$

11. **Assets**	Total
a. Cash and checking accounts, savings, credit union, money market, and other deposit accounts	$
b. Stocks, bonds, and other assets I could easily sell	$
c. All other property, ☐ real and ☐ personal *(estimate fair market value minus the debts you owe)*	$

FL-150 [Rev. January 1, 2007] **INCOME AND EXPENSE DECLARATION** Page 2 of 4

Martin Dean's ESSENTIAL FORMS™

FL-150

PETITIONER/PLAINTIFF: RESPONDENT/DEFENDANT: OTHER PARENT/CLAIMANT:	CASE NUMBER:

12. **The following people live with me:**

Name	Age	How the person is related to me? *(ex: son)*	That person's gross monthly income	Pays some of the household expenses?
a.				❑ Yes ❑ No
b.				❑ Yes ❑ No
c.				❑ Yes ❑ No
d.				❑ Yes ❑ No
e.				❑ Yes ❑ No

13. **Average monthly expenses** ❑ Estimated expenses ❑ Actual expenses ❑ Proposed needs

a. Home:
   (1) ❑ Rent or ❑ mortgage $
   If mortgage:
   (a) average principal: $
   (b) average interest: $
   (2) Real property taxes $
   (3) Homeowner's or renter's insurance (if not included above) $
   (4) Maintenance and repair $

b. Health-care costs not paid by insurance $

c. Child care $

d. Groceries and household supplies $

e. Eating out $

f. Utilities (gas, electric, water, trash) $

g. Telephone, cell phone, and e-mail $

h. Laundry and cleaning $

i. Clothes $

j. Education $

k. Entertainment, gifts, and vacation $

l. Auto expenses and transportation (insurance, gas, repairs, bus, etc.) $

m. Insurance (life, accident, etc.; do not include auto, home, or health insurance) $

n. Savings and investments $

o. Charitable contributions $

p. Monthly payments listed in item 14 *(itemize below in 14 and insert total here)* $

q. Other *(specify)* : $

r. **TOTAL EXPENSES** (a-q) *(do not add in the amounts in a(1)(a) and (b))* $

s. **Amount of expenses paid by others** $

14. **Installment payments and debts not listed above**

Paid to	For	Amount	Balance	Date of last payment
		$	$	
		$	$	
		$	$	
		$	$	
		$	$	
		$	$	

15. **Attorney fees** *(This is required if either party is requesting attorney fees.)*:
   a. To date, I have paid my attorney this amount for fees and costs *(specify)* : $
   b. The source of this money was *(specify)* :
   c. I still owe the following fees and costs to my attorney *(specify total owed)* : $
   d. My attorney's hourly rate is *(specify)* : $

I confirm this fee arrangement.

Date:

(TYPE OR PRINT NAME OF ATTORNEY) ▶ (SIGNATURE OF ATTORNEY)

FL-150 [Rev. January 1, 2007] **INCOME AND EXPENSE DECLARATION** Page 3 of 4

Martin Dean's ESSENTIAL FORMS™

FL-150

PETITIONER/PLAINTIFF: RESPONDENT/DEFENDANT: OTHER PARENT/CLAIMANT:	CASE NUMBER:

CHILD SUPPORT INFORMATION
(NOTE: Fill out this page only if your case involves child support.)

16. **Number of children**
a. I have *(specify number)*: children under the age of 18 with the other parent in this case.
b. The children spend percent of their time with me and percent of their time with the other parent.
(If you're not sure about percentage or it has not been agreed on, please describe your parenting schedule here.)

17. **Children's health-care expenses**
a. ☐ I do ☐ I do not have health insurance available to me for the children through my job.
b. Name of insurance company:
c. Address of insurance company:

d. The monthly cost for the **children's** health insurance is or would be *(specify)*: $
(Do not include the amount your employer pays.)

18. **Additional expenses for the children in this case**

	Amount per month
a. Child care so I can work or get job training	$
b. Children's health care not covered by insurance	$
c. Travel expenses for visitation	$
d. Children's educational or other special needs *(specify below)*:	$

19. **Special hardships.** I ask the court to consider the following special financial circumstances *(attach documentation of any item listed here, including court orders)*:

	Amount per month	For how many months?
a. Extraordinary health expenses not included in 18b	$	
b. Major losses not covered by insurance (examples: fire, theft, other insured loss)	$	
c. (1) Expenses for my minor children who are from other relationships and are living with me	$	

(2) Names and ages of those children *(specify)*:

(3) Child support I receive for those children $

The expenses listed in a, b and c create an extreme financial hardship because *(explain)*:

20. **Other information I want the court to know concerning support in my case** *(specify)*:

FL-150 [Rev. January 1, 2007] **INCOME AND EXPENSE DECLARATION** Page 4 of 4

Martin Dean's ESSENTIAL FORMS™

1 4. Statement of all material facts and information regarding valuation of all assets
2 that are community property or in which the community has an interest:
3
4 All material facts and information regarding valuation of
5 all assets that are community property or in which the
6 community has an interest are listed in my Schedule of
7 Assets and Debts, Form FL-142. The values are based
8 upon the most recent statements, or are my opinion as an
9 owner.
10
11 I declare under penalty of perjury under the laws of the State of California that
12 the foregoing is true and correct.
13
Executed this ______ day of ____________, 2013, at Los Angeles, California.
14
15
16 ________________________________
17
18
19
20
21
22
23
24
25
26
27
28

- 1 -

MARRIAGE OF __________ **ATTACHMENT TO DECLARATION OF DISCLOSURE**
L.A.S.C. CASE NO. ________

1 5. Statement of all material facts and information regarding obligations for which
2 the community is liable:
3
4 All material facts and information regarding obligations
5 for which the community is liable are listed in my
6 Schedule of Assets and Debts, Form FL-142.
7
8 I declare under penalty of perjury under the laws of the State of California that
9 the foregoing is true and correct.
10 Executed this _____ day of _____________, 2013, at Los Angeles, California.
11
12
13 ________________________________
14
15
16
17
18
19
20
21
22
23
24
25
26
27
28

- 2 -

MARRIAGE OF ___________ **ATTACHMENT TO DECLARATION OF DISCLOSURE**
L.A.S.C. CASE NO. _________

1 6. Accurate and complete written disclosure of any investment opportunity
2 presented since the date of separation:
3
4 Since the date of separation, I have received no
5 investment opportunities.
6
7 I declare under penalty of perjury under the laws of the State of California that
8 the foregoing is true and correct.
9 Executed this ____ day of ____________, 2013, at Los Angeles, California.
10
11
12 ______________________________
13
14
15
16
17
18
19
20
21
22
23
24
25
26
27
28

- 3 -

MARRIAGE OF __________ ATTACHMENT TO DECLARATION OF DISCLOSURE
L.A.S.C. CASE NO. ________

FL-145

ATTORNEY OR PARTY WITHOUT ATTORNEY *(Name, State Bar number, and address):* TELEPHONE NO.:

ATTORNEY FOR *(Name):*

SUPERIOR COURT OF CALIFORNIA, COUNTY OF

SHORT TITLE:

FORM INTERROGATORIES-FAMILY LAW

Asking Party:
Answering Party:
Set No.:

CASE NUMBER:

Sec. 1. Instructions to Both Parties

The interrogatories on page 2 of this form are intended to provide for the exchange of relevant information without unreasonable expense to the answering party. They do not change existing law relating to interrogatories, nor do they affect the answering party's right to assert any privilege or make any objection. **Privileges must be asserted.**

Sec. 2. Definitions

Words in **boldface** in these interrogatories are defined as follows:

(a) **Person** includes a natural person; a partnership; any kind of business, legal, or public entity; and its agents or employees.

(b) **Document** means all written, recorded, or graphic materials, however stored, produced, or reproduced.

(c) **Asset** or **property** includes any interest in real estate or personal property. It includes any interest in a pension, profit-sharing, or retirement plan.

(d) **Debt** means any obligation, including debts paid since the date of separation.

(e) **Support** means any benefit or economic contribution to the living expenses of another person, including gifts.

(f) If asked to **identify a person,** give the person's name, last known residence and business addresses, telephone numbers, and company affiliation at the date of the transaction referred to.

(g) If asked to **identify a document,** attach a copy of the document unless you explain why not. If you do not attach the copy, describe the document, including its date and nature, and give the name, address, telephone number, and occupation of the person who has the document.

Sec. 3. Instructions to the Asking Party

Check the box next to each interrogatory you want the answering party to answer.

Sec. 4. Instructions to the Answering Party

You must answer these interrogatories under oath within 30 days, in accordance with Code of Civil Procedure section 2030.260.

You must furnish all information you have or can reasonably find out, including all information (not privileged) from your attorneys or under your control. If you don't know, say so.

If an interrogatory is answered by referring to a document, the document must be attached as an exhibit to the response and referred to in the response. If the document has more than one page, refer to the page and section where the answer can be found.

If a document to be attached to the response may also be attached to the *Schedule of Assets and Debts* (form FL-142), the document should be attached only to the response, and the form should refer to the response.

If an interrogatory cannot be answered completely, answer as much as you can, state the reason you cannot answer the rest, and state any information you have about the unanswered portion.

Sec. 5. Oath

Your answers to these interrogatories must be under oath, dated, and signed. Use the following statement **at the end of your answers:**

I declare under penalty of perjury under the laws of the State of California that the foregoing answers are true and correct.

(DATE) ▶ (SIGNATURE)

Page 1 of 2

Form Approved for Optional Use
Judicial Council of California
FL-145 [Rev. January 1, 2006]

Martin Dean's ESSENTIAL FORMS™

FORM INTERROGATORIES-FAMILY LAW

Code of Civil Procedure, §§ 2030.010-2030.410, 2033.710
www.courtinfo.ca.gov

FL-145

1. **Personal history.** State your full name, current residence address and work address, social security number, any other names you have used, and the dates between which you used each name.

2. **Agreements.** Are there any agreements between you and your spouse or domestic partner, made before or during your marriage or domestic partnership or after your separation, that affect the disposition of **assets, debts,** or **support** in this proceeding? If your answer is yes, for each agreement state the date made and whether it was written or oral, and attach a copy of the agreement or describe its contents.

3. **Legal actions.** Are you a party or do you anticipate being a party to any legal or administrative proceeding other than this action? If your answer is yes, state your role and the name, jurisdiction, case number, and a brief description of each proceeding.

4. **Persons sharing residence.** State the name, age, and relationship to you of each **person** at your present address.

5. **Support provided others.** State the name, age, address, and relationship to you of each **person** for whom you have provided **support** during the past 12 months and the amount provided per month for each.

6. **Support received for others.** State the name, age, address, and relationship to you of each **person** for whom you have received **support** during the past 12 months and the amount received per month for each.

7. **Current income.** List all income you received during the past 12 months, its source, the basis for its computation, and the total amount received from each. Attach your last three paycheck stubs.

8. **Other income.** During the past three years, have you received cash or other property from any source not identified in item 7? If so, list the source, the date, and the nature and value of the property.

9. **Tax returns.** Attach copies of all tax returns and tax schedules filed by or for you in any jurisdiction for the past three calendar years.

10. **Schedule of assets and debts.** Complete the *Schedule of Assets and Debts* (form FL-142) served with these interrogatories.

11. **Separate property contentions.** State the facts that support your contention that an asset or debt is separate property.

12. **Property valuations.** During the past 12 months, have you received written offers to purchase or had written appraisals of any of the assets listed on your completed *Schedule of Assets and Debts?* If your answer is yes, **identify the document.**

13. **Property held by others.** Is there any **property** held by any third party in which you have any interest or over which you have any control? If your answer is yes, indicate whether the property is shown on the *Schedule of Assets and Debts* completed by you. If it is not, describe and identify each such asset, state its present value and the basis for your valuation, and **identify the person** holding the asset.

14. **Retirement and other benefits.** Do you have an interest in any disability, retirement, profit-sharing, or deferred compensation plan? If your answer is yes, **identify** each plan and provide the name, address, and telephone number of the administrator and custodian of records.

15. **Claims of reimbursement.** Do you claim the legal right to be reimbursed for any expenditures of your separate or community property? If your answer is yes, state all supporting facts.

16. **Credits.** Have you claimed reimbursement credits for payments of community debts since the date of separation? If your answer is yes, **identify** the source of payment, the creditor, the date paid, and the amount paid. State whether you have added to the debt since the separation.

17. **Insurance. Identify** each health, life, automobile, and disability insurance policy or plan that you now own or that covers you, your children, or your assets. State the policy type, policy number, and name of the company. **Identify** the agent and give the address.

18. **Health.** Is there any physical or emotional condition that limits your ability to work? If your answer is yes, state each fact on which you base your answer.

19. **Children's needs.** Do you contend that any of your children have any special needs? If so, identify the child with the need, the reason for the need, its cost, and its expected duration.

20. **Attorney fees.** State the total amount of attorney fees and costs incurred by you in this proceeding, the amount paid, and the source of the money paid. Describe the billing arrangements.

21. **Gifts.** List any gifts you have made without the consent of your spouse or domestic partner in the past 24 months, their values, and the recipients.

FL-145 [Rev. January 1, 2006] **FORM INTERROGATORIES-FAMILY LAW** Page 2 of 2

Martin Dean's ESSENTIAL FORMS™

Most disclosure declarations start with questions about your personal history and any other existing agreements before asking for lists of and valuations for your furnishings, jewelry, art, stocks, bonds, frequent flyer mileage, retirement pensions, IRAs, college funds. You'll have to record every insurance policy or plan that you have, every trademark or patent or copyright you have ever obtained, every piece of real estate you own. Same for debts or liabilities: any loans, credit card debt, other encumbrances. You'll be asked if you think you have any separate property; that's where you'll say that the screenplay you wrote in 1996, three years before you married, is yours, and all proceeds from it remain your separate property. You'll need to disclose how much you have paid for lawyers so far in the dissolution process, report any gifts you have received, and come clean on any health issues that might affect your ability to work.

And you'll be required to attach supporting evidence for everything you say in the declaration: tax returns, copies of property deeds or titles, bank account statements, pay stubs. The net result for both sides is an overall idea of each spouse's basic position heading into a settlement.

Obviously, you can only write down what you know. That's precisely why the lawyers exchange the information, so each can see the holes in the other's declaration. The aim is not to sniff out nefarious intentions—not yet, anyway; it's really to find facts. I long ago ceased to be even mildly surprised at the things people who live together don't know about each other—especially where money is concerned. If it's the nonworking spouse who typically handles the household accounts and writes all the checks, it won't be surprising that the working spouse has little or no idea of the family's day-to-day expenses. By the same token, the nonworking spouse may not know all the ins and outs of the working spouse's compensation package—the bonuses, perks, stock options, accumulated sick pay, or travel benefits, that all add value to the bottom-line number.

To fill in some of those holes, your lawyer may file a request for the production of documents—backup evidence that supports or fleshes out the information in the declaration of disclosure. Perhaps your spouse has disclosed an investment account of which you were unaware; you'd like to see the statement. Maybe there is no mention of frequent flyer mileage on the preliminary disclosure, so you would like to see your spouse's calendar to check on his or her travel and be sure there was none. Or maybe your spouse has always bragged that he's "worth a million bucks," yet he has declared total assets of a little under $750,000 on the disclosure form. Where is the other two-fifty? Maybe it's in that reserve he once whispered to you that he keeps in a secret account somewhere, which also did not find its way into the disclosure declaration. Time for some documentation to back up these disclosures—or lack of same.

A request—or demand in some states—for production of documents will ask, in the deadliest possible legal language, for records that may include but not be limited to "papers, contracts, agreements, drafts of agreements, books, journals, ledgers, statements, memoranda, reports, notes, letters, correspondence, balance sheets, income statements, monthly billing statements, checks, diaries, calendars, logs, drafts, recordings, instructions, minutes of meetings, orders, resolutions, telegrams, telexes, messages, résumés, summaries, tapes, computer electronic and/or digital files, magnetic backup files, and all other informal or formal writings or tangible things on which any handwriting, typing, printing, photostatic,

1 Laura A. Wasser, Esq. (SBN 173740)
WASSER, COOPERMAN & CARTER, P.C.
2 2029 Century Park East, Suite 1200
Los Angeles, California 90067-2957
3 Telephone No.: (310)277-7117
Facsimile No.: (310)553-1793
4
5 Attorneys for Petitioner
6
7
8 SUPERIOR COURT OF THE STATE OF CALIFORNIA
9 FOR THE COUNTY OF LOS ANGELES
10

11 In Re Marriage of:	CASE NO. ___________
12 Petitioner: PPPPP PPPPP	[Assigned to Dept. ____, Hon. ______________]
13 and	
14 Respondent: RRRRR RRRRR	DEMAND FOR PRODUCTION AND INSPECTION OF DOCUMENTS PURSUANT TO C.C.P. §2031.010 ET SEQ.
15	

16
17 DEMANDING PARTY: Petitioner, ___________________
18 RESPONDING PARTY: Respondent, ___________________
19 SET NO.:
20 TO [Respondent/Petitioner], [name], AND TO HIS/HER ATTORNEYS OF RECORD:
21 DEMAND IS HEREBY MADE pursuant to California Code of Civil Procedure, Section
22 2031.010 et seq. that [Respondent/Petitioner], [name], appear on ____________, at the hour of
23 10:00 a.m. at the offices of WASSER, COOPERMAN & CARTER, located at 2029 Century Park
24 East, Suite 1200, Los Angeles, California, and produce the documents described in **Exhibit "A"**
25 attached hereto and incorporated herein by reference as though fully set forth at length, for the
26 purpose of inspection, copying and photographing.
27 [Respondent/Petitioner] shall identify in a written response, SUBSCRIBED BY HIM/HER
28 UNDER OATH, and served within thirty (30) days after service of this Demand, each and every

- 1 -

MARRIAGE OF ______________ DEMAND FOR PROD. AND INSPECTION OF DOCUMENTS
L.A.S.C. CASE NO. ______________

1 document, paper, book, account, letter, photograph, object or other tangible thing of each category
2 specified in **Exhibit "A,"** and in his/her possession, custody or control.
3 A personal appearance by [Respondent/Petitioner] or counsel is not required if
4 [Respondent/Petitioner] submits copies of the requested documents **prior to** _______________
5 with a verification executed under penalty of perjury by [Respondent/Petitioner] that the copies
6 provided are accurate and true copies of the complete records requested.
7 PLEASE NOTE that Code of Civil Procedure §2031.010 et seq. requires two (2) acts for
8 compliance with this Demand for Production and Inspection of Documents:
9 1. Service of written response under oath within thirty (30) days of service of this
10 Demand [C.C.P. §2031.250]; and
11 2. Production of tangible things on or before the date set forth hereinabove,
12 which is at least thirty (30) days after service of this Demand [C.C.P. §2031.030].
13 DATED: _______________ WASSER, COOPERMAN & CARTER
Professional Corporation
14
15
16 By: ______________________
LAURA A. WASSER
Attorneys for [Respondent/Petitioner]
17
18
19
20
21
22
23
24
25
26
27
28

- 2 -

MARRIAGE OF _______________ DEMAND FOR PROD. AND INSPECTION OF DOCUMENTS
L.A.S.C. CASE NO. _______________

1 **EXHIBIT "A"**

2

3 Section I - Definitions

4 A. **"YOU"** and/or **"YOUR"** shall mean and include you, your agents, your employees,
5 your attorneys, your accountants, your investigators and anyone else acting on your behalf.

6 B. **"PERSON"** includes a natural person, firm, association, organization, partnership,
7 business, trust, corporation or public entity.

8 C. As used herein, the term **"WRITINGS"** and/or **"DOCUMENTS"** and/or
9 **"RECORDS"** includes but is not limited to papers, contracts, agreements, drafts of agreements,
10 books, journals, ledgers, statements, memoranda, reports, notes, letters, correspondence, balance
11 sheets, income statements, monthly billing statements, checks, diaries, calendars, logs, drafts,
12 recordings, instructions, minutes of meetings, orders, resolutions, telegrams, telexes, messages,
13 resumes, summaries, tapes, computer electronic and/or digital files, magnetic backup files, and all
14 other informal or formal writings or tangible things on which any handwriting, typing, printing,
15 photostatic, magnetic or electronic impulse, or other form of communication is recorded or
16 reproduced and all amendments to the foregoing.

17 D. As used herein the term **"INTEREST"** shall include, but not necessarily be limited
18 to ownership by you of any stock in a corporation, rights to or ownership by you in any general
19 partnership or limited partnership participation in profits of any business entity, or any other
20 proprietary rights.

21

22 Section II - Documents to be Produced and Time Limits

23 Unless specified within the following categories of documents, documents to be produced
24 are for the **"PERIOD"** from ______________ through and including the date of hearing or
25 continuance thereof, date of deposition or date of production of records, whichever is applicable:

26 1. Bank Records

27 Check registers, ledgers, stubs, original canceled checks, bank statements,
28 passbooks, certificates of deposit, travelers' checks, and cashiers' check acquisition records, and

- 3 -

MARRIAGE OF ______________ **DEMAND FOR PROD. AND INSPECTION OF DOCUMENTS**
L.A.S.C. CASE NO. ______________

1 any other documents reflecting deposits, withdrawals, and/or exchanges of funds at any bank or
2 financial institution having money in its possession: (a) owned by you or standing in your name,
3 individually or jointly with your spouse or any other person; (b) owned by or standing in the name
4 of your spouse, individually or jointly with you or any other person; and (c) owned by or standing in
5 the name of your spouse or any corporation, partnership, limited partnership, joint venture, trust or
6 other entity in which you and/or your spouse had any interest during the **"PERIOD."** Said records
7 include accounts where either you, your spouse or a third party, is a signator.
8 2. <u>Income Records</u>
9 Any and all documents reflecting pay, salary, wages, earnings, commissions, early
10 retirement, sick leave, vacation pay, disbursements, reimbursements, income and other monies
11 received by you from any source whatsoever (individually or jointly with your spouse or any other
12 person) during the **"PERIOD."**
13 3. <u>Financial Statements</u>
14 Any and all financial statements (including profit and loss statements, income
15 statements, balance sheets, summaries of income and expenses, net worth statements or audit
16 reports, budgets, forecasts, or financial expense analyses) prepared by or for you and prepared by or
17 for your spouse for personal or business reasons during the **"PERIOD."**
18 4. <u>Books of Account</u>
19 Books of account, cash receipt and disbursement ledgers, and all other documents
20 reflecting income, expenses and/or assets and liabilities of you and/or your spouse during the
21 **"PERIOD."**
22 5. <u>Real Property</u>
23 Contracts, escrow instructions, deeds, policies of title insurance, tax bills, loan
24 applications, promissory notes, trust deeds, escrow statements, appraisal reports, insurance policies,
25 rental income and expense records, tenant leases, maintenance records, property tax assessments,
26 capital improvements, and any other documents reflecting ownership, cost, value, obligations owed,
27 selling price, income and expenses, buyer or donee of any real property (including leaseholds)
28 presently or previously acquired, owned by or standing in your name (individually or jointly with

- 4 -

MARRIAGE OF ______________ DEMAND FOR PROD. AND INSPECTION OF DOCUMENTS
L.A.S.C. CASE NO. ______________

1 any other person or business entity) and/or owned by or standing in your spouse's name
2 (individually or jointly with any other person or business entity) during the **"PERIOD."**
3 6. Personal Property
4 Inventories, insurance policies, contracts, ownership documents, registration
5 certificates, appraisal reports and any other documents reflecting purchase, ownership, cost, value,
6 obligations owed thereon, selling price and buyer or donee and seller or donor of any furniture,
7 furnishings, art work, jewelry, automobiles, or other tangible personal property presently or
8 previously acquired, owned by or standing in your name (individually or jointly with any other
9 person or business entity) and/or owned by or standing in your spouse's name (individually or
10 jointly with any other person or business entity) during the **"PERIOD."** With regard to
11 automobiles, please also provide documentation pertaining to the source of money used to acquire
12 the vehicle(s), to pay off the vehicle(s), and documents relating to the ownership of said vehicle(s).
13 With regard to purchases of jewelry, please provide all statements, receipts, records and other
14 documents evidencing purchases of jewelry for yourself, your spouse, or any third party for the
15 **"PERIOD."**
16 7. Life Insurance
17 Life insurance policies, premium notices, loan statements and correspondence
18 relating to any policies of insurance on your life, on your spouse's life, on any third parties, or of
19 which you are, or were, the beneficiary or owner, for the **"PERIOD."**
20 8. Disability, Health, Medical Insurance
21 Disability, medical, hospital and/or dental insurance policies, summaries, statements,
22 premium notices and records with respect to any such policy under which you, your dependents
23 and/or your spouse are currently insured.
24 9. Medical Expense Reimbursement Documentation
25 All statements, check stubs, records and other documents showing the amount of
26 money reimbursed to you for medical expenses for either yourself or any third parties during the
27 **"PERIOD."**
28 ///

-5-

MARRIAGE OF ________________ **DEMAND FOR PROD. AND INSPECTION OF DOCUMENTS**
L.A.S.C. CASE NO. ____________

1 10. Safe Deposit Boxes/Vaults/Safes

2 Rental agreements and all other records reflecting the rental and right of access to
3 any safe deposit box, vault, or safe, by you during the **"PERIOD."** These documents include, but
4 are not limited to, signature cards, entry slips, and inventories of contents.

5 11. Credit Card and Charge Account Records

6 Monthly statements, billings, invoices and charge vouchers reflecting your use of any
7 charge accounts with any credit card organizations, in your name, or in the name of any other person
8 (including your spouse, any third persons, or business entities) where you have charging privileges,
9 or any account for which you have made any payment, during the **"PERIOD."**

10 12. Stock Brokerage Accounts/Securities/Stocks & Bonds

11 Monthly statements, purchase and/or sale confirmations, account agreements,
12 summary sheets, correspondence between you and any brokers or brokerage houses, transaction
13 reports, and any other records relating to securities purchased and/or sold, or pertaining to any stock,
14 commodity, or other brokerage account owned by or standing in your name (individually or jointly
15 with any other persons or business entities) and/or owned by or standing in your spouse's name
16 during the **"PERIOD."**

17 13. Employment Contracts, Etc.

18 Contracts, memoranda, correspondence and other documents relating to your
19 employment or ownership interest (as well as your spouse's employment/involvement, or ownership
20 interest) in any project or business (whether for profit or otherwise) during the **"PERIOD."**

21 14. Pension, KEOGH, IRA, Etc., Plans

22 Plan summaries, annual beneficiary statements, copies of the plan(s), periodic
23 reports, correspondence and other documents relating to any retirement, pension, profit sharing,
24 stock option, or other employee benefit plan, in which you and/or your spouse have had any interest
25 at any time during the **"PERIOD."**

26 15. Fringe Benefits

27 Vouchers, expense accounts, memoranda, books, statements, and other documents
28 reflecting obligations incurred by you, or for your benefit, and paid for by any other person, firm, or

- 6 -

MARRIAGE OF __________ **DEMAND FOR PROD. AND INSPECTION OF DOCUMENTS**
L.A.S.C. CASE NO. __________

1 entity and/or incurred by you for your spouse during the **"PERIOD"** for automobile, travel, meals,
2 lodging, insurance, entertainment, telephone, and any other expenses.
3 16. Notes Payable/Debts
4 Promissory notes, and any other documents reflecting indebtedness of any kind
5 whatsoever, and any documents executed in connection therewith, or with security therefor, and any
6 correspondence or other documents and records relating to, or reflecting monies or indebtedness
7 owed by you or your spouse during the **"PERIOD."**
8 17. Copies of Stocks, Bonds, Etc.
9 Copies of all certificates of stocks, bonds, cashier's checks, certificates of deposit and
10 other securities, in your name (individually or jointly with any other person or business entity)
11 and/or your spouse's name (individually or jointly) for the **"PERIOD."**
12 18. Social Membership, Clubs, Fraternal Organizations
13 Contracts, monthly statements, canceled checks, charge slips, invoices relating to,
14 and expenses associated with, your membership or your spouse's membership in any country club,
15 beach club, or other social organization during the **"PERIOD."**
16 19. Debts and Liabilities
17 Invoices, correspondence and other documents and records relating to any current
18 outstanding indebtedness, obligation and/or liability, including contingent liabilities of you
19 (individually or jointly) and/or your spouse (individually or jointly).
20 20. Living and Household Expenses
21 Any and all bills, invoices, receipts, canceled checks, statements and other
22 documents evidencing the current monthly and other periodic expenses incurred, claimed or paid by
23 you or on your behalf, including, but not limited to, rent, maintenance, taxes, food, clothing utilities,
24 telephone, medical and dental insurance, life, automobile and other insurance, entertainment,
25 transportation, incidentals, and any other expenses incurred during the **"PERIOD."** Said
26 documents include, but are not limited to, documents used in the preparation of any Income and
27 Expense Declaration on file in this matter.
28 ///

- 7 -

MARRIAGE OF ________________
L.A.S.C. CASE NO. ________________

DEMAND FOR PROD. AND INSPECTION OF DOCUMENTS

1 21. Travel Expenses

2 Bills, statements, invoices, receipts, canceled checks, credit card charges and any
3 other documents for airlines, hotels, rental cars, restaurants and/or stores resulting from trips outside
4 of the State of California during the **"PERIOD."**

5 22. Attorney and Expert Fees

6 Contracts, agreements, memoranda, correspondence, statements, canceled checks,
7 and any other documents reflecting fees and costs payable, and otherwise, relating to your
8 employment and/or compensation of counsel and any experts (including accountants, in connection
9 with this action).

10 23. Transmutation

11 Contracts, agreements, memoranda, correspondence, notes and all other documents
12 prepared by (and/or for) you and/or your spouse, which relate to any change in the character or title
13 of property owned, or to be acquired by, or transferred, to either of you (whether or not executed) at
14 any time during the **"PERIOD,"** including, without limitation, all prenuptial and antenuptial
15 agreements which may change the character or title of property owned, or to be acquired by or
16 transferred to either of you during the **"PERIOD."**

17 24. Property Character and Reimbursements

18 Contracts, agreements, correspondence, memoranda, any and other documents upon
19 which you base any contention that property is community, quasi-community or separate property of
20 you and/or your spouse, or upon which you claim that you and/or any other person are entitled to
21 reimbursement or a return of any portion of the value or purchase price of that property.

22 25. Inheritance/Gifts Received/Receivable

23 Wills, trust agreements, deeds, and any other documents reflecting your prior, or
24 future, inheritance or gift of monies, or other property from any person, trust or estate.

25 26. Trust, Estates

26 Trust agreements, fiduciary income tax returns, correspondence, periodic
27 accountings, and any other documents relating to any trust in which you have or had any interest
28 whatsoever during the **"PERIOD,"** including, but not limited to, any trust agreement prepared on

1 behalf of your former spouse. Said documents include, but are not limited to, checks, stubs,
2 vouchers, bank drafts and any other written materials.

3 27. Gifts to Others

4 A. Gift tax returns (both State and Federal) filed by you, or your spouse and any
5 documents reflecting gifts made by you, or your spouse, to one another, or any third person or
6 business entity, during the **"PERIOD."**

7 B. Any and all documents, including, but not limited to, notes, agreements, or
8 memoranda evidencing any cash, cash-in-kind, gifts, or other monies paid to any third person or
9 business entity during the **"PERIOD."**

10 28. Partnership Tax Return

11 Partnership income tax returns (both Federal and State) filed by any partnership,
12 limited partnership, or joint venture, in which you or your spouse had any interest whatsoever
13 during the **"PERIOD"**and any amendments, adjustments and/or correspondence relating thereto.

14 29. Corporate Tax Returns

15 Corporate income tax returns (both Federal and State) filed by any corporation in
16 which you or your spouse has had any interest during the **"PERIOD"** and any amendments,
17 adjustments and/or correspondence relating thereto.

18 30. Business Financial Statements

19 Financial statements (including balance sheets, income statements, and profit and
20 loss statements) received by you or your spouse, with respect to, or prepared by or for, any
21 proprietorship, joint venture, partnership, closely held corporation and/or other legal entity in which
22 you or your spouse has had any interest whatsoever during the **"PERIOD."**

23 31. Business Books of Account

24 Books of account, cash received and disbursement ledgers, and all other documents
25 reflecting income, expenses, and/or assets and liabilities, of any proprietorship, joint venture,
26 partnership, closely held corporation and/or other legal entity in which you or your spouse has any
27 interest during the **"PERIOD."**

28 ///

- 9 -

MARRIAGE OF ______________ **DEMAND FOR PROD. AND INSPECTION OF DOCUMENTS**
L.A.S.C. CASE NO. ______________

1 32. Corporate Minutes, Etc.
2 Articles of incorporation, corporate minute books, by-laws, stockholder agreements
3 and stock certificate ledgers of any closely held corporation in which you or your spouse have any
4 interest from the date of incorporation, to the date of production.
5 33. Business Agreements
6 Partnership, limited partnership, joint venture, shareholder agreements, and any
7 buy/sell and/or other agreements, reflecting ownership, limitations and transferability, the value of
8 any interest in any partnership, limited partnership, joint venture, and/or corporate shares, in which
9 you or your spouse have had any interest at any time during the **"PERIOD."**
10 34. Employee Records
11 During the **"PERIOD,"** all employment records pertaining to persons employed by
12 you, including without limitation, the names and addresses of such employees, the amounts paid to
13 such employees, the date of such payment, and the nature and extent of the services performed by
14 each employee.
15 35. Bank Records of Business
16 Check registers, ledgers, stubs, canceled checks, bank statements, passbooks,
17 certificates of deposit, traveler's checks and cashier's check acquisition records, and other
18 documents reflecting deposits, withdrawals and/or exchange of funds, at any bank or financial
19 institution having money in its possession belong to, or standing in the name of, any business in
20 which you or your spouse have had any interest during the **"PERIOD."**
21 36. Efforts Regarding Employment
22 Any and all documents, records, notes, and materials reflecting your efforts,
23 attempts and/or successes in establishing a business venture during the **"PERIOD."**
24 37. Efforts Regarding Writing Career
25 Any and all documents, records, notes, writing samples, screenplays, works in
26 progress, and any materials reflecting your effort, attempts and/or success in establishing your
27 writing career during the **"PERIOD."**
28 ///

- 10 -

MARRIAGE OF ____________ DEMAND FOR PROD. AND INSPECTION OF DOCUMENTS
L.A.S.C. CASE NO. ____________

1 38. Cash from Friends

2 Any and all documents, records, notes and materials reflecting monies (i.e., cash)
3 which you have received from third parties during the **"PERIOD."**

4 39. Bills and Debts at Separation

5 Any and all bills, statements of account, and other documents evidencing community
6 obligations and debts existing at the time of your separation from your spouse, and all statements,
7 receipts, and documents reflecting the payment by you of such community obligations after
8 separation.

9 40. Loan Applications

10 Any and all loans or credit applications made by you or for you with respect to any
11 business entity, person, association, bank, savings and loan, or credit union (whether or not said
12 loan or credit was, in effect, granted) during the **"PERIOD."**

13 41. Passports

14 Any and all passports, whether issued by the United States of America, or any other
15 country, issued in your name during the **"PERIOD."**

16 42. Income Tax Returns

17 Any and all federal and state income tax returns that you and/or your spouse filed
18 during the **"PERIOD."** If you have not yet prepared your income tax returns for the immediate past
19 calendar year, then please provide copies of all backup and source material which you have for the
20 preparation of said returns.

21
22
23
24
25
26
27
28

- 11 -

MARRIAGE OF ______________ DEMAND FOR PROD. AND INSPECTION OF DOCUMENTS
L.A.S.C. CASE NO. ______________

magnetic or electronic impulse, or other form of communication is recorded or reproduced and all amendments to the foregoing."

And that's just the opening shot. Each category of asset, liability, income, or expense requested—real estate, personal property, credit card records, employment contract, etc.—will be further defined with a similar list of precise terms that seek to ensure total compliance by leaving out absolutely nothing.

This still may not be enough. Special interrogatories may also be necessary, especially where records are murky or nonexistent. Businesses that deal in cash fit the bill: the hair stylist who is paid in greenbacks and silver, the restaurant that takes no credit cards, the performer who agrees to receive some of his or her pay under the table because it's really easier for everybody that way—not to mention the numbered account in Switzerland or the offshore holdings of foreign currency and precious metals. A special interrogatory might ask a spouse whether he or she has been paid in cash from any clients; if so, how much per client, and by how many clients per day? Another might inquire if the party has any financial holdings in locations that are beyond the reach of U.S. law. All answers, of course, are on penalty of perjury, which is often a compelling incentive for producing the documentation requested.

Yet another possible path to discovery is the deposition. We've all seen depositions played out in the movies, and that's pretty much what they're like. Their aim is to elicit or clarify information, and the transcript that emerges from a deposition session is both a tool for arguing your case for settlement and a possible weapon to impeach the credibility of one party or the other if and when a story changes later. Both parties and their lawyers are of course present at the deposition; a court reporter is at the ready; and a videographer captures the whole thing digitally. Talk about a

1 Laura A. Wasser, Esq. [SBN 173740]
WASSER, COOPERMAN & CARTER, P.C.
2 2029 Century Park East, Suite 1200
Los Angeles, California 90067-2957
3 Telephone No.: (310)277-7117
4 Facsimile No.: (310)553-1793
5 Attorneys for Respondent
6
7
8 SUPERIOR COURT OF THE STATE OF CALIFORNIA
9 FOR THE COUNTY OF LOS ANGELES
10

11 In re the Marriage of	) CASE NO. ___________
12 Petitioner: PPPPP PPPPP	) [Reassigned to Dept. ____, Hon. _______________]
13 and	) NOTICE OF TAKING DEPOSITION OF PETITIONER AND REQUEST FOR PRODUCTION OF DOCUMENTS PURSUANT TO CODE OF CIVIL PROCEDURE §2025.010 ET SEQ.
14 Respondent: RRRRR RRRRR	
15–18	) DATE: _______________ TIME: _______________ PLACE: WASSER, COOPERMAN & CARTER 2029 Century Park East, Suite 1200 Los Angeles, CA 90067

19
20 TO PETITIONER, _______________, AND TO HER ATTORNEY OF RECORD:
21 PLEASE TAKE NOTICE that the deposition of Petitioner, _____________, will be taken
22 by Respondent, ______________, through his attorneys of record, Wasser, Cooperman & Carter,
23 on ________________, at ________, at the law offices of Wasser, Cooperman & Carter,
24 Professional Corporation, 2029 Century Park East, Suite 1200, Los Angeles, California 90067, upon
25 oral examination before a notary public, certified court reporter, or such other officer authorized to
26 administer oaths that may be present at the time and place.
27 The deposition will be taken pursuant to the provisions of C.C.P. §2025.010 et seq. and will
28 continue from day to day, excluding holidays and weekends, until completed.

- 1 -

MARRIAGE OF ________________
L.A.S.C. CASE NO. ________________

NOTICE OF TAKING DEPOSITION AND REQUEST FOR PRODUCTION OF DOCUMENTS

1 **PLEASE TAKE FURTHER NOTICE** that pursuant to the provisions of C.C.P.
2 §2025.220(5) and 2025.330(c), the Respondent may record said deposition testimony by audiotape
3 or videotape in addition to recording the testimony by stenographic method, through the instant
4 visual display of the testimony, with the Certified Shorthand Reporter.
5 **NOTICE IS HEREBY FURTHER GIVEN** that Petitioner, ______________, will be
6 required to produce then and there at the taking of her deposition, for inspection, examination and
7 copying, all of the books, records, and other things that are set forth as follows: Please refer to
8 **Exhibit "A"** attached hereto and incorporated herein by this reference as though set forth in full.
9 This request for production and inspection of documents is pursuant to the provisions of C.C.P.
10 §2025.010 et seq.
11 DATED: ____________________

WASSER, COOPERMAN & CARTER
Professional Corporation

12
13

By: ____________________________
LAURA A. WASSER
Attorney for Respondent

14
15
16
17
18
19
20
21
22
23
24
25
26
27
28

- 2 -

MARRIAGE OF ____________________
L.A.S.C. CASE NO. ________________

NOTICE OF TAKING DEPOSITION AND REQUEST
FOR PRODUCTION OF DOCUMENTS

picture being worth a thousand words! Few things are more satisfying than when your ex swears in court that she never tried to conceal the online brokerage account she opened under her maiden name, and your lawyer then says, in effect, "Roll tape!" and there's your ex in the deposition session, claiming that she never deals in stocks, wouldn't feel comfortable acting as an individual investor, and of course has no brokerage account of her own.

Be an Active Participant

The aim of gathering and compiling all this information is to give the lawyers the comprehensive understanding they need to frame the argument for an advantageous settlement. This is the very heart of the work you have hired an attorney to do for you. It is exacting work, typically time-consuming, often requiring the participation of other experts—forensic accountants, for example, or a range of experts in various aspects of financial evaluation and calculation. Among them are appraisers who specialize in every conceivable area of expertise—real estate, jewelry, art and antiques, musical instruments, even pinball machines. The specialization can be highly fine-tuned; it is *Antiques Roadshow* without the charm or goodwill. I once had to deal with an appraiser skilled in appraising Birkin bags, the leather handbags by Hermès, the French fashion enterprise, that can range in value from $15,000 for what might be called a "standard" Birkin bag to $40,000 and up for a crocodile satchel tote. At least two of my clients have owned collections of more than fifteen of these bags each.

In addition to these experts with their exquisite aesthetic sense, the discovery process may also need to call upon the most mundane actuarial skills, drawing on experts in financial probabilities and contingencies who can figure out total payouts over time and the impact on all sides of the financial equation. Vocational evaluators may be called in to assess the value of a party's future earnings potential. Experts in how royalties and residuals work—and how they diminish over time—or gurus who understand the real estate market may be summoned to contribute their expertise.

To determine child support for children of high earners—an amount limited only by what the paying spouse is willing to shell out—your lawyer may turn to experts who understand exactly what level of wealth is at issue and who can tell you, for that level of wealth, exactly what would be appropriate expenditures for a child's food, clothing, camp, school, and entertainment. Obviously, these kids are not chowing down at Mickey D's or wearing fashions by Target, but somebody has to come up with the actual dollar figures for what's appropriate, and believe it or not, there are experts who do just that.

So the discovery process can be complex and complicated, as your lawyer reaches out for whatever may be needed to elicit needed data. Still, the best way to ensure that the process works is for the client to be an active participant in it. Again, keeping in mind that the case your lawyer makes for you will rest in large measure on the information you provide, you are not going to want that information to be anything less than complete and correct in every part. Therefore, it behooves you not just to inundate your lawyer with everything you have, but also to organize, codify, and catalog the inundation.

First, you need to gather everything. For the type-A personalities among us, that probably means sliding open a file drawer or clicking on a few folders on the laptop. For most people, it means running around the house trying to remember where you put whatsis and did you file whosis under "House" or "Important Records"? One thing to remember is that if you don't have the stuff you need, someone else probably will. A lot of my clients have business managers; their job is to keep such records. You may not have a business manager, but you probably have used an accountant to help with your tax preparation. Call him or her. Part of the service you pay for is the timely receipt of a copy of your tax returns or other records.

Maybe you're the type of person who just routinely tosses her bank statements into the trash. Your lawyer has assured you that your spouse is going to subpoena these from the bank anyway, so not to worry if you can't produce them yourself. Yes, they can be subpoenaed, and they will be, and there will be a charge for the subpoena order, when all you really have to do is head into the bank and ask for copies of the statements you need. These days, you can even log on to your account online and download your statements, although you may not be able to access all the ones you need. Why wait for the subpoena and why make it another bone in an already contentious process?

It isn't always easy to do this pulling together of data; it's often inconvenient, and it's sometimes downright impossible. If one of you is off filming in Asia or the other of you is crashing on a do-or-die project at work, the process may have to wait. And if it's anywhere near April 15 or October 15, no business manager or accountant is going to look favorably on a request for copies of paperwork. Time can pass before you are able to compile everything you need to compile.

And in some instances, you may really have to chase the information, which can also take time. One area where sleuthing is often required is in proving that separate property has not been commingled during the marriage—that is, has not been put into a joint account or asset. Let's say you owned your own home before your marriage and then you both moved into it when you married. When your growing family needed a bigger place, you sold the house, realizing a profit of $200,000. That $200,000 then became the down payment on the second, bigger house. If you can bring evidence tracing that down payment and showing that it derived from a separate property that was solely yours, you can prove the $200,000 is separate property, too. But you have to bring the evidence.

A client of mine missed out in just such a transaction. He had inherited half a million from his father twenty years back and had used the money as the down payment on the house he bought when he married. But he didn't have records showing that; he couldn't trace the down payment on the house back to his inheritance from his father. The result was that his wife and kids are living in the house, along with the stunningly good-looking semipro soccer player his wife left him for, and all my client can do is grind his teeth in frustration and keep on writing checks. The moral of the story? Follow Chanelle's lead: Keep records.

And as you prepare to hand the records over to your lawyer, keep an inventory as well—a written list of everything you have gathered. Note the type of document it is—communication, bank statement, bill of sale. And to the extent possible, keep a copy of everything for yourself also.

I get documentation from clients in a variety of styles, typically corresponding to their styles of gathering the data: The type As of course have everything in tidy, color-coded file folders—whether the files are paper or digital. The folks who are fairly loosely wound show up with a grab-bag assortment of random pieces of information in a shoebox. Most people are somewhere in between. But there is little doubt that the more ordered and orderly the client's offering, the better for me as the lawyer—and therefore, eventually, the better for the client.

The actual exchange of information typically happens these days via CD. When you factor in everything from both parties—e-mail correspondence plus financial statements plus everything else—there can be tens of thousands of documents on multiple CDs. Right now, for example, there sits on my desk a set of three CDs containing some 25,000 documents. This is a case that will require the expertise of a forensic accountant, so both of us will be going over all of these documents with a fine-tooth comb as my office prepares the legal case for my client.

Making Your Case

Making your case for what you believe you're entitled to is of course your lawyer's job. But it is also your responsibility, and the discovery process is your opportunity to figure out what your argument ought to be. You and your lawyer together should establish the argument your lawyer will make and concur on the evidentiary story that will frame that argument.

As part of that, you are of course entitled to see what the other side has come up with during discovery. Everything your lawyer receives from your spouse's lawyer in the exchange of information also goes back to you. The three-CD set on my desk has already been duly copied and transmitted to the client so she can do her own due diligence. It can be a daunting prospect, and it is one few clients relish. But I know most of them feel as I would if I were in their shoes—that this is a process that directly affects their lives and the lives of their children, and that they have a duty to review the information on which they will base their settlement claim. You may well be the one to spot a smoking-gun transaction because it seems irregular or inconsistent with your family's normal spending.

So go over stuff, both on your own and with your lawyer. It's an attorney's job—and our obligation—to help clients understand what the law is and how it applies to their case. Again, the more the client knows and the deeper his or her understanding, the better the lawyer can do his or her job of finding and framing the premise of the argument.

The day is coming when everybody will walk into a room together, and, through your lawyer, you will state just what it is you believe you are entitled to in the dissolution settlement. When you do so, you want to feel confident that the case you are making is persuasive, that your reasoning is sound, and that the information to back up your claim is correct and complete.

And I will promise you this: Once you have gone through the discovery process and have forced yourself to understand, maybe for the first time, exactly where you stand financially, you'll never again allow yourself to become ignorant about money issues. Laborious as the discovery process may seem, it really is an opportunity, as you break with the past, to set foot on a new path of staying involved in your finances and participating fully in your own economic future.

IN BRIEF

The purpose of the discovery process is to enable you to build the case for the settlement you will ask for and to provide you with the hard evidence that supports your case.

1. Disclose all. Withhold nothing; it is virtually impossible to do so in this day and age in any case.
2. Organize and catalog all supporting evidence.
3. Remember that depositions, interrogatory and document production responses, and declarations of disclosure are all given under penalty of perjury.
4. Review what has been disclosed by the other side. You will often be the one to spot something irregular and relevant.

12

Resolution—and Settlement

You are now ready to proceed to the final phase of the dissolution process—resolving all the differences between you and your spouse or partner so you can come to a final settlement, sign it, file it with the appropriate court to make it legally binding, and move on. In this final phase, whether it proceeds through mediation or negotiation or in court, another law of divorce in the twenty-first century should prevail—namely, keep your eyes on the prize.

The prize is closure—saying good-bye to a relationship that has soured your existence so you can say hello to the next stage of your life. The bonds between you and your spouse or partner that *can* be dissolved *will* be dissolved; any others—coparenting, or joint financial interests—will be limited or qualified by the rules and protocols you agree to now.

Remember what I promised you at the beginning of this book about the victory you really want? The prize of great worth you're really struggling for is to get out of this relationship with both yourself and your children safe, sound, and emotionally healthy—and with your sanity, your wallet, and your dignity intact. Keep that in mind, and the process of resolving and settling will be a lot more tolerable—because, frankly, you're going to have to give in order to get.

Pigs Get Fat, Hogs Get Slaughtered

There's a classic Jewish joke that tells of a grandmother walking with her little grandson on the beach. Quintessentially overprotective, she has made sure he is wearing sunscreen, a jacket, and his little hat, and her grip on his hand is vise-tight. Suddenly a huge tsunamilike wave rolls in, rips the grandson's hand from hers, and sweeps the little boy out to sea. Weeping and wailing, the distraught grandmother appeals to the heavens. "What will I do? How will I live? How can I face my daughter? Bring him back! I'll do anything. Only bring him back! I'll never ask You for anything again."

As if on cue, another tsunamilike wave rolls in—and deposits the grandson back beside his grandmother. She enfolds him in her arms, sets him down, and gazes at him—alive and well and right there before her.

Then she looks toward heaven again. "He was wearing a hat," she says. "Where's the hat?"

Which brings us to another law of twenty-first-century divorce: Be reasonable. Don't overreach. Striving for all you can get is understandable, but when it crosses the line into hoggishness, you can lose out—big time. Accept that you are probably not going to achieve the perfect deal, the one in which you get everything you want. Understand that legally ending a marriage or partnership is not like suing for an injury. In the latter, you ask a court to tell you that you deserve an almost infinite payback for all you've been through and everything you put up with, you poor thing. But ending a marriage is like bargaining for something you can live with—an acceptable portion of finite resources. In the best settlement resolution possible, no one is entirely happy.

The Process

You and your lawyer should have come out of the discovery process with sufficient knowledge and understanding of the facts to have worked out your positions on all the issues to be resolved in your case: spousal support, child support, division of property, attorneys' fees, and the like. Your lawyer has synthesized these positions in a mediation or settlement brief—a precise, lawyerly articulation of the case you want made on your behalf. Now the time seems right to make a deal, and you're ready to do that very thing.

Are you ready?

Timing is important. Sometimes, one of you is ready and the other is not. I recently went into what I thought was to be a voluntary settlement conference with my client, the husband in the dissolving marriage, who was, admittedly, a serial adulterer. When I extended my hand across the conference table to shake the hand of his wronged wife, whom I had not met before, and she looked at her husband and said, "Are you fucking *her* too, Steve?" I formed the distinct impression that she wasn't as psyched up to make a deal as we would have liked. Bingo. That was indeed the case. But her lawyer had persuaded her that this was Steve's "window of contrition," as a wise judge once called it—a moment when Steve still felt guilty enough to be generous to her, but a moment that wasn't going to last forever. We went ahead with the conference and in due course achieved a settlement.

So the fact that "now is the time" is really the biggest incentive to proceed toward settlement. When that window is open—of contrition maybe, but of opportunity definitely—you really do need to seize the moment. And when you do so, you need to be primed and predisposed to compromise and prepared, in mind and heart, to get to a final settlement that probably won't give you exactly what you want—except an open door to the rest of your life.

Keep in mind that you are armed with one particularly powerful weapon that may help achieve that settlement—namely, your knowledge of your spouse or partner. You know, far better than your lawyer could, what really matters to this person. You know his or her fault lines, funny bones, hot buttons, sore spots. Better than anyone else on earth, most likely, you can guess what will set him or her off into thunderous anger or sneering disdain or howls of laughter or even benign acceptance. Clue your lawyer in. He or she knows the law and knows the process, but when it comes to reading the opposing side in the discussions coming up, you are the font of wisdom from which your lawyer should draw to help move you to a settlement.

You'll get to the resolution either through mediation, or in a settlement conference, or in court, or in a combination of some or all of the above. That's a big change from the way things used to be. Back in the day, most divorcing couples went to court. Period.

For one thing, with fewer divorces, it was simply easier to go to court; there just weren't that many litigants. Today, the dockets are so full of divorce litigation that courts are horribly backlogged. Moreover, back then, a scorched-earth policy was the norm for divorce litigation. The aim was to assign blame and achieve victory, defined as basically annihilating the other party. In today's no-fault family law environment, however, blame isn't an issue, and victory is more about making sure you can stomach the idea of running into each other at your kids' graduations. Most victories win you considerably more than that, but if that's all you get, it's still a win. That makes for a very different ball game from what past generations played—a much better ball game—and it is therefore little wonder that the vast majority of divorces are negotiated settlements that never go to court at all except to file the papers both parties have signed.

Mediation

It's safe to say that divorce mediation—an agreement arrived at by the two of you working with a neutral mediator—was almost unheard of a generation ago. Today, it is on the rise. It is probably not for everybody. If trust has been utterly shattered, if you know you're not at your best in an unstructured situation, if the number or complexity of the issues you're dealing with just seems too overwhelming, or if the power dynamics in the relationship have been such that you fear you'll cave just to avoid direct confrontation or to get it over with, mediation is probably not the best option. But where both parties are comfortable with the idea and want to make it work, it can be a very good option indeed.

You'll typically meet with the mediator on a preliminary basis to see if you and your ex have an equal interest in pursuing this form of resolution and settlement. If so, the mediator will likely ask to see all the documents from the discovery process so he or she can get up to speed on the issues. Then you'll start meeting; the mediator may ask to see each of you separately as well as the two of you together. That's it—the two of you and the mediator, reviewing ideas, brainstorming, with the mediator proposing and the two of you disposing as you work toward a plan you can agree on.

Don't think you cannot have a lawyer if you mediate. You may consult your lawyer at any time; in fact, it is probably a good idea to check with your lawyer before or during the mediation to get some advice, coaching, or to run you through the legal options. And in many cases, at the end of the process, the mediator will suggest that you ask your lawyer to review any draft settlement. If the mediator does not suggest it, you should ask your lawyer to do so anyway.

Mediation typically takes a number of sessions over the course of several days and possibly weeks. All discussions are considered privileged—i.e., confidential—so that you can feel fully protected to speak freely. It makes for a very comfortable environment in which, among other things, you can vent all you want—something you cannot do in a courtroom.

The value of this venting should not be underestimated. For one thing, this is likely to be your only chance to tell your story—and to spill all your emotions—to an objective third party. It's different from the venting you do with your friends, who love you, or your lawyer, who is paid to be on your side. A professional mediator has absolutely no ax to grind, no skin in the game, no dog in this fight; choose your cliché. And sometimes, the very act of speaking your narrative and having it heard by such a person is enough; it's all that is needed to bring about a settlement.

That's because the mediator is trained to keep the lines of communication open and to keep you both on track as much as possible. Mediators are problem-solvers; they know how to help you formulate ideas that can lead to agreements. What's more, experienced mediators have seen a wide range of disputes, levels of contention, and solutions, so they are often able to lead a couple to a resolution they might never have thought of otherwise.

And nothing about mediation is binding—unless and until an agreement is signed. If the mediation falls apart beforehand, you haven't lost anything but time (and money of course, although mediators tend to be less expensive than lawyers). And if the mediation does bring you to an agreement, you just sign on the dotted line, file the agreement with the court, and walk away. You're done.

Negotiations: The Voluntary Settlement Conference

But most people, it seems, still feel more comfortable with lawyers leading the negotiations. Dissolving a relationship is a matter of law, after all, and the issues can be complicated. I estimate that 75 to 80 percent of the cases I handle are resolved through negotiation in voluntary settlement conferences, where both sides can bring in other needed expertise to support their positions on any and all issues.

It's a negotiation. That means that you are there to work at the difficult task of give-and-take. Remember that there is only a certain amount of money to be divided, however great or small the amount, so the giving and taking will need offers and counteroffers in disparate currencies—i.e., in things other than money. Remember also that negotiation is a process with numerous moving parts. So keep in mind that it's almost impossible to put the toothpaste back in the tube—that is, to go back on an offer once it is made. So squeeze things out gradually and in small amounts, and hold on to your reserves as long as you can.

Although intentionally informal, settlement conferences are serious business meetings, so you should look and dress the part—that is, serious, businesslike, and as good as you can look. Be prepared for the lawyers and judge/mediator sometimes to speak in terms you may not understand entirely; on occasion, the judge may ask to speak to the lawyers alone. This is standard procedure, so don't panic, but you are going to need to trust your lawyer when it happens. It's my practice always to announce to a judge in such a case that I intend to tell my client the substance of what transpires, even if the sidebar conference concerns technical matters of law or procedure.

Sometimes, when the process hits a snag, the two parties may themselves be able to effect a solution that seems to be beyond the ability of the lawyers. That's not surprising. You know each other very well, and as you are going to be coparenting with each other for the rest of your lives; you may well be better positioned to figure out a solution than anybody else. It's worth trying. And if you succeed, it's a lot cheaper than paying lawyers to keep on tussling.

Settlement conferences can be crowded. Typically, they take place in a law office, and anyone can attend such a conference. My own view is that it's probably a really bad idea to ask your new boyfriend to show up, and almost the same can be said of your best friend from fifth grade, whom you asked along for moral support. Lovers and confidantes should probably not attend, but if they do, they should certainly wait in another room and leave the settlement conference to those who are there to come to terms.

That includes you and your soon-to-be-ex, the lawyers for both of you, your accountants, and any other professional experts necessary—all of whom are on the clock and being paid by the hour. It's one reason that the question of who pays the attorneys' fees—including the fees of the experts the attorneys have summoned—is often an issue to be settled in the conference.

At the head of this crowded table—a neutral party, on neither side—is the divorce mediator, typically a retired judge, who will guide the discussion. He or she has been hired by both parties and, by the time the conference is scheduled, has received all the mediation or settlement conference briefs laying out each party's positions. Despite the juridical nature of legal briefs and despite the presence of a judge, the tone of a settlement conference is, as noted, as informal as possible. That's by design, the aim being to distinguish this from a courtroom proceeding, with its gowns and armed guards and court reporters and oaths taken on penalty of perjury. There's none of that in a voluntary settlement conference; it's why it's called "voluntary"—there is no compulsion of law. And the judge/mediator will typically kick off a settlement conference by talking about all this, delivering a preamble about the aim of the conference, the manner of it, and how his or her experience and expertise can help guide the proceedings.

Then the parties will almost invariably go into separate rooms, and the judge/mediator will begin a process not unlike that of shuttle diplomacy. "Look," the judge/mediator might say to the soon-to-be-ex-husband—call him Jeremy—"I don't think you're really offering her enough in spousal support, especially given the size of your annual compensation." To which Jeremy—or Jeremy's lawyer—might reply that half of that annual compensation actually goes to his soon-to-be-ex-wife, Gina, in the form of community property residuals. "Even though it's not imputed to her," says Jeremy's lawyer, "Gina is actually receiving that money over and above the spousal support we've agreed to."

"Uh-huh," the judge might say, in that jurisprudential way of judges, just before offering another idea—just a small tweak on Jeremy's position that Jeremy and his lawyer find unobjectionable, if they get something else in return.

With that, the judge will summon Gina's group and present the idea. "How about, in exchange for a bit more in spousal support, you give a little on the child care payment issue?"

And so it will go, hour after hour. Lunch will be brought in. The new boyfriend may leave for an appointment; the fifth-grade pal may fall asleep on one of the Barcelona chairs. Judge, lawyers, and the divorcing pair keep working at it. At one point, Gina's side offers to sign off on the child custody issue *only;* Gina, they say, is still not comfortable with the money arrangements but wants custody settled. A deal memo will be drawn up, pending final resolution of all other issues.

It's always amazing how much gets accomplished during the last two hours of the day—say, from 4:00 to 6:00 P.M., just up against the time the judge must leave. But a fatigue factor can often be at work by then as well, and I caution my clients—and you, Dear Reader—not to sign anything while tired, and certainly not to sign anything unless you're completely comfortable with every part of it. Another day won't hurt.

Often, there is one key issue that cannot be settled but is the key to all the rest. If you could settle that single holdout bone of contention, it seems likely that everything else would fall into place. In many such cases, it makes sense to separate that issue, slice it away from negotiations in the conference room, and take it to court.

Once a judgment has been reached there, the parties can come back to the table to negotiate a complete settlement.

Sometimes, reluctance to sign a final settlement is a matter of letting sensitivities settle, for this can be an emotional process as well as a diplomatic and legal one. Old feelings are stirred; anger and resentment can bubble up again. Moreover, when you look at a final draft settlement, you are looking at the definitive ending to a big part of your life. It can be scary, can make you hesitate, can prompt you perhaps to want just one more look before you dot the last *i* and cross the last *t*. Good idea.

In fact, in the last two daylong settlement conferences I was involved in, parties ready to settle stopped just short of it, and the conferences ended in failure. All the pieces were in place to sign off on item after item, but it just didn't happen.

In one case, the wife pitched a stiletto heel at the conference room door just as it closed behind her departing husband; fortunately, no blood was spilled. In the other case, the day simply dribbled away, and along with, it seemed, the will to find closure.

Yet in both cases, closure was achieved the very next day. Who knows just what it took—one more talk between the two parties, another reassurance by a lawyer, or just a night to sleep on it—but what couldn't be achieved in the room was achieved just hours later. So it does not always work in a day or get settled in the room; it may need to simmer in the parties' minds and hearts for a few more hours, even days. Still, a negotiated settlement achieved through mediation in a voluntary settlement conference or a divorce mediator's office remains the best way to dissolve a relationship and resolve all its issues in detail.

And it may also offer a precedent for the way future issues between the two of you could be handled. In that sense, negotiating a settlement can actually be a key step toward both parties' emotional healing.

Easy Out

Remember the term POSSLQ—pronounced "possle-cue"? It was invented by the U.S. Census Bureau to cover the rising tide of couples living together but not married, and it stood for Person Of Opposite Sex Sharing Living Quarters, a euphemism of stunning dullness. CBS commentator Charles Osgood gave the term some life and warmth with a bit of poetry:

> **You live with me, and I with you,**
> **And you will be my POSSLQ**
> **I'll be your friend and so much more;**
> **That's what a POSSLQ is for.**

That was certainly the case with Emma and Byron. They had been POSSLQs for seven wonderful years. They were in love and overtly enjoyed the life they lived together—a life of travel, of delving into exotic cuisines, of intellectual adventures they shared by taking courses together at the local university, and of common beliefs, including a disinclination to have children.

For reasons never quite made clear, after this seven-year idyll, they decided to get married. Had they married because they suspected their relationship was in trouble? Or had they decided that because the relationship was so good they should take it to an-

other level? No one knows, but what was clear was that after eighteen months of marriage, they realized they had made a mistake, and they sought a divorce.

Although the marriage had been brief, the two had commingled many of their assets during the seven years prior to the marriage, and the untangling was clearly going to be difficult. They had jointly owned their home before marrying but had refinanced it and changed the title just a few months after the wedding. They had also amassed a somewhat valuable art collection, had years of shared purchases to split up, and were co-owners of a three-year-old Border collie named Jezebel, on whom both of them doted.

This might have been a truly complicated, sticky proceeding except that Emma and Byron were totally committed to preserving not just their friendship, but the regard in which each held the other. They did not want to sully the value of their years together and their love for each other.

They put the commitment into action by sitting down with their business manager, listing all their assets, then mediating an amicable division of everything. Emma took the bulk of the cash and investments, while Byron realized equal value by keeping the apartment. They devised a custody schedule for Jezebel, alternating weeks. They set aside an afternoon, got a bottle of wine and a couple of packs of Post-its—green for Emma, yellow for Byron, and flipped a coin to determine who would get first pick. Byron won the toss and slapped the first Post-it on the Balinese basket they dropped their keys into in the hallway. They moved on from there, dividing their belongings until each had an equal portion of both actual and sentimental value. They

finished the wine, wept a little, then went out to dinner. They still do, from time to time.

Oh, that all settlements could be like this. . . .

IN BRIEF

Remember what you came for—ending a relationship that has soured your existence so you can say hello to the next stage of your life. To get to a settlement, you both need to set rules and protocols that define that ending and the links—namely, children and/or any joint property—that still bind you.

1. There is no such thing as a perfect deal in which you get 100 percent of what you want.
2. Use what you know—knowledge of your ex.
3. Seize the moment. If the door to a settlement is open, now is the time to walk through it.
4. Consider mediation if you thrive in an unstructured situation, if you're dealing with a limited number of issues, if the issues are fairly simple, or if the balance of power in the relationship is equal.
5. Be reasonable. In negotiating a settlement, you will have to give to get.

13

Court—the Last Resort

There is no winning in this. It's only degrees of losing.

—GAVIN D'AMATO,
DANNY DEVITO'S CHARACTER IN *THE WAR OF THE ROSES*

The judge had scheduled our courtroom appearance for 8:30 A.M., an hour of the day my rock-musician client hadn't seen in decades, and I had been on the phone since 7:00 asking his manager for assurances that he was on his way. As 8:30 rolled around, then slid toward 9:00, the only saving grace was that while my client hadn't showed up, neither had his soon-to-be-ex-wife. And neither was answering the phone.

By late morning, the judge rescheduled our hearing for after lunch, and it was around then that the couple arrived—together and disheveled-looking. I whisked my client off to the other end of the courtroom hallway and asked what had held him up. "Well," he said sheepishly, "we were shagging in the back of her car."

An unusual way to usher in a final dissolution decree, but it worked: The soon-to-be-ex-husband and wife were both in such a dreamy mood of benevolence toward the world as a whole that we were able to dismiss most outstanding issues right away, and we resolved some fraught points—length of spousal support and division of some publishing royalties for my client's music catalog—by midafternoon. The atmosphere was sweetness and light as I read the marital settlement agreement into the record and the judge pronounced the two well and truly divorced.

But boy, is that rare. Court is, in general, an unpleasant experience for both parties. For one thing, it really is the last resort, which means no more kidding around, no more trying to pull a fast one, no more weaseling away from the facts. This is the endgame and the last stop. And it looks it. There is something utterly unsmiling about a courtroom. Its trappings—the flag, the judge's black robe, the no-nonsense clerk, the court reporter recording your every word, including hemming, hawing, grammatical mistakes, and a thousand "umms," and the gun-toting bailiff, not to mention the bar separating you from the judge's raised bench—deliberately make you aware that this is the home of justice-with-a-capital-*J* and the place where judgments are handed down. So going to court tends to be uncomfortable during the course of the proceedings.

But of course it is particularly uncomfortable for the losing party, which could be you. That is the nature of a court proceeding, and it is the whole point of going to court—namely, one of you wins, and one of you loses. And as a lawyer who is pretty successful in court, I will say this: There is no guarantee that you are going to win. I have known many a client who insisted on his or her day in court and ended up ruing the day.

Moreover, even if you do win, the victory is rarely total or outright or unequivocal. For the most part, courtroom orders leave both sides unhappy in some respect about some issue or other.

So staying out of court altogether is always a better choice in my view. Settling on the courthouse steps, a not infrequent occurrence, is the next best thing. But sometimes, you just run out of options. Even when you yourself consistently answer your spouse's anger or spite with patience and maturity, clenching your teeth and checking your rage despite every provocation, you still can't control what said spouse will say and do. And if your spouse or partner insists on being a jerk, or if and when mediation and negotiation simply run out of steam with dissolution issues still unresolved, then it will indeed be time to go to court—at least, in the case of a failed mediation, for those issues still outstanding.

Not that you're stuck in court forever. Sometimes, getting even a tentative decision issued by a judge or an order made on one issue will be enough to make an unbending spouse rethink the austerity of his or her upright stance, especially if the courthouse skirmish has demonstrated that he or she really does have something to lose by going this route. Then everybody comes scurrying back into the conference room to start negotiating all over again. Of the 75 or so percent of my cases that are negotiated, I estimate that 60 percent have gone to court first—usually resulting in a temporary order on some particularly niggling issue like support. Getting a whiff of what it is like to put your fate in the hands of a judge and to hear your case "told" by witnesses under oath can send the most unyielding spouse racing back to the negotiating table.

But whether court is a temporary detour or the final road to dissolution, you should know and understand its realities.

First of all, remember that this is the twenty-first century. Unlike divorce court a generation ago, no-fault is the rule today. It means that judges are not interested in and will not indulge attempts to ascribe blame, sling mud, or elicit sympathy. It simply isn't relevant. They are there to resolve issues and divvy up the assets, often just splitting everything down the middle, and they need to do it fast. That is because despite the growing use of mediation, court dockets just about everywhere are overcrowded. This may also mean that you will wait all day, paying your lawyer and your expert witnesses by the hour, and then either not be heard at all or get little more than a brief hearing for your case. It's worth keeping in mind.

Second, going to court is not a quick fix. Because of crowded dockets, you will probably have to wait a considerable time—on average, four to six weeks—before a judge can be freed up and a date set for your hearing. In California, the backlogged dockets mean you'll wait an average of six months for a trial date, but California is hardly unique, especially with Great Recession budget cuts exacerbating already straitened state resources. Just ask the folks trying to get a divorce in New Jersey or Alabama, where some counties report a two-year backlog for divorce and custody cases, thanks to staff reductions forced by budget cuts. So the chances are that whatever your jurisdiction, you will be twiddling your thumbs and cooling your heels for some extended period of time before your case is heard.

Once you are before a judge, however—there are no jury trials in family law cases, by the way, except in Georgia, where a jury trial is an *option*—a hearing proceeding on a single issue may indeed take only a day, albeit usually a long day. But if you are preparing a full-blown, multi-issue trial, it could drag on for weeks.

During those weeks, of course, you must be present—which could wreak havoc with your job, profession, and indeed with your family responsibilities—while at the same time you are paying by the hour for your lawyers and the other experts who must of course be on hand. And you could still lose. Besides, win or lose, this isn't like a personal injury case, where you take your money if you win, pay it if you lose, and in either case go home and forget about it. If you have kids, remember that you will be connected to the person you beat or lost to for years of coparenting. A victory could be Pyrrhic, while a loss could hang around your neck like an albatross.

Therefore, even if you have both decided that you have had it with mediation and it is time to go to court, do one more thing before you actually pull the plug and make it official. One more time, have a talk with your spouse. Just the two of you. Leave the anger and the threats outside the door and try to make sure that you both understand that what is coming up is going to be tougher, more acrimonious, and more expensive than the already tough, acrimonious, and expensive negotiation you think is not working. Remind each other that in today's world, the judicial tendency is to split the baby in half, giving each of you a share but at a price both will have to pay; a nuanced, delicate threading of the needle is not what court decisions are known for. You may think you have passed the point of no return, but take this one further step before you jump off this cliff into an unknown, uncertain, ambiguous future.

Your Lawyer

But if you do decide to go to court, your first move should be to take another look at your attorney. Back in chapter 6, when I offered advice on what to look for in a lawyer, I said you should find someone who would be "a problem-solver, an advocate, an expert advisor on the law and on your rights and responsibilities, a strategist, a negotiator, and a litigator." It's not all that easy to find all those attributes in a single person. Not infrequently, an attorney who is an ace at explaining the ins and outs of dissolution, educating you about the law, guiding you through the process, negotiating on your behalf, and, nine times out of ten, getting a good settlement, is not so good at what you want if negotiation fails—namely, crushing the opposition.

In truth, mediation and litigation are sufficiently different skills as to constitute separate specialties. Just think of Great Britain, where the two types of practice constitute distinct professions—solicitors for legal transactions, barristers for going to court. On this side of the pond, your very good settlement attorney may not be a litigation specialist; litigation may not be his or her bent or interest, and if that is the case, he or she is likely to have less experience of it, if any. Lots of lawyers will make that clear up front, letting you know in advance that they are mediation-based and that if mediation fails and the case goes to court, you're going to need someone else. But if your lawyer did not offer such information up front, now is the time to find out just how good a litigator he or she is—or is not.

Let me be clear: A great many family lawyers are skilled and experienced in both mediation and litigation. Solo practitioners of family law will typically be skilled in both aspects of the practice, while law firms with family law practitioners will have specialists in both, so if your lawyer is not the best choice to take the case to court, the firm will be able quickly to find a replacement or associate to carry your case forward.

Obviously, you can't afford to be thin-skinned about changing lawyers if you need to go to court and you feel that your mediation attorney is just not suited to what is a whole new ball game. Nor will your mediation attorney be thin-skinned about being replaced; this is the way the world works, and no mediation attorney wants to fail in the litigation arena.

Changing lawyers loses you nothing except time as your new attorney gets up to speed on the issues. You may even request of your mediation lawyer that he or she spend a few hours with your newly hired litigation specialist to go over the facts, the issues, the mediation lawyer's insights. It seems little enough to ask, especially since the mediation failed.

Getting a new lawyer up to speed in this instance is not an overly lengthy process. On a number of occasions, I have been called in to litigate cases that others mediated, and just about everything I needed was at hand: The discovery was done, the voluntary settlement conference brief had been written, and the facts were all there. We were soon up and running.

Know Before You Go

Your lawyer will prep you about how court works and what is expected of you, but the more homework you can do on your own, the better. Familiarize yourself ahead of time as best you can with two central players in this next phase of the dissolution of your marriage or partnership: the judge, and the courtroom itself—that is, its look and feel and atmosphere. The less exotic a place the courtroom is to you, the more comfortable you will feel and the smoother and more efficient the process can be.

Once you know the name of the judge who will hear your case, you can find out basic information online. Your lawyer is likely to have access to Lexis/Nexis and its array of search engines on judges, but it is probably just as easy to run a search on the judge's name or on "find a judge [YOUR STATE]." That should lead you to one or more links to the state's judicial directory or to different courts within the state. There, you can usually learn the judge's pre-judicial-appointment background, education, length of experience, professional and civic activities, and so forth.

Armed with the basics, you want to find out from your lawyer exactly what he or she knows about the judge, what his or her experience is litigating before the judge—if any—and failing any direct experience, what the lawyer has heard about the judge from colleagues. Lawyers routinely attend state bar functions, where they are introduced to judges, or where judges make presentations, or where, at the very least, there is plenty of gossip about judges. Lawyers also talk to one another, and their shop talk is bound to include stories of their own court experience and of the judges that presided. There are thus a number of sources from which lawyers can get some sort of perception of the judge. Judge A, for example, is perceived as tending to rule in favor of women over men. Judge B is known as a stickler for court decorum but counts on oral arguments more than the pleadings he has failed to read. Judge C is easygoing—even a bit of a jokester—during proceedings but a strict constructionist when it comes to rendering judgment.

An even better way to get a sense of the person who will be rendering judgment on you is to experience him or her in person. In other words, do your own trial run of your upcoming litigation. This is also a great way to familiarize yourself with the courthouse so that you don't get lost and show up late on your actual day of reckoning, and it is something I advise all my clients to do—namely, an advance trip to court. You'll learn how long it takes you to get yourself there, where to park, how to find your way to the right courtroom, what the security procedures are like. (Recently, appearing in a branch court I had not been to before, I was relieved of a silver-plated spoon I had brought from home with a carton of yogurt; it had set off the metal detector. I got it back at the end of the day.) You may be surprised by what you find. The elegantly imposing courtrooms you've seen in all those Hollywood movies may turn out to be a good deal more utilitarian than inspirational, and the judge is most probably not going to have the craggy looks or homespun wisdom of Spencer Tracy, but better to find out all this now. Public access to courtroom proceedings is of course a cherished principle of our republic, so slip on in and take a seat so you can watch in real time the judge you will soon come before as petitioner or respondent.

You will see where you'll be seated and where that puts you relative to the judge, the table at which your ex will be seated, the court reporter, the bailiff. You can check out how the proceedings advance, the small rituals, the required breaks for the court reporter and other staff, the hallways where people wait. You can search out the restroom and the water fountain and the nearest place to get a cup of coffee or a snack. It may sound frivolous, but in fact it means that on the day of your own hearing, there will be fewer butterflies in your stomach and a bit more confidence in your manner.

On the other hand, if your advance trip reveals to you a judge you think is likely to be unsympathetic to your cause, you still have time to try to convince your ex to go back into negotiation mode.

What Your Lawyer Should Tell You

At some point before your court date, your attorney will have drafted and filed pleadings setting forth your arguments, evidence, and relief requests. Often, a declaration from you will also be submitted, so you will have had to read, approve, and sign it well before your court date. You should also read the full set of pleadings before your day in court—that's really highly advisable. Then your lawyer will confer with you at length about what to expect on the day of the hearing, what will happen, how things are likely to go, and your role in the proceedings. (If your lawyer does not schedule such a conference, request one; if a lawyer sees no need for such a conference, you may have the wrong lawyer.)

He or she will walk you through the entire process, starting with what time to arrive at the courthouse, where to meet, and how you should dress. Attire is not unimportant. For a courtroom appearance, more than for a deposition, it is appropriate and customary to dress up a little. For one thing, court is a more formal setting. For another, what you wear and how you look will reflect how you approach the proceedings, and it's a good idea to show a certain level of respect for our system of law and for the dispensing of justice—*and* for the judge who will be making decisions that will affect your destiny. That means dressing right. I have many clients who are dreadlocked, tattooed, and pierced from head to toe, but they understand that respect means not showing up in a torn T-shirt. They are their natural selves in a suit and tie. I have other clients who are among the most glamorous people on earth, and they understand that they are not at a Hollywood premiere but in a public courtroom. For both men and women, suits are the ideal attire, and for women, a nice dress—maybe leaning toward business formal—is always appropriate.

Your lawyer will instruct you on how the day will go—from waiting for your number on the docket to be called, to possible sidebars between judge and lawyers, to lawyers and judge going into chambers to confer privately. You'll learn about the daily schedule; although this may differ from jurisdiction to jurisdiction, you can probably count on a ten- to fifteen-minute break around midmorning, an hour or an hour and a half for lunch, and another break in midafternoon. Courtroom staff need these breaks. The court reporter's fingers must be breaking off at this point, and everybody could use a trip to the bathroom and/or the water-cooler. The breaks are also a chance for judges to do some quick research or review the pleadings in the privacy of their chambers and for lawyers to take a breath and assess for just a moment or two. Essential—because every other minute of the day will be the hard work of the proceedings. If there is an emergency hearing regarding domestic violence or custody, these may take precedence and be heard before your matter. Also, attorneys with hearings scheduled in other departments or courtrooms may ask for priority of their matter to be heard first or request to be put on "second call"—meaning the late-morning calendar call.

Perhaps most important, your lawyer will go over with you the scenario of those proceedings—what you hope to gain, your chances of getting the outcome you want, the positions you are taking on each issue before the court.

If you will be testifying, your lawyer will prep you about what to answer and how to answer. If you have testified under oath in a deposition, you know the basic rules: Don't say too much, don't say too little, don't offend. But a major distinction between a deposition and a court hearing is that in a deposition, only the opposing lawyer questions you, so a different style of response is warranted when you are questioned in court by your own lawyer. You'll want to pay close heed to these instructions, and you and your lawyer will probably want to work out a set of signals—typically via eye contact—that can help you navigate your way through your testimony.

In Court

Avoid courthouse contact with your ex if you can. By now, everything that could be said has been said, and there is little point in rehashing old arguments in the hallway. That approach failed, which is why you're here today. So give it up, don't let yourself be drawn into it, keep your eyes forward, and walk right past a possible reiteration of recriminations.

When your case is called, you will take a seat next to your lawyer at what is called counsel table. Do so quietly and with dignity, and by all means turn off your cell phone and spit out your gum (not in the judge's direction). I routinely advise my clients to take what is called the STFU pill each morning before court; it stands for Shut The Fuck Up. No judge wants to hear from you except when you are on the witness stand or are replying to a direct question the judge may pose. Everything else is off limits and out of place: whispering, eye-rolling, grimacing, gestures or noises of any kind, staring—or glaring—at your soon-to-be-ex at the other table or when he or she is on the stand. It is often difficult for the parties to restrain themselves, and I understand how frustrating it can be to remain mute and unmoving while your ex-spouse rattles off accusations a mile a minute from the elevated and protected bastion of the witness stand. But remember that the judge is watching you. Gesturing or glaring or an outburst can only harm your case and your cause, so I tell clients to bring a notebook to court and vent their emotions in pen and ink.

Watch your body language and your actions as well. You're in court to listen and perhaps to testify—nothing more. I cannot emphasize too strongly how off-putting any kind of showboating is in a courtroom. The petitioner in a recent case insisted on bringing in coffee and doughnuts for everybody during a proceeding scheduled to run for a week—the bailiff; the clerk; the court reporter; the respondent, who was my client; and me as opposing counsel. It smacked of grandstanding and of trying to own the courtroom—or to turn it into an informal gathering of pals, which it most definitely is not—and the judge finally put a halt to it. It was just inappropriate.

If you are to testify, remember that you don't need to understand the rules of evidence; that's your lawyer's job. All you have to do is answer questions. Remember also that your ex's lawyer is there to win and that one way to do that is to try to rattle you so that your answer either doesn't help or actually harms your case. So when opposing counsel asks a question, stop, breathe, and wait a beat for your lawyer to object. That will happen if your lawyer believes that the answer to the question as posed is something the judge should not hear—not if you want to win your case. "Did you see a doctor about your insomnia in the spring of 2012?" your ex's attorney might ask with the sincerity of a concerned and sympathetic buddy. "Objection!" your lawyer shouts. "Move to strike! My client does not waive the physician-patient privilege!" Just relax.

Wait for another question, and again, take a beat before you respond. Only when it is clear that your lawyer has no objection should you go ahead and answer—simply, briefly, succinctly.

On direct examination, with your own lawyer asking the questions, keep in mind that this is your chance to tell your story. Your lawyer has crafted a set of questions consistent with the pleadings submitted to the court on your behalf. These questions are designed to elicit from you the narrative that presents your case in the strongest possible way and that you can convincingly uphold during any cross-examination by your ex's lawyer. So say what you have to say—again, as simply, briefly, and succinctly as possible.

What Will Happen

The outcome of a court proceeding depends entirely on what is being decided and on how complex the evidence is. Your day in court may trail into two days, or more, although a proceeding expected to last longer than five days is usually so scheduled at the outset when the judge asks the lawyers for time estimates, and such a trial is often moved to a different courtroom. But however long the proceeding lasts, its ending may not necessarily mean a decision; it could be a while before the judge renders judgment. Or, the judge may rule on a particular motion and order the clerk to draft and issue a minute order, as it is called, from the bench. Such an order might require that from this moment, or starting the next day, or on the Monday morning following the weekend, a particular custody arrangement goes into effect, or the petitioner must pay the respondent's legal fees, or something similar. Even that order may have to be e-mailed or faxed or transmitted in some way, so don't expect complete resolution—not to mention final judgment—as a result of your day in court. It's rarely that crisp and unequivocal.

Remember too that court cases don't actually finish up as portrayed on *Law and Order* or the old *Perry Mason* shows. Family law has very few crushing moments; with the one well-known exception of a famous ballplayer's wife, you're rarely led away in handcuffs. Rather, for the most part, neither party is ever totally happy.

There is an alternative to going to court, and that is binding arbitration. It means you and your spouse or partner sign an agreement to accept the arbitrator's ruling, whatever it may be. Obviously, you both agree on the choice of arbitrator—again, typically a retired judge, preferably one with a background in family law—and the process is exactly the same as in a courtroom. That is, rules of evidence prevail, testimony is sworn under oath on pain of perjury, objections are raised and motions put forth. The single difference is that that you are not in a courtroom, and that the arbitrator is not a sitting judge. Theoretically, that means the case can be heard more quickly and, even more important, that the proceedings may be kept private. But they are no less formal, and as with a court proceeding, arbitration is unlikely to produce a clear winner.

Either way, whether in or out of a courtroom, such proceedings are the fallback only when all else has failed. The court of last resort is not for sissies.

IN BRIEF

A court proceeding is typically an unpleasant and difficult experience for both parties. And you could lose. So think hard about going to court and prepare well.

1. Spend a day in court as an observer—preferably before the judge who will preside at your proceeding—in order to familiarize yourself with the environment, procedures, and the judge.
2. Ask your attorney to brief you on what to expect.
3. Show respect for the court in your appearance, attire, and manner.
4. Binding arbitration can be a faster, more private alternative to a court proceeding, but is equally a win-or-lose proposition.

14

Wrapping It Up

So it's done. Issues resolved, settlement agreed upon, judgment delivered. You're divorced, right? This no-longer-viable relationship is now truly dissolved?

Well, no. Not really. What the mediation process or a court of justice proposes, lawyers and perhaps other expert professionals must still dispose, and there are a lot of details to attend to in actually executing the deal that has been hammered out. That means there is typically a lag between the doing of the deal and the implementation of its every particular. For both parties, that downtime can be an anticlimactic and frustrating sort of limbo.

Chances are that the broad terms of your settlement have been set down in a deal memo. The next step is to fine-tune those broad terms into explicit details and elucidate said details in a long-form judgment. That judgment form must then be presented to the court, stamped by a clerk so that it is properly filed, and signed by a judge, which is what gives the deal its legal force.

It sounds simple and straightforward, but of course the fine-tuning and elucidating of the details can take time. As always, it depends on the volume and complexity of the details. Certainly, some judgments may be prepared and filed in as little as a day—although in many backlogged jurisdictions, it may take a while before a clerk is available to stamp the document or a judge to sign off on it. More often, it will take longer than a day.

It is time during which both parties' lawyers are—or should be—hard at work crossing every *t* and dotting every *i* of the settlement. For example, they are immediately transferring your medical insurance to COBRA, giving you temporary continued group health coverage under the Consolidated Omnibus Budget Reconciliation Act pending you getting your own coverage in six months, or eighteen months, or as much as thirty-six months. That's because any joint medical insurance coverage you had ends the moment the settlement is official.

This is also the time when the lawyers determine which party gets to take the dependency tax deduction for the children in which year, decide when filing singly with the IRS will replace the joint filing that once prevailed, calculate the exact amount down to the penny of any equalization payment to balance or offset a disparity in the division of property and assets, and finalize the language of the agreement as only lawyers can.

It's exacting work, and a pair of lawyers already feeling pretty exhausted from tough negotiations or a difficult court proceeding may believe they need a day or two, maybe a week, maybe more to take a break from your case, recharge their batteries, and clear their heads.

For the clients who have been through the wrenching process of ending the central relationship of their lives, this added delay often seems like insult added to injury. You've worked it all out, and now here you are, waiting while the lawyers do what lawyers do.

Nor are you dependent solely on lawyers to get it done. Keep in mind that an agreement on dividing assets is not the same as dividing assets. Your broker may have to do the actual deed—split the portfolio, divvy up the shares, roll over the IRA, transfer ownership of stocks, all of which requires paperwork for the parties, for the companies that issued the stock, for the IRS, and possibly for a zillion other regulatory and compliance authorities. Your settlement agreement may have set a date for the dividing of assets, or it may have said that the settlement division won't be final until the division settlement is complete. Either way, the ball needs to start rolling.

One of you may be moving out of what used to be your joint home while the other of you takes sole possession, in which case you are likely to need to change ownership title in what is called an interspousal transfer deed. That may require some sort of real estate expert as well as a lawyer. Then the one of you moving out needs to move out, which means arranging the removal, setting a date, hiring the moving company, and paying that bill as well.

And sometimes, one party or another drags his or her feet. I've known husbands who agreed to community property splits but couldn't seem to get around to actually writing the check for their ex-spouse's half. I've known wives who signed off on agreements only to decide that by dawdling a bit longer—delaying a clean ending and thereby annoying or angering their ex—they just might be able to extract a bit more loot.

The bottom line is that settled is not finished. And the work of getting it finished is pretty much out of your hands and in the hands of a lawyer or mediator whose mind may now be focusing on the next case, and of a broker, accountant, financial planner, etc., for whom you are one of numerous clients.

What can you do?

The Punch List

Take a tip from the construction industry and get together with your ex and your lawyer to draw up a punch list. For those of you not familiar with the term—I guess you have never renovated your kitchen or lived next door to people adding a room to their house—a punch list is a list of tasks still to do to complete the job. In most construction contracts, the contractor asks the architect to do a "pre-final" inspection when the job is *substantially* completed, after which the two draw up a list of what still has to be done to fully complete the work for final inspection. In the old days, two copies of the list were made, and both contractor and architect would punch a hole next to each task when it was done. Hence: punch list.

It's a great phrase, and it's precisely the apt mechanism for getting through the downtime between deal and done. Start the next phase of your relationship with your ex-spouse or former partner by jointly coming up with such a list—what needs to happen and who or what can make it happen for this dissolution to be fully realized. Assign each task; for example, decide jointly that your ex will handle the closing on the transfer of the house title while you deal with the broker and finalize the division of the portfolio. And as for the tasks your lawyer still must do, set a deadline for getting them done, with the understanding that final payment will of course be dependent on the final judgment being filed.

Key to all this, as to everything this book is about, is communication—between you and your lawyer and between you and your ex. The fastest route to the fat lady's song is through talking to each other on a regular basis and in a civil manner.

Parting Ways

My client, the husband, offered $50,000 per month in spousal support. His wife demanded $75,000. The judge awarded her $30,000. Once the divorce decree was filed, the two parties joined up to sue the ex-wife's lawyer for malpractice because he had assured her they could do better than the $50,000 originally offered. It was somewhat bizarre, and they did not prevail, and had she been the master of her own destiny and acted reasonably, she would not have taken her lawyer's litigious advice. But the very fact of the two of them taking up this joint action is indicative of two realities of dissolving a relationship: (1) the finality of a dissolution often tends to defuse the acrimony and ignite a different and better relationship between the two spouses or partners, and (2) as I always say to my clients, your relationship with your ex will last a lot longer than your relationship with your lawyer.

That latter relationship can often seem close. After all, your lawyer has probably heard some of the more intimate details of your life. He or she has seen you display a range of emotions, has been there when you wept with frustration or sadness, has calmed you down when you were furious, has sympathized with your regrets and supported you in your recriminations. Some clients see their lawyers as saviors—as people who have emancipated them from an untenable situation and are therefore worthy of veneration.

We're not, and the feeling that we might be is, I assure you, temporary. So is the feeling that you and your lawyer have become soul mates. Yes, dissolving a marriage or partnership is a life-changing, life-defining event, and the lawyer who has steered you through it may seem like your besty. But as the saying goes, he or she really was just doing the job you hired him or her to do. I can promise you with certainty that a year from now, if you and your lawyer pass each other on the street, a hello and a handshake will be just the level of contact you'll feel up to.

Where your ex is concerned, however, parting ways is far less precise, and if you are coparents, you will be involved in each other's lives one way or another for years to come. Take some courage from the fact that you have now made it through the hard part. By hook or by crook—and sometimes by both—you have managed to resolve what needed resolving. It's an indication that you *can* work out whatever may need to be worked out, and that seems like a good precedent and solid starting point for the future.

IN BRIEF

Settled is not necessarily finished. And the work of getting it finished is pretty much out of your hands.

1. With your ex and your lawyers, create a punch list that details the tasks to be done and assigns responsibility for each task.
2. Keep the lines of communication open.

15

This Really Is the First Day of the Rest of Your Life

Bravo!

You've gone through a life-changing process—in less time than your parents did a generation ago—and have survived it and learned something from it. So here you are—bruised but not broken, and experiencing a civil, even respectful relationship with your ex. Congratulate yourself; you deserve it. Mission accomplished.

Now what?

Refer back to the list of five things your spouse or marriage holds you back from doing that I asked you to make in chapter 1 and go for it. If you don't accomplish at least three of the five things now, you'll have no one to blame but yourself.

This really is time for you. Yes, you may in due course find another rewarding relationship. Men in particular seem eager to jump back into the comfort of partnership, while women—certainly those with school-age children, at any rate—tend to revel for a while in the freedom derived from having far fewer responsibilities and in the license to do things that the freedom makes possible. But both sexes in time may gravitate toward new relationships, although my advice is: not just yet. Wait a while. As in Alcoholics Anonymous, which suggests twelve months of sobriety before getting into a new relationship—a suggestion nobody heeds—wait a while. Give it some time anyway.

You *need* time to find and get acquainted with the identity of what we might call You 2.0. This is particularly true if you married very young; if you did, you probably spent little enough time finding and identifying with You 1.0. Once you were embroiled in the relationship with your spouse, your identity became inextricably tied up with being someone's partner; you were half of a couple. During your divorce you were able—were forced—to represent yourself as master of your own destiny. It is now time to re-present yourself as you. It may feel odd at first, so give yourself time to ease into it til the oddness passes and you feel at home with it.

Remember that you have a built-in babysitter—your ex, during his or her custodial time—so yes, you should take that weekend trip to New York, hit the museums, see a Broadway show every night, eat yourself sick, shop yourself silly, and come home exhausted. Or maybe you prefer Rome, or trekking in Nepal, or pulling a Julia Child and taking cooking classes in Paris.

Actually, you don't have to go to Paris to take a cooking class; there is undoubtedly a good one at the nearby community college, which probably also offers a range of extension courses you could sign up for. But don't stop there. You can easily arrange your custody schedule to accommodate computer workshops at the library, dinner and drinks with friends, salsa dancing evenings at the Y, the book club at the local bookstore, the community chorus that meets in the school gym, film screening and review workshops, even a post-divorce support group meeting. The point of these undertakings is to do things you didn't know how to do before. But it is also true that you will meet people who share at least one interest with you—learning the computer or salsa dancing or reading or singing choral works or getting over getting divorced. Sharing an interest is the best opening move there can be toward connecting the new You 2.0 with others.

Healing?

Can divorce be "an opportunity for personal growth and a new life?" An outfit known as Divorce Detox certainly believes so, and it offers workshops, coaching sessions, newsletters, and workbooks to help you "let go of the past and create a better future." Based in Southern California—where else?—and charging substantial fees for its services, Divorce Detox in effect repackages many of the emotional processing techniques of traditional therapy and aims them at the recently or about-to-be divorced.

This doesn't mean that the techniques don't work or that the workshops and coaching are not valuable. Testimonials from satisfied customers insist otherwise. And certainly, the existence of Divorce Detox speaks to the very real emotional turmoil that many people feel when they dissolve the central relationship of their lives and to the emotional toll such a dissolution can take.

That is one reason why there are so many avenues for emotional healing following divorce, as even a brief search on the Internet (www.divorcecare.org, www.healingfromdivorce.com, etc.) or in your local bookstore makes clear. In this as in everything having to do with divorce, assess clearly and choose wisely among a range of choices.

Dating

I once had a great idea for a reality TV game show. With apologies to the late, great Henny Youngman, I was going to call it *Take My Wife, Please!* As you can guess, it would have been aimed at ex-husbands so annoyed at paying spousal support that they were ready to do anything—even go on a TV game show—to find new spouses for their former wives.

I hope it isn't necessary to add that I'm kidding. Which doesn't mean that the fact of your ex dating someone else, publicly, isn't somewhat fraught. Jealousy, a bruised ego, envy that your ex is moving on in life when you just don't yet seem to be able to: A range of negative emotions is likely. Maybe that he or she was having an affair is what precipitated the divorce, but now here it is, out in the open. Maybe it's that seeing your ex with someone else places a finality on the dissolution of your relationship that even a court document couldn't quite achieve. Or maybe you're not angry or hurt or jealous but actually glad for your ex, yet the fact of him or her with another stirs memories of what you and your ex experienced back when you were first in love.

Put it away or let it wash over you. Either way, experience the feeling and move on. Don't dwell on any of these emotions. Draw back and remember why you ended this relationship and what you have ahead of you. And among the things ahead of you is your own almost certain foray into the world of dating—again.

Okay, if you're a man, the love handles are clear physical evidence that you don't have the body you had when you won a starting position on your college hockey team. If you're a woman, you're not thrilled about the stretch marks or the C-section scar. In both cases, the only other people who have ever clapped eyes on these imperfections are your ex-spouses, now no longer in the picture. Are you really willing to expose your post-disso self to a possible suitor—and how much wine do you have to drink to prepare yourself to do so?

Dating again is not easy. But at some point, you are almost surely going to be ready.

The Internet, which proved so useful during your dissolution process, is of course the present-day portal into the world of hooking up. Match.com, eHarmony, and JDate are just the beginning; a simple search returns numerous sites dedicated specifically to people who are divorced. Of course, you're equally likely to meet someone on the salsa dance floor or in the computer workshop or the cooking class. Remember the statistics? There are plenty of newly single—or still-single—people around, and like you, they're trying to branch out and go where they can connect with others.

Granted, the first actual date you go on after two or five or ten or twenty years of not dating can be positively intimidating. If the date is absolutely awful, you can make the telling of it a recitation to amuse your friends the next time you're all out together. If it's not so bad or maybe kind of nice, keep in mind that it was a date—a first date at that—and nothing more. You don't need to commit just yet. Remember that it is not actually necessary to remarry. It is not even necessary to be in a relationship; many people live full, rich, productive, and happy lives all on their own. But keep in mind also that just because one relationship has ended does not doom you to never having another.

Next . . .

Do you remember that moment when you realized that it would be better to be alone with a shot at happiness than together with your spouse and miserable? That was your personal aha! moment, the instant of psychic shift that prompted you to pursue the dissolution you have just gone through. So now you are alone with your very own shot at happiness. This is your chance.

As much as you can, try out new firsts—things that stretch the mind, the body, the imagination, things that wake up the perspective that may have been napping over these last few unhappy months or years. There are more options for doing so today than at any time in history. You have just benefited from a transforming evolution in the way central human relationships are dissolved. Now just think of all the other evolutions that have taken place in your lifetime, over the course of a single generation: evolutions in self-knowledge, in scientific understanding of health and longevity, in diversity, in the nature of relationships, in the power opportunities open to women, in the speed of transfer of information, in travel, education, technology. Here's your chance to benefit from any or all of those evolutions as well, as you wade into anything and everything that interests you.

Another very important evolution has been in the nature and very definition of aging. As I write this, I have just finished reading *Grace*, the delicious memoir by Grace Coddington, the creative director of *Vogue* magazine. Ms. Coddington tells us that "seventy is the new fifty." It seems just a few minutes ago that we were told "fifty is the new thirty," so it's not unlikely that by the time this book comes out, seventy will be the new thirty. It means that whatever your age, you are "younger"—more vital, more open to the new—than your parents were at the same age. You also have access to more opportunities for gaining happiness than earlier generations—partly because in our prosperous nation, you are probably not overly burdened by a daily struggle to find food and shelter, and partly because you inherit a legacy of self-examination and self-discovery that has opened new doors to happiness for all. Let me put it simply: Where our parents' generation went home from divorce court and closed the curtains, you have the chance to divide and conquer. Stride out into a whole new world of things to do and learn and experience in the search for your own happiness.

I wish you luck as you take the first step.

Keep Your Perspective

Let me end where I began, with a reminder that I've been where you are right now. As I told you early on, I have two sons, each by a different father, and I am not "with" either father but rather coparent with both. I think we all manage pretty successfully; our most important barometer for that assessment is our kids, who are healthy, happy, and certainly confident in the love of both their parents.

From my own vantage, however, it sometimes takes enormous willpower, a level of patience I have had to work hard to achieve, and above all a sense of irony about life in general to keep my perspective, my sanity, and my wits about me. So if I were asked for advice for getting through a divorce, with all its permutations and complications, I would offer this: Try to remember that what seems awkward, difficult, or impossible today is very likely something you will laugh at a year from now, five years from now, maybe even a month from now. Here's a moment that illustrates what I mean:

I had been separated from my ex—we'll call him Baby Daddy One—for about two years and was hugely pregnant with my second child, by Baby Daddy Two. I have a "beach house"—actually a trailer in a gated trailer park high above the beach—but a wonderful getaway for a day or a weekend, and on this day, that's where we all had gone. "We" in this instance was me, Baby Daddy Two, my older son, and his father, Baby Daddy One, whom I had invited so he could spend time with our son and with some of our mutual friends who were coming to spend the day. Because the park is at the top of a hill, I use a GEM electric golf cart to transport kids, towels, beach toys, and snacks to and from the beach. And because the park is gated and locked, there is a coded sticker on the GEM that automatically opens the gates.

So we had driven down the hill to the beach, and there we all were, enjoying the day, until about 3:00 in the afternoon, when Baby Daddy One said he had to leave. Since his car was up at the house and he had no way of getting through the gate, Baby Daddy Two offered to take him up in the GEM. BD1 politely declined—their relationship has always been civil but strained at best—so I said, "Okay, let's all go. We'll run you up to your car and come back." BD1 said good-bye to our son, who stayed behind with the friends, and off we went—me wearing a black bikini, my seven-months-pregnant stomach, and no shoes. BD2 took the wheel and started zipping up the hill, with me wedged in the middle, flanked by my two dudes. I felt moved to put a hand on each of their knees. "See," I said, "isn't this nice? The three of us getting along, hanging out like this?"

BD1 grunted, and BD2 nodded, and then, as if on cue, the GEM cart slowed, sputtered, ran out of battery, and stopped. We were about a quarter of the way up the hill, and there was nothing for it but to push the cart all the way up and into the trailer park. So we did—the three of us, sweating, pissed off, supremely uncomfortable, and, I am sure, regretting the idea of spending the day together, let alone agreeing to the driving arrangement.

So much for hanging out together being "nice."

But that was then; this is now. A lot has changed. Both Baby Daddies are intermittently present in my life as coparents, and we've all moved on in our lives. So when we think back on that idyllic beach day turning into a sweaty trudge up the hill, we laugh about it.

Well, *I* do, anyway.

ACKNOWLEDGMENTS

I would like to thank the following individuals for their support and assistance with this book . . . and life in general:

My awesome sons, Luke Emerson Weber and Jack Northcutt Childers, and the amazing Alix Antonia Childers—you guys are my reason for EVERYTHING!

My brother, Andrew; sister-in-law (the other Laura A. Wasser); nephew, Cooper; and as of yet unborn niece, Ruby.

Thank you to my "baby daddies," David Weber and Minor Childers;

David—for telling me it was time to grow up; teaching me how to diaper (albeit left-handed); giving me perspective where I sometimes lack it; and for providing Luke with athletic ability, a sense of direction, and outstanding musical taste;

Minor—for showing me how to have some fun again; replacing all of the lightbulbs; letting me be right (almost always) still; and the genetic contributions of Jack's gorgeous blue eyes, charming demeanor, and unstoppable dance moves.

Howard and Ruth, for being stepparents not at all like in the fairytales.

My "sister" Melissa, who is due to begin the roller coaster we call parenthood the very same week this book is released.

Erica, Linda, and Jean for keeping me mentally, professionally, and financially sound—in that order.

Mandi, Irma, and Laney for making it possible for me to keep all of the balls in the air at home . . . most of the time.

My goddess girlfriends: Katherine, Mary, Erica (again), Suzy, Melanie, Bonnie, Deb, Christy, Leslie, Julia, Cathy, Natasha, Andrea, Kaye, Samantha, Nan, Parima, and Johnnie for showing me how to be a better mom and sharing so much over so many glasses of wine throughout the years.

My partners and colleagues at Wasser, Cooperman and Carter for the support and guidance, and for generally making me look better than I otherwise would. I am so proud to work with all of you—my extended family.

Susanna, Geoffrey, Andy, Jennifer, Mollie, and Matthew, this book would not have been possible without you. Thank you for the education regarding the prestigious industry of book publication.

The clients who have shared your stories, your emotions, your trust, your angst, your heartache, your relief, and your new beginnings with me over the past twenty years; each of you has taught me something very valuable.